# SEARCH FOR SANCTUARY

## BRIGHAM YOUNG AND THE
## WHITE MOUNTAIN EXPEDITION

# SEARCH FOR SANCTUARY

## BRIGHAM YOUNG AND THE WHITE MOUNTAIN EXPEDITION

by

Clifford L. Stott

University of Utah Publications in the American West

University of Utah Press
Salt Lake City

Volume Nineteen
of the

University of Utah Publications in the American West
under the Editorial Direction of the American West Center

S. Lyman Tyler, Director
Brigham D. Madsen, General Editor

**Library of Congress Cataloging in Publication Data**

Stott, Clifford L. (Clifford Lyle), 1949–
  Search for sanctuary.

  (University of Utah publications in the American
West ; v. 19)
  Bibliography: p.
  Includes index.
  1. Mormons—Utah—History—19th century.  2. Young,
Brigham, 1801–1877.  3. Great Basin—Description and
travel.  4. Utah—History.  5. Utah Expedition, 1857–
1858.  I. Title.  II. Series.
F826.S757  1984          979.2'02          84–15250
ISBN 0–87480–237–7

F
826
.5757
1984

*to Vicki*

# CONTENTS

# ILLUSTRATIONS

# MAPS

# PREFACE

The White Mountain Expedition, although an integral part of Utah War history, is a little-known, little-understood, and largely neglected facet of Brigham Young's war strategy. Previous histories focused primarily on the military operations and political maneuvers of the United States and the Mormon theocracy in Utah Territory, and generally overlooked this episode of the Utah War. Early in 1858, as the nation awaited news of the hostilities in Utah, Mormon leaders in Salt Lake City formulated contingency plans in the event of the collapse of their defenses. Although predicting a military victory, Brigham Young conceived a large-scale resettlement scheme should the Mormon militia fail to halt the advance of U.S. troops into the territory. The move south—when Salt Lake City and other northern Utah communities were evacuated into Utah's southern counties—is generally dismissed as a mere safety precaution or political ploy. It is the author's finding, however, that it was also the first step of Brigham Young's alternative strategy, which would have uprooted the Mormons to resettle them in a series of desert oases hundreds of miles to the west of Utah's southern settlements.

Evidence shows that as Young observed his deteriorating military position and floundering diplomatic efforts during the late winter of 1857–58, he despaired of a military solution, and began the move south. His apparent intention was to remove the Saints to a sanctuary deep within the southwest deserts of Utah Territory. The White Mountain Expedition was to spearhead the new exodus. Its charge was to search out the unexplored reaches of the Great Basin deserts and locate the first settlements. For months the White Mountain companies explored the inhospitable deserts of Utah and Nevada in an attempt to locate a refuge for the Saints. In the process, these men encountered some of the last uncharted territory in the continental United States.

In this work I have attempted to examine Brigham Young's alternative plans and offer some new perspectives of the Utah War.

Few historians of the Utah War have given more than a passing mention to the White Mountain Expedition; some fail to mention it at all. Historians of the early exploration of the Great Basin have similarly overlooked the contributions of the Mormons in 1858. With very few exceptions, the expedition's records have lain unexamined in the archives of the Church of Jesus Christ of Latter-day Saints for well over a century. Typical of the oversight is Houghton's recent summary of early exploration in the central valleys of the Great Basin:

> Certainly he [Jedediah S. Smith] was the first white man to make the Great Basin transit. . . . The 1830s did not constitute a time of discovery. The Walker and Bartleson-Bidwell parties skirted these valleys to the north, and it was not until 1845 that the inquisitive John C. Frémont . . . came this way . . . , but his was a very swift and limited observation, and it added very little to the public knowledge of this *terra incognita*.
>
> Thereafter, the land from Walker Lake to the Utah deserts lay undisturbed while emigrants and forty-niners passed it by, either to the north along the Humboldt River or far to the south. Its mineral wealth was not to be sought or exploited until the 1860s. . . . But one man was to change all this—in 1859 the Army sent Capt. James H. Simpson of the Topographical Engineers on an expedition to find a wagon route across this territory.[1]

Houghton's brief statement conforms to the accepted understanding of Great Basin exploration. Nevertheless, the White Mountain Expedition was completed before Simpson and his army engineers ever set foot west of the Wasatch Mountains. This work, therefore, will assess the expedition's role in Utah War strategy, and analyze its considerable achievements in Great Basin exploration. The routes of the White Mountain Expedition have been established and examined in light of previous Great Basin explorations, and White Mountain geography has consequently been clarified.[2]

Finally, the story of the White Mountain Expedition is an interesting one and deserves to be told if for no other reason.

I wish to express my sincere appreciation for the help and patience of all who aided in the production of this work. The research was assisted by the librarians, directors, and staff members of the following institutions: the Church Historian's Archives of the Church of Jesus Christ of Latter-day Saints, Salt Lake City; Marriott Library, University of Utah, Salt Lake City; Harold B. Lee Library, particularly the departments of Archives and Manuscripts, and Special Collections, Brigham Young University, Provo, Utah; Utah State Historical Society, Salt Lake City; Utah State Archives, Salt Lake City; and Lehman Caves National Monument, Baker, Nevada. I also wish to acknowledge Todd I. Berens for reading the manu-

script, for his helpful suggestions, and for liberally sharing the
results of his own considerable fieldwork on the White Mountain
trails in Nevada; John F. Bluth for his suggestions and encouragement; and Richard D. Poll and David L. Bigler for their careful
reviews of the manuscript and many valuable comments. Finally, I
would like to thank the people of western Utah and southeast
Nevada, whose hospitality and willingness to share their knowledge
of the land was of invaluable assistance in discovering the routes of
the White Mountain explorers.

Clifford L. Stott

Orem, Utah
September 1983

# SEARCH FOR SANCTUARY

## BRIGHAM YOUNG AND THE
## WHITE MOUNTAIN EXPEDITION

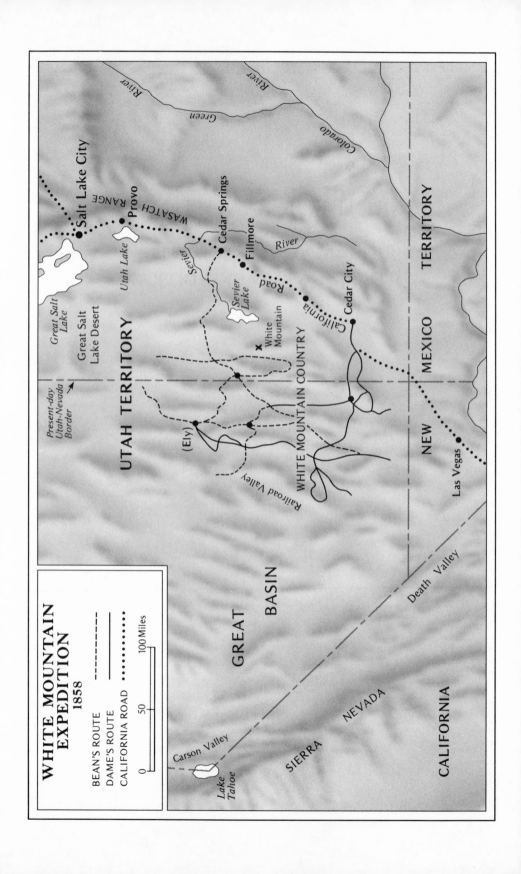

# I

# AN INTRODUCTION TO EXPLORATION IN THE GREAT BASIN

When the Mormons planted the seeds of their theocratic empire on the western slope of the Wasatch Mountains, establishing the first permanent settlements in the Great Basin, they had little authentic geographical knowledge of much of the country. The proposed Mormon "State of Deseret"—centered squarely over the Great Basin—was larger in area than present-day Texas, and much of it was lesser known than any portion of North America south of arctic latitudes.[1] Although Brigham Young and other church leaders had carefully studied the reports of John C. Frémont and other early explorers of the Great Basin, they were largely ignorant of the great tracts of land lying to the west of the Wasatch Mountains. Especially primitive in its state of exploration was the central region of the basin between the Humboldt River and the Spanish Trail. This was an area extremely remote from any civilized outpost, trail, or navigable waterway, and was virtually unknown to civilized man. Eleven years after the first Mormon settlement of Utah, the White Mountain Expedition took a great stride toward filling this gap. The history of the White Mountain Expedition is the story of an attempt to explore and colonize one of the last unknown lands in America.

The American Great Basin, which constitutes the geographical framework of this study, is a vast network of mountains and deserts lying primarily between the Wasatch range of Utah and the Sierra Nevada of California, and from the Snake River country in the north to Baja California's Laguna Salada in the south. It comprises most of the state of Nevada, western Utah, the Mojave region of southern California, and parts of southern Oregon, as well as smaller portions of Idaho and Wyoming. But the Great Basin is a hydrographic entity more accurately described by the division of watersheds. It is called a basin because its waters have no outlet to the sea. Trapped between two of the great mountain ranges of the

North American continent, rivers and streams of the Great Basin flow into the dead lakes, playas, and sinks in the lower valleys of their respective watersheds, actually forming well over one hundred individual basins connected at their rims. The entire eastern flank of the Great Basin, from Wyoming to Mexico, is bordered by the Colorado River system. In the north the basin is bordered by the Snake River system; in the west the Sacramento-San Joaquin River watershed provides the border. In the northwest corner it is the Klamath River system.

All of the major river systems of the Great Basin, with the exception of the Humboldt, are born in the high mountains on its periphery—the Wasatch and the Sierra Nevada. Along the basin's eastern flank, the Wasatch gives rise to the Bear, Weber, Provo, and Sevier rivers. The perennial snows of the Sierra Nevada feed the Walker, Truckee, Carson, and Owens rivers on the western flank. None of these streams flow far into the basin before terminating in a sink or lake, thus depriving the deep interior of the precious liquid. Most of the lakes in the Great Basin are brackish. Since these lakes have insufficient or no outlets, except through evaporation, mineral deposits become concentrated. Freshwater lakes, such as Lake Tahoe and Utah Lake, are most likely to be found near the perimeter where there is sufficient drainage into lower reservoirs. But the system is closed; the waters of the Great Basin will never flow to the sea. Deep in the interior valleys of the basin, where the plentiful snow of the outer rims is lacking and the climate drier, playa lakes are abundant. During the wetter winter months, large shallow sheets of water form in the bottoms of many of the valleys. As summer approaches, the streams that feed these shallow lakes cease to flow, and the playa lakes evaporate leaving a fresh layer of mineral deposits—mud, salt, or alkali. Few rivers in the interior valleys sustain a permanent flow.

Aridity is the common factor in all of the valleys of the Great Basin. The extremes are found in opposite corners of the region, with northern Utah's Cache Valley receiving about seventeen inches of precipitation annually, and California's Death Valley less than five.

The geophysical structure of the basin is one of alternating mountain ranges and broad, flat valleys. The mountain ranges generally run from north to south, with many summits in excess of 10,000 feet above sea level. These craggy peaks are relatively barren except in the canyons. Some slopes are nearly naked of vegetation, while others are clothed with piñon pine, cedar, and juniper, especially in the northern valleys. The high mountains on the periphery are the exception, where aspen, fir, and spruce are abundant. The valleys of the Great Basin are predominantly desert or near-desert. The northern valleys are thick with sagebrush and greasewood, except where alkali prevents its growth. Rushes and willows are often found near water, and grasses are found in some of the wetter areas. In the hotter climate of the low-lying southern valleys, vegetation is markedly different. Here creosote bushes, cacti, and yucca varieties (such as Spanish bayonets and the gnarled joshua trees) prevail.

Animal life in the Great Basin is also severely restricted by the harsh environment. Only small mammals, reptiles, and an occasional antelope band are found in these valleys. A wider variety of wildlife, including deer, are found in the mountains.[2]

Prior to 1858, infrequent attempts were made to penetrate the Great Basin's interior. Of particular interest are explorations into the central Great Basin and adjacent territory lying across southwestern Utah and southern Nevada. Roughly defined, this region encompasses the land between western Utah's Sevier Lake and central Nevada's Railroad Valley, from Steptoe Valley in the north to Pahranagat Valley in the south. Far from the perennial snows of the Wasatch and Sierra Nevada, it is an area containing no major river systems and only a scattering of springs and small streams—many of which are dry during parts of the year. To the Mormons of the 1850s, it was the White Mountain country—a mysterious, uncharted desert region to the west of Utah's southern settlements. The term "White Mountain" had its origins in vague reports from the Indians who described to the Mormons a mystical white mountain far to the west of Fillmore, Utah. By the outbreak of the Utah War this term was being applied to the entire southwestern desert of Utah Territory (which then included all of present-day Nevada north of the 37th parallel). Before the White Mountain Expedition of 1858, this ground had scarcely been touched by pre-Mormon Great Basin explorers.

The Mojave region was the first area of the Great Basin to be penetrated. These early intrusions were attempts by the Catholic Fathers of the Sonora and Santa Fe regions to make overland contact with the newly established missions of San Gabriel and Monterey on the coast of upper California. The Franciscan friars, serving as missionaries to the Indians, were the first Europeans known to penetrate the borders of the Great Basin. Beginning in 1771 Father Francisco Garcés of Tubac (present-day Arizona) entered the basin near its southern extremity, establishing the Sonora-California trail.[3] Over the next decade the Spaniards familiarized themselves with the Mojave region as numerous expeditions were conducted across the desert between the Sonora and California missions by Garcés and Juan Bautista de Anza, commander of the garrison at Tubac.[4]

The Catholic priests were also the first to explore the eastern flank of the basin as they attempted to forge a new trail from Santa Fe to the mission at Monterey. Proceeding north and west in 1776, Fathers Francisco Domínguez and Silvestre Vélez de Escalante penetrated the Great Basin east of Utah Lake and explored south to the vicinity of modern Cedar City, Utah. Upon discovering the Sevier River in central Utah, they postulated it was a lower segment of the Green River, which they had previously discovered and named the Río San Buenaventura. With the true hydrography of the basin a mystery to them, they advanced the theory that the Buenaventura flowed to the Pacific. Although the expedition failed to reach Monterey, the ambitious Catholic fathers were successful in establishing much of the geography of the eastern Great Basin.[5] And their one enormous error—creating the Buenaventura River, the mythical waterway to the Pacific—proved to be one of the expedition's greatest contributions to further exploration of the Great Basin. In the first half of the nineteenth century, belief in the legendary Buenaventura renewed interest in locating the Northwest Passage, inducing some of America's most talented explorers and mountaineers to investigate the basin. Jedediah S. Smith and John C. Frémont both sought the apocryphal stream. The myth was not laid to rest until Frémont's second expedition of 1843–44.

The Domínguez-Escalante expedition ended Spanish exploration in the Great Basin on an official level; however, trading parties and punitive expeditions continued to probe the basin. The most notable of these was the Arze-Garcia party of 1813, which discovered a direct route between the Green and Sevier rivers.[6] In 1821 the Mexican revolution succeeded in overthrowing Spanish rule, and few explorations of any consequence appear to have been undertaken by the new government.

The era of the Far West fur trade was a time of intense exploration in the Great Basin. The promise of rich supplies of furs in the Wasatch and the possibility of an outlet to the Pacific lured trappers into the northern Wasatch as early as 1810 when a contingent of Jacob Astor's Pacific Fur Company penetrated the Bear River country from the north.[7] The North West Fur Company's Snake Country expeditions first reached the same area in 1818, subsequently carrying out further exploration under the command of the daring Donald Mackenzie.[8]

By the early 1820s there were several powerful fur companies competing in the trans-Mississippi West. The Hudson's Bay Company, successor to the North West Company, gave command of the profitable Snake Country expeditions to Peter Skene Ogden in 1824. The intrepid and capable Ogden soon became famous for his frequent exploring tours and numerous discoveries. Between 1824 and 1830 Ogden led his brigade of trappers on six major exploring enterprises in the Great Basin.[9] He was soon familiar with the northeast quadrant of the basin—the northern Wasatch and Great Salt Lake region—as well as the northwest Great Basin in Oregon. But Ogden's discovery of the Humboldt River in 1828 was perhaps his most significant contribution to Great Basin exploration. Stretching from east to west across the northern part of the present state of Nevada, the Humboldt would become the overland highway of the nation across the Great Basin to the Pacific Coast.

During 1829–30 Ogden's brigade completed its sixth and final Snake Country expedition; the trappers explored the entire western flank of the Great Basin to the Mojave Desert. But with all of Ogden's extensive exploration, he never penetrated the central Great Basin region. As a trapper, he saw the dry interior valleys as of little value. Instead, it was Jedediah Smith and the Rocky Mountain Fur Company who first explored the deep interior.

The American fur trappers descended upon the Great Basin in the fall of 1824. Foremost among these companies was the Rocky Mountain Fur Company organized in 1822. When Indian depredations along the upper Missouri brought the fur trade to a near standstill early in the 1820s, the Rocky Mountain Fur Company moved its center of operations south to the Wasatch Mountains. The company included such notables as Jedediah S. Smith, James Bridger, Daniel Potts, John Weber, Thomas Fitzpatrick, William Sublette, and Etienne Provost, all of whom became intimately associated with exploration in the Great Basin, as did the Rocky Mountain Fur

Company itself. Like Ogden, who entered the basin at practically the same time, these men quickly made themselves familiar with the streams issuing from the Wasatch in the northeast quarter of the Great Basin and proceeded over the next half-dozen years to trap the area almost to extinction. Unaware that the region was a great hydrographic basin without connection to the Pacific slope, the company was particularly interested in ascertaining the truth of the Buenaventura's supposed outlet to the sea. After several fruitless attempts to locate the stream by following the Green River and circumnavigating the Great Salt Lake,[10] Jedediah Smith set out on his famous southwest expedition to California in 1826. Smith was a firm believer in the existence of the Buenaventura. Hoping to locate the mythical stream and a source of fur, he planned to push operations farther to the west and export pelts from the West Coast. Marching southwest the Smith party followed the Wasatch to its terminus, eventually leaving the basin and following the Virgin and Colorado rivers to the Needles (site of present-day Needles, California). Striking west across the Mojave Desert, Smith finally found his way to the California missions. The following year Smith worked his way north up the San Joaquin Valley of California searching the western ramparts of the Sierra Nevada for the Buenaventura River in hopes of following the legendary stream back to the Great Salt Lake region. After several months of disappointment, he traversed the Sierras at Ebbetts Pass and penetrated the harsh interior deserts of the Great Basin. The northeast trek to the Great Salt Lake cut directly across the central region, which Smith described only as a great "sandy plain."[11] Three decades later the Mormons called it the White Mountain country.

Although the areas along the Wasatch were nearly trapped out by 1830, another major fur-trapping venture was undertaken during the decade. Benjamin L. E. Bonneville, a captain in the U.S. Army, became obsessed with ideas of making a fortune in the Far West fur trade. Guided by Joseph R. Walker and M. S. Cerré, Bonneville plunged his company of 110 men into the Rocky Mountains in the summer of 1832, apparently oblivious to the fact that the area had been trapped nearly to extinction. In 1833 Bonneville sent Walker with forty men across the Wasatch into the Salt Lake Basin. After making a swift reconnaissance of the lake, however, the Walker party struck out instead for California. Rounding the northern shore of the Great Salt Lake, they crossed the intervening desert to the

Humboldt River and followed it west to its sink near modern Lovelock, Nevada. The Walker party then crossed the Sierra Nevada near present-day Yosemite National Park, establishing the first overland trail to California.[12]

In 1841 the Bartleson-Bidwell company became the first emigrant party to use the new trail to California.[13] Over the next few years the route was refined, with most notable improvements being the use of Donner Pass in the Sierra Nevada and the Hastings Cutoff, which diverted California-bound traffic south of the Great Salt Lake for a time. The cutoff was shorter but extremely difficult across the extensive salt flats.

The other prominent corridor to California through the Great Basin was the Old Spanish Trail. Although the groundwork for this route had been laid by Domínguez and Escalante, Garcés, and Jedediah Smith, the route was not traveled in its entirety until the Wolfskill-Yount company followed it in the winter of 1830–31.[14] The route went through a long metamorphosis over many years, but was basically a trail from Santa Fe to Los Angeles—the highway of the lucrative Santa Fe trade and Indian slave trade that was replacing fur in importance during the decades of the 1840s and 1850s. The trail cut across the Mojave region after entering the basin east of present-day Cedar City. By 1849 the trail had also become an important emigrant route to the West Coast. But the area that lay between these northern and southern overland trails was practically unknown.

The decade of the 1840s saw the commencement of U.S. government surveys in the Great Basin. Although the region was a part of the Republic of Mexico at the time, to the American mind such delineations were at best temporary. The first of the surveys to probe the basin was led by Captain John C. Frémont of the U.S. Topographical Engineers. Frémont entered the basin in 1843 seduced by the myth of the Buenaventura. His report indicates that he expected to find the stream at any moment:

> In our journey across the desert, Mary's Lake [the Humboldt Sink] and the famous Buenaventura River were two points on which I relied to recruit the animals and repose the party. Forming, agreeable to the best map in my possession, a connected water-line from the Rocky Mountains to the Pacific Ocean, I felt no other anxiety than to pass safely across the intervening desert to the banks of the Buenaventura, where, in the softer climate of a more southern latitude, our horses might find grass to sustain them and ourselves be sheltered from the rigors of winter and from the inhospitable desert.[15]

Frémont's belief in the Buenaventura seems odd in light of the previous discoveries by Jedediah Smith, Peter Skene Ogden, and Joseph R. Walker who found no such river in these regions. Frémont either chose to ignore their reports or was ignorant of them. But after encircling most of the basin in 1843–44, Frémont was the first to completely reject the idea of the Buenaventura and declare the region to be a great basin, and so it was named.[16] Ironically, while exploding the myth of the Buenaventura and in general interpreting the hydrographic nature of the Great Basin, Frémont became responsible for the creation of a new myth which was to have a profound impact on the exploration of the Great Basin in the years to follow. This was the myth of a great east-west mountain range connecting the eastern rim of the Great Basin near present-day Cedar City to the Sierra Nevada. Operating under an apparent misconception, Frémont believed that for the streams of the Great Basin to be isolated from the sea, the basin must be surrounded by a high chain of mountains. Having thus convinced himself, he apparently imagined seeing the hypothetical range on the northern horizon while in the Las Vegas area in 1844:

> And in returning from California along the Spanish trail, as far as the head of the Santa Clara fork of the Rio Virgen, I crossed only small streams making their way south to the Colorado, or lost in the sand—as the Mo-hah-ve; while to the left, lofty mountains, their summits white with snow, were often visible, and which must have turned water to the north as well as to the south, and thus constituted . . . the southern rim of the Basin.[17]

Frémont's reports of his first two expeditions were widely circulated and read by an American public anxious to move west.[18] Because of the credibility accorded the "Pathfinder," some readers would eventually be lured into the central Great Basin region by the implications of the great east-west range. It was Frémont's misconception of the mountain structure of the Great Basin's interior (which he had not visited) that enticed pioneers, gold seekers, and explorers into the region for well over a decade. Frémont's map of 1848, which illustrated the legendary mountains in detail, was also widely circulated. Seeing the mountains on the map made the myth all the more difficult to dispel. The Death Valley company of 1849, the backers of the central railroad route to the Pacific, and the White Mountain Expedition of 1858 were all mislead by Frémont's Great Basin theory.

John C. Frémont returned to the Great Basin in 1845 intending to map the California Trail. Frémont was accompanied by Joseph R. Walker, the man who guided Bonneville and established the overland trail to California a decade before. Using Hastings's Cutoff south of the Great Salt Lake, the company crossed the salt flats and arrived at Mound Springs near present-day Wells, Nevada. From this point Frémont pivoted to the southwest and explored a new route to Walker Lake on the western flank of the basin thus exploring a large slice of new territory, but skirting well to the north of the White Mountain country.[19]

The Mormons established their sanctuary in the Great Basin in 1847 and built their first settlements along the fertile base of the Wasatch Mountains. By the time of the White Mountain Expedition eleven years later, over forty settlements had been founded from Cache Valley in the north to Washington in the south. In addition, the Mormons had fanned out, establishing the distant settlements of Carson Valley at the foot of the Sierra Nevada, San Bernardino, Las Vegas, and Fort Limhi in present-day Idaho. During the first years of the Mormon occupation of the Great Basin their enterprises were conducted largely in areas that had been previously explored.

By 1849 exploration west of the Wasatch Mountains by both Mormons and non-Mormons was focused primarily on finding a suitable shortcut to California and the goldfields. Two basic ideas were advanced by advocates of a direct route. The first was the same as proposed by Hastings—a trail south of the Great Salt Lake which would eliminate the long detour around the north side of the lake. The difficulty was to get over the treacherous salt flats south and west of the lake. The other plan was to radically shorten the long and tedious Spanish Trail by forging a route directly across the desert west of present-day Cedar City, Utah, to Walker Pass in the Sierra Nevada. Such a trail would eliminate the agonizing southern bend through the Mojave Desert. Some of those who attempted the southern passage, or "Walker's Cutoff," penetrated the White Mountain country for the first time since Jedediah Smith's southwest expedition in 1826–27.

In 1849 a company of packers on the California road south of Salt Lake City decided to attempt Walker's Cutoff. The company was composed of a party of gentile packers heading for the goldfields under the leadership of Captain O. K. Smith, and an equal number of Mormon missionaries lead by James M. Flake. It was probably in Sevier Valley in central Utah that the company encountered Elijah

Barney Ward, a mountain man who had lived in the Wasatch for years and who later became a Mormon with a prominent role in the White Mountain Expedition story. It was Ward's firm belief that a shortcut route from southern Utah to the gentle Walker Pass in the Sierra Nevada was not only possible but indeed existed. Ward urged the company to try the new route, giving them a map with the route marked out on it. He also alleged that the route was well stocked with grass and water and claimed that he had been over the ground three times himself.[20]

On Beaver Creek in southern Utah the company overtook a large wagon train of forty-niners guided by the Mormon Jefferson Hunt. Totally captivated by the so-called cutoff, Captain Smith's enthusiasm infected the others. But it was Frémont's mythical east-west mountain range that became the deciding factor. After listening to Smith's favorable recommendations for the new route, someone pulled out a copy of Frémont's 1848 map. W. B. Lorton, a member of the forty-niners' train, recorded the incident in 1850:

> Fremont's map was perused by the knowing, and sure enough, he had seen a high range stretching east and west, but did not explore it, and then they consulted the matter thus:
> Now, says they, wherever there is a chain of high mountains there must be snow, and wherever there is snow there must be streams eminating therefrom—so we will not go the out of the way, the Spanish trail, but the short and expeditious route to the mines. . . .[21]

Almost the entire wagon train turned from the Spanish Trail near present Newcastle, Utah, and many of the company perished in the deserts of Death Valley. In the process these gold seekers cut a trail through the southern portion of the White Mountain region, the first in over two decades. It had only been a matter of time before someone tested Frémont's theories; but the forty-niners would not be the last. In the decade to follow many, including Brigham Young, would become deluded by the same myth, just as Frémont and an earlier generation of explorers had been fooled by the Buenaventura. Coincidentally, it was a member of the Death Valley company, Asahel Bennett, who guided the White Mountain Expedition over a portion of the same ground nine years after his own close brush with death.

Others to attempt a southern shortcut passage to California included a party of U.S. Army Topographical Engineers commanded by Captain John W. Gunnison. But Gunnison and seven of his men were massacred by the Indians in 1853 before passing west of Sevier Lake.[22] In the following year John C. Frémont led his fifth and final expedition to the Far West. This time he was a civilian representing the interests of the central railroad route to the Pacific. Frémont closely followed the steps of the forty-niners, again penetrating the White Mountain country in the same area as the Death Valley company. Steering to the north of Death Valley, he struck the Owens River near the 37th parallel and avoided much of the difficulty of his predecessors.[23]

The search for a direct route to California immediately south of the Great Salt Lake was begun by Hastings in 1844. Hastings's Cutoff was difficult and dangerous, but it was used by several forty-niner companies and others including the ill-fated Donner party. In 1854 Lt. Edward G. Beckwith, successor to the Pacific railroad surveys after the death of Captain Gunnison, was successful in establishing a new trail to California across the salt flats at roughly the 40th parallel. But according to James H. Simpson, a fellow engineer, "it was too far north and too torturous to be of great value."[24] The route was rarely used.

Later in the year, Colonel Edward J. Steptoe arrived in Salt Lake City on his way to California with two artillery batteries and a company of dragoons. Having heard of Beckwith's recent survey, Steptoe hired Oliver B. Huntington, a Mormon, to scout the trail, shorten it if he could, and guide his men across it in the spring. Huntington's party set out from Salt Lake City in September and returned two months later claiming to have reached Carson Valley in just twenty-seven days. The route was said to follow Beckwith's trail for 200 miles, then veer to the southwest cutting 150 miles from the Beckwith route.[25] But thinking Huntington had tricked him, Steptoe hired Orrin Porter Rockwell to resurvey the route in the spring of 1855. Rockwell and four other Mormon scouts returned shortly, asserting that wagon travel across the salt flats was all but impossible at that season.[26] Now, convinced that he had been duped by Huntington, Steptoe departed for California by the traditional Humboldt River route north of the Great Salt Lake.[27] But the Mormons, meanwhile, received considerable new knowledge of an unfamiliar portion of the Great Basin. George W. Bean, a member of Rockwell's party, led a contingent of the White Mountain Expedition three years later.

Among other Mormons to attempt a direct route to California

during the 1850s was Howard Egan, a prominent guide and mountaineer. Egan went south of the salt flats in 1855 then connected to the Humboldt route near present-day Elko, Nevada.[28] The following year Brigham Young sent Seth Blair, U.S. Attorney for Utah and a Mormon, to locate a direct route to Carson Valley where a colony of the church had been established. Blair, however, failed in the attempt, probably going no further than the Deep Creek Mountains on the present Utah–Nevada border.[29]

By the mid-1850s reports of a strange white mountain west of Fillmore had been carried into the Mormon settlements by the desert tribes. In 1855 Brigham Young decided to open an Indian mission in the vicinity of the White Mountain, selecting Bishop David Evans of Lehi to lead the expedition and plant the settlement. Twelve White Mountain missionaries left Fillmore on May 28 and struck across the desert in a northwest direction to Antelope Springs thirty miles west of present-day Delta, Utah. Crossing the House Range at Dome Canyon Pass, the expedition traversed Tule Valley, and descended the smaller Confusion Range into Snake Valley on the present Utah–Nevada border. It was in Snake Valley on June 1 that Evans recorded: "Here for the first time I got sight of the White Mountain, which lies from this place about 35 miles southeast. The lower the sun got the whiter this mountain appeared until about sunset or a little before it looked like a great pile of dirty snow."[30] Considering Evans's vantage point, about twenty miles north of present-day Garrison, Utah, the mysterious mountain peak would have been in the Wah Wah Range of western Millard County. A further description by E. G. Williams, a member of Evans's company, reveals the identity of the mountain. On June 6 Williams reached the foot of the White Mountain. "Here we halted a few moments," wrote Williams,

> to gaze at the mysterious wonder which was only known by a faint, meagre description by the Indians. This mountain is a white sandstone rock, interspersed with bastard diamonds. . . . These small diamonds almost cover the ground for some distance before we reach the mountain, so much so as to dazzle the eye of the traveler on a sunny day. There are some who say they have been to the White Mountain, but I think not excepting the red men. I claim that I was the first white man who ever stepped upon it and I have been the highest up its rugged slopes.[31]

From the descriptions of Evans and Williams, there can be little doubt that the White Mountain was Crystal Peak in the Wah Wah Range. Williams's "bastard diamonds" eventually gave Crystal

Fig. 1. Crystal Peak—the original "White Mountain." Western Millard County, Utah. *Courtesy Utah State Historical Society.*

Peak its name. Evans did not think much of the country, but he did concede the possibility of success for a small settlement on Snake Creek at the foot of the snow-capped Snake Range. For want of proper supplies, however, the men set out for home and never returned.

Two years later a Mormon, Chauncey Webb, tracked his stolen horses into Snake Valley, where he treated with a band of hostile Snake Indians for the return of his herd.[32] Even prior to this, Mormon punitive expeditions had been launched onto the western deserts in an unsuccessful bid to capture the murderers of the Gunnison party in 1853. Ironically, the Pauvan Ute war chief Mashoquab, the one generally blamed for the massacre, was Webb's guide in 1857, and the following year he guided the White Mountain Expedition over some of the same ground.[33]

By the late 1850s White Mountain came to mean the entire desert region west of Utah's southern settlements, as is clear from the journals of the 1858 White Mountain explorers, who applied the name of this single peak in the Wah Wah Range to many mountains and places in the remote central basin region. Contemporary diary accounts testify that the White Mountain terminology was widely known in Utah prior to the Utah War.[34]

Exploration in the Great Basin before the Utah War was extensive, but it was far from thorough. The Spaniards explored the Mojave region and the eastern flank of the basin from Utah Lake south. The trappers, who first appeared in the Great Basin in the mid-1820s, thoroughly explored the Wasatch region and discovered the Humboldt River. Jedediah Smith, boldly cutting a path across the interior valleys of the Basin in 1827 while attempting to locate the Buenaventura, was the first to penetrate the central region. Ogden was the first to explore the western flank of the basin, and the Bonneville–Walker expedition of 1832–33 established the Humboldt River as an overland route to California. Trading parties then connected the explorations of Garcés, Smith, and Escalante to form the Spanish Trail in the 1830s.

Between these two overland trails to the West Coast lay a vast area, little of which had been seen by white men. The several groups which explored north and south along the eastern and western flanks of the Great Basin had largely avoided the hostile interior. John C. Frémont filled a portion of this gap during his third expedition of 1845–46. By this time emphasis on exploration had shifted to locating a direct route to California south of the Great Salt Lake. Hastings, Gunnison, Beckwith, Huntington, Rockwell, Blair, Frémont, forty-niners, and Mormon missionaries all attempted to find the elusive shortcut with varying degrees of success during the 1840s and 1850s. Only the Mormons looked upon the region as a place to attempt settlement. Their first expedition to the eastern fringes of the White Mountain region went only as far as Snake Valley. Their next expedition took up where the first left off.

After more than eight decades of exploration in the Great Basin, non-Indian encroachment into the central valleys was minimal. Only Jedediah S. Smith, John C. Frémont, the Death Valley company, and to a lesser extent the few Mormons who had reached Snake Valley, had as yet ventured into any part of the deep interior between the Spanish Trail and the Humboldt River—known to the Mormons as the White Mountain country. In 1858 Brigham Young's quest for a refuge for the embattled Latter-day Saints resulted in the organization of the White Mountain Expedition, one of the largest Great Basin exploring companies ever assembled, to penetrate, observe, and map this long-neglected region.

# II

# THE GATHERING STORM

Unlike previous attempts to probe the Great Basin, the White Mountain Expedition of 1858 was a desperate measure—a calculated response by Brigham Young to a United States military expedition marching on Utah to depose him as governor and suppress an alleged rebellion in the territory. For a few desperate weeks in the spring of 1858, Brigham Young saw the expedition as a last hope of survival for the Mormon people as a gathered body.

The causes of the Utah War and ultimately the White Mountain Expedition were unique in American history. The territory of Utah was inhabited during the 1850s almost exclusively by members of the Church of Jesus Christ of Latter-day Saints—or Mormons— who numbered nearly 40,000 by 1857.[1] The Mormons were not only separated from their countrymen by hundreds of miles of prairies and deserts, but by a body of religious doctrine, institutions, and policies which threw them into frequent conflict with nonbelievers and governments alike. Since the organization of the sect in 1830, persecution and tragedy had almost become a way of life for the Saints, as they called themselves. Early in its existence the church had abandoned its ground in New York and Ohio in the face of opposition. The Saints had been violently ejected from Missouri in 1839 under threat of extermination, and were expelled from Illinois in 1846. In Utah little more than a decade passed before the Mormons found themselves preparing to defend their homes again. With their backs to the Great Basin deserts, they faced what appeared to be their gravest threat—the U.S. Army.

The seeds of nineteenth-century Mormon–gentile conflict lay deeply seated within the religion itself.[2] It was the basic purpose and challenge of Mormonism to prepare the way for the return of Jesus Christ—an event which the Saints expected momentarily. Under the direction of Joseph Smith, and later under Brigham Young, the Mormons were busily engaged in the noble task of constructing a physical as well as a spiritual kingdom of God on earth—a project not altogether unlike the Puritan settlement of Boston two centuries before. The "gathering of Israel" was a necessary component of this kingdom-building process and resulted in large-scale emigration to Utah in the decade preceding the Utah War. From its roots as an obscure and scattered sect the church became a force to be reckoned with; Mormons dominated the economic, political, and social life of Utah Territory in their quest for the establishment of Zion. Unfortunately, the construction and preservation of a physical kingdom of God proved to be incompatible with almost any form of government recognized within the jurisdiction of the United States.

In forming the physical kingdom, as in all other matters, the Mormon church claimed to act under divine powers and guidance. All Mormon church presidents have asserted their right to the title of "prophet" with the authority and power to speak for God. As no earthly law could take precedence over the word of God, the introduction of this prophetic priesthood order created a "higher law" which devout followers responded to enthusiastically in all things. It was the Mormon claim of a superior religion—in fact, "the only true Church"—coupled with their supreme allegiance to their prophets, which initially brought persecution to the surface.[3] When the church openly embraced polygamy in 1852, the Mormons further exposed themselves to persecution.[4] Polygamy became a rallying point for the opposition, and nonbelievers soon developed a suspicion of Mormons and Mormon institutions.

The Mormons, meanwhile, set about to accomplish their grand designs for the Great Basin with their characteristic vigor and sense of destiny and high purpose. After three years of relative peace, however, Brigham Young found his Great Basin kingdom within the jurisdiction of a U.S. territorial government that could easily place the Mormons at the mercy of their enemies and impede or destroy the kingdom as they envisioned it. As a federal territory, Utah's officers would be appointed by the president of the United States rather than elected by the citizens of Utah. Although Millard Fillmore was persuaded to appoint Young governor of Utah, the Saints soon locked horns with the federal judges and other non-Mormon territorial appointees. The causes of the Utah War of 1857–58 are to be found in the Mormons' attempts to neutralize federal authority in Utah Territory and in the almost universal disdain for Mormonism in the East.

Brigham Young was an open advocate of theocratic government, "one in which all laws are enacted and executed in righteousness, and whose officers possess that power which proceedeth from the Almighty [the priesthood]."[5] Although such a government was impossible in a federal territory, Young used his overwhelming influence among his followers to reduce the effectiveness of gentile officeholders, a situation that soon exasperated federal appointees. Since Mormons looked to their prophet for guidance in all things, juries and voters were easily influenced.[6] With the entire Utah legislature composed of Mormons (mostly prominent churchmen), Brigham Young effectively controlled the legislative as well as executive branches of government.

The Mormons met with sustained opposition when the church hierarchy attempted to control the judiciary of the territory. In 1852 the Utah legislature established a system of "probate" courts endowed with extraordinary powers. The Mormon-controlled probate courts were given jurisdiction over criminal and civil cases and were in direct conflict with federal courts. The legislature also created the office of territorial marshal with powers that largely overlapped the duties of the federal marshal, usually a gentile.[7]

Several gentile officials in the territory complained bitterly of shabby treatment at the hands of the Mormons. In the fall of 1851, Chief Justice Lemuel Brandebury, Associate Justice Perry Brocchus, and Secretary Broughton Harris abandoned their posts in Utah claiming to fear for their safety. Their charges against the Mormons included treason, assassination, and political despotism.[8] When Judge George P. Stiles struck down the excessive powers of the territorial marshal in 1856, he was threatened with violence. Shortly after, Stiles's office was ransacked, the papers of the court removed, and some law books burned.[9] In 1857 David H. Burr, surveyor general of Utah Territory, surrendered his appointment insisting that his life was in immediate peril. The church, he said, had openly censured him, and one of his assistants had been beaten, perhaps crippled, by the Mormons. Burr claimed he had been rendered ineffective in his appointment by intimidation and violence. Furthermore, the surveyor alleged redress was an impossibility in the Mormon-controlled courts. After Burr's departure from the territory, three of his former assistants claimed to have been threatened and hounded from Utah. In a similar incident, Indian agent Garland Hurt fled the territory later in the year believing his life was in danger.[10]

The most celebrated clash between the Mormons and federal

officers, and probably the one with the most far-reaching consequences, was the case of W. W. Drummond, who was appointed Associate Justice for Utah by President Pierce in 1854. Drummond's
attacks on the Mormon probate courts quickly brought him into
conflict with the church. After experiencing the frustrations of
Utah's theocratic power structure, the judge fled to California early
in 1857 where he delivered scathing attacks against the Mormons. In
his letter of resignation to Attorney General Jeremiah S. Black,
Drummond outlined numerous charges against the Saints. He alleged that Brigham Young was the only law in the territory; federal
law was not considered binding, and a secret order existed among all
male members of the church to resist federal authority; the church
was guilty of eliminating its enemies by murder; the papers and
records of the Supreme Court had been destroyed by order of the
church; federal officers of the territory were insulted, harassed, and
annoyed by the Mormons; and justice was administered differently
to Mormons and gentiles.[11]

The Indian agents appointed to posts in Utah similarly accused
the Mormons of perfidy in their dealings with the Indians by attempting to create a distinction between Americans and Mormons
among the several tribes with which they came into contact. Agents
Garland Hurt, Henry R. Day, and Jacob Holeman all agreed,
along with Perry Brocchus, that the Mormons were endeavoring to
turn the Indians against the government.[12] These indictments
served to inflame public opinion against the Mormons to the flash
point in 1857.

The Mormons' willful disregard of federal authority was not entirely without provocation. Frequently government officers dispatched to Utah were of limited ability and doubtful character.
While most were insensitive or indifferent to Mormon problems,
some were openly anti-Mormon. Brocchus was a pompous, foolish
man whose desire to lecture the Mormons on their morals was
largely responsible for his persecution.[13] Justice Drummond was an
unsavory character and many of his non-Mormon colleagues considered him totally unfit for federal service. He arrived in Utah with
a prostitute from the streets of Washington whom he introduced as
his wife, occasionally seating her next to him on the bench as he administered justice. The Mormons, themselves objects of much an-
tipathy for their peculiar system of marriage, were understandably
outraged.[14]

Another sore point between the church and federal government was the small amount of money Congress appropriated for Utah. In addition, tight-fisted federal officers were unnecessarily slow in dispersing the funds.[15]

The issue of land ownership was another annoying problem. Since the church had established its gathering on the public domain, Mormons could not receive legal title to their lands until the Indian title had been extinguished and the area surveyed. While Indian treaties had been enacted in other federal territories, the Mormons felt slighted by the government's failure to act in Utah. Without a legal claim to their lands, the enemies of the church could threaten expulsion. It was this fear that prompted the Mormons to disrupt the activities of Surveyor General Burr.[16]

The Mormons saw all of these issues as a continuation of the persecution they had endured for nearly three decades. In all of this perceived treachery, they viewed the gentiles as tools of Satan in a dark, evil plot designed to destroy the New Zion and crush the priesthood. To save the kingdom, resistance was justifiable. At one point the Utah legislature even claimed the right to disobey federal officers and laws that were inconsistent with Mormon views.[17] Apostle John Taylor summed up the Mormon opinion of federal officers and federal authority in 1857:

> I do not believe in their right constitutionally to appoint our officers. Still they have done it, and we have submitted to it. And they have sent some of the most miserable scoundrels here that ever existed on the earth. Instead of being fathers, they have tried every influence they could bring to bear in order to destroy us.[18]

The reformation that swept across Utah in 1856–57 also had a significant impact on the Utah War. Church leaders attempted to cleanse the body of the church by launching an intensive revival of religious values—essentially another step in the kingdom-building process. Those who were unwilling to conform were purged from church membership. Speeches by church leaders during the reformation often carried violent assaults on the character and purposes of the government and its officers, as well as gentiles in general. The emotionalism resulted in occasional violence toward backsliders and apostates in the territory, which further goaded Utah's federal officers and contributed to their anti-Mormon behavior.

While the reformation outraged the gentiles, its effects consolidated the church's power by weeding out dissenters and forcefully reminding loyal members of their duties, thus emboldening the church hierarchy and contributing to its troubles with Stiles, Drummond, and others. As such, the reformation was at least a catalyst in opening hostilities between the Mormons and the government.[19]

By the spring of 1857 Utah was a powder keg. Incensed over polygamy and alleged political despotism in Utah, Easterners demanded the government take action against the Mormons. Public opinion against the Saints was virtually universal.[20] Just months prior to the outbreak of the Utah War, Mormon Apostle Parley P. Pratt wrote from his mission headquarters in New York that "the whole country is being overwhelmed with the most lying, mockery, and hatred of the Saints."[21] The Eastern press claimed that Mormons were murdering gentiles by the score, arming the Indians, and plotting war against the United States.[22] By the spring of 1857 powerful editors were urging the government to militarily intervene in Utah and install a gentile governor at the point of a bayonet.[23]

The recently elected James Buchanan administration concluded no later than May that the Mormons were indeed in a state of insurrection and in need of chastisement. Some historians contend the public outcry for military intervention was so great as to make Buchanan's actions almost mandatory.[24] While the bitter complaints of past and present federal officials in Utah provided the primary justification for armed intervention, Buchanan may also have been compelled to settle the Mormon question to save his Democratic party from embarrassment. Having been rebuffed by the Republicans' anti-polygamy plank in their platform in 1856, the Mormons had been driven into the seemingly less hostile camp of the Democrats. When the Republicans accused their rival of being soft on polygamy, the Democrats found it politically expedient to denounce the Mormons. Buchanan's Utah expedition provided a convenient way for the president to vindicate his party.[25]

Initial orders for assembling and outfitting the expeditionary force at Fort Leavenworth were drawn up on May 28, and the first elements of the 2,500-man army marched west on July 18. Original command of the expedition was given to Brigadier General William S. Harney. Part of Harney's instructions from the War Department stated: "The community and, in part, the civil government of Utah Territory are in a substantial state of rebellion against the laws and authority of the United States." The army was to be a *posse comitatus* to be called upon when "the ordinary course of judicial proceedings or the power vested in the United States' marshals and other proper officers" was found to be "inadequate for the preservation of the peace and the due execution of the laws."[26]

A multitude of new federal officers were appointed to territorial posts and assigned to accompany the army to Utah. Among them was Alfred Cumming, the new governor of Utah Territory. Cumming's instructions from Secretary of State Lewis Cass told him to "take care that the laws are faithfully executed and to maintain peace and good order in the Territory." Cass instructed the governor not to interfere with the Mormons' religious practices, but resistance to the law "must be met with firmness." In such an event he was authorized to call for as many troops as the situation required.[27]

On July 24 Brigham Young and 2,500 of his followers were assembled in Big Cottonwood Canyon southeast of Salt Lake City for the tenth annual Pioneer Day celebration, when three weary horsemen galloped into the midst of the festivities for a consultation with Young. Abraham O. Smoot, Judson L. Stoddard, and Orrin Porter Rockwell, just twenty days from Fort Leavenworth, brought the news of an army marching toward Utah. This was the first news of the expedition for most Utahns. When it was remembered that President Young had said just ten years earlier to the day, "If the people of the United States will let us alone for ten years we will ask no odds of them," the news acquired a prophetic ring. There is ample evidence, however, that church leaders knew about the government's actions for some days and probably weeks before the dramatic events of July 24 at Big Cottonwood, which must now be viewed as having been staged for effect.[28]

From the beginning, the Mormons were convinced they were the innocent victims of an army sent to destroy them or hold them still while their old enemies killed them off. According to Brigham Young on September 13, 1857, the Mormons

are in a Government whose administrators are always trying to injure us . . . and they are organizing their forces to come here, and protect infernal scamps who are anxious to come here and kill whom they please, destroy whom they please, and finally exterminate the "Mormons."

. . . The Government . . . had ordered 2,500 troops to come here and hold the "Mormons" still, while priests, politicians, speculators, whoremongers, and every mean, filthy character that could be raked up should come here and kill off the "Mormons."[29]

The Mormons were not alone in their belief that the army was sent to Utah with hostile intent. Many in the army seemed bent on the destruction of the Mormons. Capt. Jesse Gove of the Utah expedition wrote to his wife that "we have got to give them a sound whipping, hang about 100 of them, and the rest will submit."[30]

The conflict rapidly assumed the status of a holy war in the Mormon community. It seemed perfectly clear to the Saints that the *real* enemy was not the government, nor even the gentiles; the real war was between God and the devil. Typical was the assessment of George Laub: "Our enemies . . . are now determined through the power of the Devil that worketh in their hearts to make war upon the saints & desire to destroy us from of[f] the face of the Earth and thus obliterat[e] the Kingdom & Priesthood of God."[31] And Heber C. Kimball argued that "the day has come when the Devil is coming with all his combined forces: he has laid siege to the kingdom of God, and it will never cease till this kingdom triumphs."[32]

Another peculiar view of the projected war with the gentiles was the Saints' belief that the approach of U.S. soldiers was a prelude to Armageddon, the last great battle to pave the way for the return of Christ. To the Mormons, the coming struggles were the beginning of a process which would ultimately liberate the kingdom and prove the destruction of the wicked. The speeches of church leaders during the early days of the war boldly proclaimed the fearful result of the government's attitude toward them.[33] Even as late as May 6, 1858, when the crisis with the government was drawing to a close, Brigham Young seemed convinced that the nation was on the verge of collapse. "You know the nation cannot last long in its present capacity," wrote the Mormon prophet to John M. Bernhisel, Utah's congressional delegate. "She is liable to perish in an hour—at any moment she may be dismembered and rent asunder. The only wonder is that the slender thread which holds her together has not already parted."[34] Clearly, President Buchanan's simple *posse comitatus* was seen in Utah as a development with ramifications having global impact, setting in motion events that would revolutionize the world.

Although the Mormons did not consider themselves to be rebels, they perceived their "hour of deliverance" drawing near.[35] Historian Thomas B. H. Stenhouse, president of the church's Eastern States mission during the Utah War, affirmed that "for years previous, the people had been taught to look forward to the time when 'the Kingdom' should throw off its allegiance to all earthly power, and now they concluded that 'the long-expected blessed day' had arrived, when they beheld on the one side of the mountains the national army advancing to their homes, and on the other side the Prophet with the armies of Israel determined to dispute their entrance into the valleys."[36] But declaring independence from the United States was a delicate business, for if the bid for freedom failed, Mormon leaders would be vulnerable to the penalties for treason. Brigham Young moved along cautiously. As early as August 2 he toyed with the notion in his Sunday sermon. Asking his followers if they were "prepared to have the thread cut today," he noted that he would "take a hostile move by our enemies as an evidence that it is time for the thread to be cut."[37] Four weeks later, Heber C. Kimball, Young's impetuous first counselor, delivered a flaming discourse from the Bowery in Salt Lake City with remarks tantamount to a declaration of independence for the Mormon kingdom. Perhaps influenced by the hysteria of the times, Kimball asserted that he would "never be subject to them again—no never."

> Do you hear it? Do you think we will submit to them? No, never. They have cut the thread themselves. . . .
>
> We are the Kingdom of God; we are STATE OF DESERET; and we will have you, brother Brigham, as our Governor just so long as you live. We will not have any other Governor.[38]

The speech drew thunderous approval. When Brigham Young rose to the pulpit, he could do little more than offer his sanction to the course now laid before them. On October 18 Young declared from the Tabernacle, "We are free. There is no yoke upon us now, and we will never put it on again."[39] The unavoidable question now facing Young, however, was how the besieged kingdom could enforce its flamboyant claims.

Brigham Young was fifty-six years old at the onset of the Utah War. In actual fact, he did not appear to be the religious fanatic his enemies portrayed. "He shows no signs of dogmatism, bigotry or fanaticism," Richard Burton said of him in 1862. "There is a total absence of pretension in his manner, and he has been so long used to power that he cares nothing for its display."[40] But few men in Utah questioned the authority of the Mormon prophet. Brigham Young was riding the crest of power in 1857. The recent reformation had weeded out dissenters and solidified his power as never before. The millennial traditions of the people and the constant sabre-rattling of the anti-Mormon faction in the East kept Mormons sharply atuned to the leadership of the church. As historian Edward Tullidge recalled: "Great as Brigham Young was in the exodus of this people from their Egypt, his power seems to have found its culmination in the Utah War."[41] As an acknowledged prophet of God he wielded almost unlimited influence, and as territorial governor, he controlled the militia. Although the governor was accountable to the president, Young's overwhelming command of the Mormon people made his grip on Utah extremely tight during the early years of the territory.

In designing a plan to deal with the invasion threat, Young viewed the safety of the Saints as of primary importance. He believed it was impossible to introduce an army into Utah Territory without incurring hostilities,[42] and from the beginning he vowed to deny the federal troops entrance. But even if conflict could be avoided there were other reasons for keeping the soldiers out of the territory. Admitting a corrupt and wanton soldiery, as they were perceived, would be a serious blow to the aspirations of the Mormons. To allow the "heathen" to pollute and destroy the kingdom from within would be to forfeit its destiny as the kingdom of God, for the purity of Zion was essential. As Brigham Young affirmed, "With us it is the kingdom of God or nothing; and we will maintain it or die in trying."[43] The supposed immorality of the U.S. troops, asserted Mormon historian B. H. Roberts, was, in part, justification for Mormon resistance.[44]

Brigham Young's defense strategy was well matured by early August. The strategy was two-pronged. The primary plan would employ the Utah militia—the Nauvoo Legion—in an active but bloodless campaign of harassment. Ideally the army's advance would be halted by a series of delaying tactics. It was anticipated the army would be unable to reach Salt Lake City before the winter snow sealed off the mountain passes by annoying the troops in every way possible—stampeding the stock, burning off the prairie grass, destroying supply trains. If the army could be stopped for the winter, it was thought the public furor would subside to the point where a peaceful settlement could be effected. Should these tactics fail to bring the desired results, the legion was prepared to make a stand in Echo Canyon and at other principal entry points into the territory.[45] Large numbers of Mormon militiamen were engaged in fortifying Echo Canyon and patrolling the mountains east of the settlements as a corps of observation during the late summer and fall of 1857.

The lesser-known secondary plan culminated in the expedition to the White Mountain country the following spring. As a last resort a tactical retreat into the deserts or mountains, leaving behind nothing but scorched earth, would ultimately defeat the army. According to this strategy, should the Utah expedition force its way into the settlements, everything was to be put to the torch, leaving nothing of value, not even the grass, for the invading army. The citizens would then flee to preselected locations for resettlement while the Mormon troops fought a guerrilla war, taking advantage of the familiar narrow mountain defiles and wide, waterless deserts. It was thought the army, destitute of provisions, would be forced to retreat or seek quarter. Brigham Young frequently mentioned his willingness to "burn up and flee" should the situation make it necessary. Speaking to his followers from the Bowery on September 13, Young proclaimed:

> Before I will suffer what I have in times gone by, there shall not be one building, nor one foot of lumber, nor a stick, nor a tree, nor a particle of grass and hay, that will burn, left in reach of our enemies. I am sworn, if driven to extremity, to utterly lay waste, in the name of Israel's God. . . .
>
> Suppose that our enemies send 50,000 troops here, they will have to transport all that will be requisite to sustain them over the winter; for I will promise them, before they come, that there shall not be one particle of forage, nor one mouthful of food for them. . . .
>
> They might stay amid blackened desolation till they had ate up what they had brought, and then they would have to go back.[46]

Throughout the fall the Mormon prophet continued to reveal more of this strategy. On October 18, while claiming "we will waste our enemies by millions . . . and not a man of us hurt," Young admitted he was going "to prepare for the worst." "I want you to prepare to cache our grain and lay waste this Territory," he admonished the Saints in the Tabernacle,

> for I am determined, if driven to extremity, that our enemies shall find nothing but heaps of ashes and ruins. We will be so prepared that in a few days all can be consumed. I shall request the Bishops to see that the people in their wards are provided with two or three years provisions.[47]

The plan to desolate Zion, if necessary, was no secret. In fact Brigham Young believed that such a policy would wring sympathy out of the Eastern gentiles with positive results in the government's policy. Indicative of the church's attempts to reap public relations benefits from its defiant policies was the manipulation of Capt. Stewart Van Vliet. As an assistant quartermaster for the U.S. Army, Van Vliet was sent to Utah in early September to procure supplies and make arrangements for the arrival of the army. The captain was astonished, however, to find the Mormons anxious to resist the government troops and refusing to sell supplies. Young also used the captain's visit to make a public demonstration of Mormon solidarity on the plan to desolate the territory rather than submit to oppression. With Van Vliet seated in the Bowery, Apostle Taylor stood before the congregation and asked, "All you that are willing to set fire to your property and lay it in ashes, rather than submit to their military rule and oppression, manifest it by raising your hands." As might be expected, there was not a dissenting vote in the crowd.[48] Newspapers eagerly picked up reports of Mormon plans for scorched earth and guerrilla war.[49]

While Young was insisting that "we are fully able to defend ourselves, and that our enemies will not be able to come within a hundred miles of us,"[50] the Saints were being directed to mobilize and prepare to fire the territory. In the early stages of the war, the primary thrust of this alternative strategy was to secure the grain and keep a lookout for suitable locations in the mountains where it might be cached and the women and children safely hidden. Maj. David Evans, of Lehi, was instructed to

> Drop other business and thrash the grain, and secure it first thing. This is the first business to attend to. The time may come when we shall have to lay everything waste, and group into the mountains; therefore be prepared for such an event. . . .
>
> Find safe retreats in the mountains for stock as well as families, and cache some grain to learn how to do it so it will keep. . . .[51]

The Mormons faithfully patrolled the mountains and located places for grain caches. Joseph Fish, a Parowan resident, wrote that he went on two such expeditions. One exploring tour of four days in late August took him into the mountains west and northwest of his home. Again in early September Fish spent another eight days scouring the mountains northeast of Parowan, even penetrating some little-known country in the upper Sevier Valley and Otter Creek region.[52] By early April it had been learned at Fort Bridger that "large caches of provisions" had been secreted at the head of City Creek Canyon east of Salt Lake City, according to a *New York*

*Herald* correspondent traveling with the army.[53] Other reconnaissance and caching expeditions were dispatched throughout the territory.[54] But for all the time and energy expended on these
measures, the implementation of this alternative strategy was
deemed remote. Throughout the fall and early winter of 1857 church
leaders never failed to assert their confidence in the ability of the
Mormons to stop the army on the field.

As for the military campaign, the first step was to muster the
legion, arm it, and bring all units to full strength. On August 1 Lt.
Gen. Daniel H. Wells issued a communication to all district military
commanders officially notifying them of the invasion and ordering
all units to be held in readiness to march at a moment's notice to any
part of the territory to repel the enemy. "Avoid all excitement, but
be ready," read the instructions.[55] The strength of the legion was
reported by Adj. Gen. James Ferguson at 6,101 militiamen,
although early returns showed gaping holes in the ranks of many
units.[56]

By the time Captain Van Vliet arrived in Salt Lake City on September 8, preparations for war were well under way. Although the
captain attempted to allay the fears of church leaders by affirming
the peaceful intentions of the expedition, Brigham Young remained
unconvinced. He was suspicious of the army's "sealed orders" (a
reference to the president's failure to notify him of the existence and
purposes of the march), and he insisted that the expedition was bent
on the destruction of a peaceful religious community. No sooner had
Van Vliet departed than Brigham Young issued his now-famous
"Proclamation," bearing the date of September 15. The document
began: "Citizens of Utah; We are invaded by a hostile force who are
evidently assailing us to accomplish our overthrow and destruction." By virtue of the authority he still claimed as territorial governor, Young forbade all armed forces from entering the territory and
instructed the militia to maintain a constant state of readiness. Furthermore, martial law was imposed throughout Utah Territory.[57]
Copies of the document were immediately sent to every part of the
Mormon domain and beyond. Military commanders in Utah received the proclamation with a cover letter containing the "plan of
operations" dated September 16 and signed by both Daniel H. Wells
and Brigham Young. The instructions again referred to both of the
plans devised by the church. While military commanders were advised to be ready for "a big fight next year," the possibility of being

overpowered was also considered. In such an event, instructions were given to "desolate the Territory, and conceal our families, stock and all effects in the fastness of the mountains, where they will be safe, while the men waylay our enemies, attack them from ambush, stampede their animals, take the supply trains, cut off detachments . . . to lay waste everything that will burn."[58]

Young's proclamation and other events during the fall of 1857 had a tremendous effect on the growth of the legion. Col. William H. Dame, commander of the Iron military district, reported on August 23 he could field two hundred effective men with ample arms and ammunition. But his return of October 10 indicates the ranks of his regiment were almost entirely filled with 440 officers and men.[59] These returns, however, point out a serious weakness in the militia's readiness. While the number of troops in Dame's regiment more than doubled, there was no increase in amounts of arms and ammunition at its disposal.

To solve the problem of arms and ammunition shortages, a gunpowder mill was erected at Cedar City. Several men were "called" to the so-called "Saltpetre Mission" to mine the mineral from a recently discovered deposit in a cave in Washington County. Another powder mill was established in Provo during the winter and still another in Salt Lake City. A gun shop was erected on Temple Square that turned out about twenty revolvers per week. But the Saints' efforts to manufacture their own war munitions were inadequate. Five hundred revolvers were shipped into the valley from the church's colony at San Bernardino, and the Saints in Carson Valley sent 2,700 pounds of ammunition and "a large amount of arms." An additional $800 worth of war munitions was purchased in San Francisco and forwarded to Utah.[60]

Not all preparations in Utah were military. Church leaders, ever mindful of the value of a solid propaganda campaign, soon unleashed a tirade of vitriolic speeches apparently designed to inculcate a sense of duty and obedience. The campaign was unnecessary, however. Solidarity seems to have been the one commodity that the Saints were not lacking. Nevertheless, church leaders persisted with a series of anti-administration war sermons, many of which carried a violent undercurrent. "There is high treason in Washington," exclaimed Young on September 13, "and if the law was carried out it would hang up many of them. . . . And now, if they can send a force against this people, we have every constitutional and legal right to send them to hell and we calculate to send them there."[61] Heber C. Kimball cried from the pulpit: "Send 2,500 troops here . . . to make a desolation of this people! God Almighty helping me, I will fight until there is not a drop of blood in my veins."[62] The frequent result of such speeches was the intensification of the already high emotional state of the Mormon people.

The Mountain Meadows Massacre was a result of such emotionalism. Caught up in the unusually fervent war hysteria in the south, elements of the Iron County militia and a band of Paiute Indians massacred a large company of Arkansas immigrants encamped at the Meadows forty miles west of Cedar City on September 11, 1857. To the perpetrators of this calamity, this was but the opening round of a general conflagration they perceived as descending upon them. Ironically, the first blood of the Utah War was shed on a lonely meadow four hundred miles from the anticipated scene of conflict or the nearest enemy soldier. The massacre had important repercussions in the development of Mormon defense strategy.[63]

During the fall the Mormons commenced their military operations on the eastern front. By mid-October over one thousand men were in the mountains in Echo Canyon, and a force of three thousand was available within fifteen hours.[64] Later in the winter a standing army of one thousand mounted riflemen was organized and outfitted at a cost of one million dollars.[65] The Utah troops constructed numerous forts and breastworks in Echo Canyon, which was considered the primary battleground. The Mormon defenders contended their bulwarks were almost impregnable, but most soldiers of the Utah expedition were anxious to test them. After viewing the works at the conclusion of hostilities with the Mormons, one U.S. soldier claimed the Mormon defenses "resemble boys' play things more than fortifications."[66] And an officer of the expedition commented that Echo Canyon "could have been turned easily by 500 troops."[67]

Nevertheless, the fall campaign of harassment seemed to go well for the Mormons. Without the loss of a single man, Maj. Lot Smith's company burned three of the government's forty-one supply trains containing enough food to supply the entire expedition for three months. The Mormons were also successful in running off nearly 1,400 head of government cattle and driving them to Salt Lake Valley.[68] One U.S. soldier recalled the Mormons' tactics:

Every day when coming into camp they [the Mormons] would set the grass on fire, using long torches, and riding swift horses, so that before pitching tents we always had to fight fire. They destroyed so much of it that the animals had to be driven some distance to get feed. One morning, just before daybreak, they rushed through the camp, firing guns and yelling like Indians, driving off all our mules and horses, numbering about a thousand, and before we could get into line they were safely out of reach of our rifles. It was ten o'clock before we recovered our animals. They hovered around daily, watching and taking every advantage of us, feeling safe in their tactics, knowing our inability to cope with them, as we had no cavalry, while they had the swiftest of horses.[69]

To some extent the Mormons succeeded in holding the army at bay until winter could halt its further advance. Running off the government cattle and burning supply trains made some rations a bit scanty, to be sure. But the expedition's greatest enemies appear to have been its late start from Fort Leavenworth and the onset of an early winter on the high plains. Compounding these liabilities was Col. Edmund B. Alexander's conviction that the Mormons' fortifications in Echo Canyon were formidable. Despite the soldiers' later contempt for the makeshift defenses, they served their purpose well. Convinced that the Mormons had created a deathtrap in the canyon, Alexander spent what little time he had remaining before the first snow trying to bypass the canyon and enter the territory via Bear River far to the north.[70] Blundering its way northwest up Ham's Fork, the expedition became bogged down by impassable roads and an early snowstorm. Forced to retreat, the Army for Utah went into winter quarters in November near the burnt-out ruins of Fort Bridger, previously destroyed by the Mormons to keep it from falling into enemy hands.[71]

The trials of the soldiers were just beginning, however, as they faced a long, brutal winter on the high plains. Three thousand head of cattle died from cold and starvation in October and November with others perishing daily.[72] By November temperatures at Camp Scott, as winter quarters was designated, had dipped far below zero. Charles Scott, a U.S. soldier, wrote in his diary that the thermometer stood at minus sixteen on the night of November 7.[73] About this time the army received a temporary morale boost when Colonel (later General) Albert Sidney Johnston arrived with additional troops to take command of the expedition. Johnston was well liked by his men, but the soldiers were deeply disappointed by their failure to penetrate Salt Lake City in 1857. As the discomfort of the soldiers increased, their disappointment was translated into hate and bitterness toward the Mormons. After spending the winter at Camp Scott, a *New York Herald* correspondent wrote on May 22:

> If there is one thing that would please this little army more than another it is to meet the Mormons in battle array. For six long months they have been lying in these mountains of snow, subsisting on the flesh of cattle so poor that they could not live, hauling the wood they burned with their own hands through pathless snows, suffering all, enduring all, without a murmur or word of complaint, hoping only for spring and the time for revenge. The soldiers have already expressed their willingness to their officers, if there was not animals enough here to draw the batteries, to harness themselves to the guns, thus advance to fight the Mormons. Each man feels that he has been made to suffer, been wronged, been insulted, been dishonorably assailed, and longs to vindicate himself and pay back the account with interest. They wish to fight the Mormons not because the government sent them here, but from personal reasons the contest with them is individual.[74]

The Mormons were all too familiar with the soldiers' contempt for them, but they were confident God would not allow their defeat. The army's inability to reach the Valley in 1857 was seen by the Mormons as purely prophetic. So it was that John Taylor summed up the misfortunes of the Utah expedition: "Brigham Young has said, Stop, and they have stopped. Why? Because Brigham said so."[75]

# III

# THE CRISIS

In contrast to the dreary winter at Camp Scott, the winter of 1857 in Utah was one of the gayest ever seen. While the U.S. forces were suffering the cold and privations of their winter encampment, the Mormons called in their troops. Singing, dancing, and celebrations were everywhere. The Lord had heard the pleas of his children; while he protected his Saints, he was humiliating the enemy.[1] As the U.S. forces were lamenting sub-zero temperatures and scanty rations at Camp Scott on January 1, Apostle Woodruff addressed a large New Year's Day social gathering in Salt Lake City:

> The blessings which you are enjoying this evening are from the hand of God. We all should acknowledge the hand of God in all things. We have had to hew our necks to the yoke of tyrants and our persecutors in days gone by. The seen [sic] is past; the yoke is now upon the necks of our enemies in a measure. They have to stop East of the mountains in the snow while we have the privilege of living still in our homes. It depends on our conduct whether we still enjoy our own homes or have to flee to the mountains.[2]

Such was the feeling as the Saints enjoyed their brief flirtation with independence. Mormon contingency plans were laid, however; grain was secured, and the territory readied for the torch. But the Saints were convinced if they would but remain faithful, they would not have to flee. One thing was certain: Unless a diplomatic solution was struck, the Mormons were going to have to deal with the army when the spring sun melted the snow in the passes.

Shortly after New Year's a crack developed in the Mormons' defense shield. The breach threatened to alter the entire military strategy of the Mormons. On January 3 the California mail arrived in Salt Lake City,[3] and included was a communication from Jesse N. Smith to his cousin, George A. Smith. In this letter, dated at Parowan, December 27, a rumor was reported that "there are a party of 300 troops exploring the Colorado conducted by an old mountaineer who says there can be a more practical road made up the headwaters of the Virgin and down the Sevier than the one presently travelled."[4] The information had probably reached southern Utah by way of the Saints returning from the recently abandoned San Bernardino colony or from missionaries returning from the coast. The mail also contained the December 5 edition of the *Los Angeles Star*, which published an article about an expedition being conducted on the Colorado by the U.S. Army Topographical Engineers.[5] Lt. Joseph C. Ives was said to be commanding a steamboat up the river to determine the upper extent of its navigability. The party totalled 100 men, including fifty soldiers from Fort Yuma under the command of Lieutenant Tipton. Although the expedition was billed as a scientific one, it must have been viewed with suspicion by the Mormons. If steamers could be brought up the Colorado to the mouth of the Virgin River, the government could put soldiers within twenty-five miles of the California road (Spanish Trail) near Las Vegas on an all-weather highway at the southern entrance to the territory. The long Mormon defense perimeter might have to be extended, and in an area far from where the bulk of the army was presently garrisoned.

Reactions were mixed among Mormon leaders. The invasion from the south was a topic for discussion in a joint session of the Territorial Legislature on the following day. John D. Lee, a member of the House, wrote on the same day, "All hell is in commotion, government intends sending ten thousand troops by the south rowt and as many by the north rowt."[6] But if the Mormons were being outflanked by their enemies, Brigham Young did not seem overly concerned about it. On January 3, 1858, he told his followers in the Tabernacle that "I think we shall use this room yet for a few years to come yet I mean to be ready."[7] The threat from the south does not appear to have been taken seriously by the churchman for some time. Adj. Gen. James Ferguson wrote to Young on January 7 desscribing such threats as "idle."[8] Brigham Young took no official action for at least a month, when more credible evidence was received.

By midautumn word of Mormon participation in the Mountain Meadows Massacre leaked out and reached California. The indignation of the Californians was fierce. "The blood of American citizens cries for vengeance from the barren sands of the Great Basin," decreed the San Francisco *Daily Evening Bulletin* on October 27. "From this state alone," continued the *Bulletin*, "thousands of volunteers could be drawn, who would ask no better employment than the extermination of the Mormons at the call of the government."[9]

Many of the Mormons passing through California on their way to

Utah found it necessary to travel incognito for fear of their lives. Elder William Wall, who was returning from a mission in Australia, nearly became the victim of the California mob. Not until a noose was around his neck did a man step forward and prevail upon the mob to spare Wall, as he had not been in Utah at the time of the massacre. He was released. In another instance, it was only through the display of "a splendid double-barrelled shotgun, 3 revolvers, a good bowie knife, and a legging knife, all in sight" that the peace was preserved. "They looked very savage at me but said nothing," claimed Wall.[10]

While on the Mojave Desert in November, Wall made another suspicious discovery. On the 10th or 11th he witnessed the procession of the U.S. Army Camel Corps under the command of Lt. Edward F. Beale. Wall reported in Salt Lake that the "camels performed well in sand in crossing the desert but they were no account at all in mud."[11] Although it was not known in Utah what the Camel Corps was to be used for, it could only be viewed as an evil omen. Later newspaper accounts confirmed the use of the corps in the Utah campaign, but these reports came out too late to influence the decisions of Brigham Young in the days before the commencement of the White Mountain Expedition.[12] With rumors running rampant and communications cut to a minimum during the winter, church leaders were left to form their own conclusions about such events, often from fragmented or unreliable data.

Reports of the army plying the Colorado and experimenting with camels in the Mojave along with thousands of outraged Californians at their rear must have occupied the thoughts of Brigham Young to some degree, but he was not yet sufficiently alarmed, in this first week of January, to order troops to march south or even investigate the rumors.

The Saints in the south were not so sanguine about the matter. They were the ones who would feel the full weight of a southern invasion, and they were becoming uneasy. Reacting to rumors he picked up from the Indians, Jacob Hamblin, the well-known Mormon frontiersman and Indian missionary, acted on his own. Hamblin operated the Indian mission at Fort Clara in southwestern Utah and was well acquainted with the rugged southern country. It was probably here that he acquired the same information that Jesse N. Smith had forwarded to Salt Lake City in his letter of December 27. Accordingly, in December Hamblin sent two fellow missionaries,

Ira Hatch and Dudley Leavitt, to the Colorado River to ascertain the truth of the invasion rumors and line up the support of the Mojave Indians who lived near the Needles should the rumors prove true. Unfortunately, Hatch and Leavitt found the Mojaves in a hostile state, and the two missionaries barely escaped with their lives.

On January 17, near the Virgin River, Hamblin came across a company of explorers led by Mormon Apostle Amasa Lyman. Lyman, who had recently left his home in San Bernardino, was in the company of eight prominent Iron County men[13] and was in the process of returning to California to aid in the San Bernardino evacuation while making a reconnaissance under the direction of President Young to find "water and feed away from the present travelled road."[14] Brigham Young was apparently taking steps to avoid a collision between the Saints returning from California and any troops that might be on the road. Hamblin fully advised Lyman of the latest reports from the Colorado, and three days later the apostle reported the situation to Brigham Young:

> The Indians have brought us the news that the "Americats" are coming up the Colorado to kill off the Mormons and Indians. Of this we expect to learn more, as we intend, so soon as we shall return from the present excursion, (which we hope will not be longer than three weeks) to visit the Colorado and that portion of the country occupied by the "Hyatts" [Mojaves] with a party of twenty men and four missionaries, some, or all of whom we propose to leave there if circumstances are favorable.[15]

The Lyman party continued south and west along the line of the California road to examine the country. On January 31 Lyman arrived at the Mojave River where he met a detachment of U.S. soldiers under the command of Maj. George Blake. Blake had recently been in the Colorado River region with his men to escort Beale's Camel Corps through the Mojave Indian country. It was only by coincidence that Beale and Blake encountered the river expedition coming downstream on January 23 above the Needles. From them Blake learned of government intentions to penetrate the Mormon country from the river. In his meeting with Lyman, however, Blake took the opportunity to greatly exaggerate the real condition of affairs on the Colorado in an obvious attempt to boast of the army's success in the region and alarm the apostle. "He informed us that the expedition to explore the Colorado had been perfectly successful," wrote Lyman in his diary:

there was three steamers on the river, that another of 5 feet draught was to be placed on it in a short time, that they had ascended within 70 ms of the mouth of the Virgin, & that they expected to be able to reach its mouth with vessels of that draught. He also hinted that 3000 men w[ould] be sent up that way.[16]

Needless to say, Lyman was greatly shaken by this supposed confirmation of the evil rumors they had been hearing. As soon as possible the party began its return to Utah.

In the Las Vegas area on February 13, the Lyman party encountered an old friend, Col. Thomas L. Kane, of Philadelphia.[17] Traveling incognito as Dr. Osbourne for his safety, Kane was en route to Salt Lake City on his own initiative with the unofficial blessings of President Buchanan to attempt a mediated settlement of the war. At this point, Kane and Lyman separated themselves from their companions and made haste for the Mormon capital. It was a weary but unique twosome who rode into Salt Lake City twelve days later. One man carried the hope for peace, the other the key to the southern defense.

Actually, the threat of a strike from the Colorado was not as grave as the Mormons had been led to believe. While the menace indeed existed, the Colorado as an invasion route was highly impractical. The Mormons, however, could only react to the knowledge they had and conditions as they perceived them to be.

Originally the exploration of the Colorado was, as reported, a scientific expedition, having little to do with the Mormons. A contract had been awarded to the adventurous Capt. George A. Johnson, who operated two river steamers between the mouth of the Colorado and Fort Yuma, fifty miles upstream. Johnson longed to prowl the river's upper reaches, but before the approved funds arrived he discovered that a government exploring party had landed on the river in November 1857 and was making preparations to survey the Colorado under command of Lt. Joseph C. Ives. Apparently President Buchanan canceled Johnson's appropriation thinking it too expensive and decided to proceed with the Ives expedition.[18]

Insulted by the government action and fearing he would be deprived of the honor of being the first to navigate the upper Colorado, Johnson proceeded immediately to outfit his steamer the *General Jesup* and assemble an impressive group of scouts, trappers, and interpreters to accompany him up the river. The most notable of these was the old mountain man Powell "Pauline" Weaver, who had trapped along the Colorado for years and was well known throughout the Southwest. Weaver was no doubt the "old mountaineer" that Jesse N. Smith had written to George A. Smith about, who was said to be leading a party of 300 troops up the Colorado into the Mormon country.[19] With a detachment of fifteen soldiers from Fort Yuma commanded by Lt. James L. White, the 105-foot sidewheeler began its ascent of the Colorado on December 20. It was on the return trip, after reaching Cottonwood Valley, two hundred miles north of Yuma, that the expedition was discovered by Beale's Camel Corps, resulting in Major Blake's exaggerated report to Lyman eight days later.

With his steamer *Explorer* finally fitted out, Lieutenant Ives belatedly challenged the river on January 11 accompanied by a contingent of fifty soldiers commanded by Lieutenant Tipton. Although *Explorer* was slow, it was able to penetrate thirty miles closer to the mouth of the Virgin than Johnson's high mark. From Eldorado Canyon a skiff was launched and rowed as far as Vegas Wash, where a reconnaissance connected their navigation with the Salt Lake road just twenty-five miles to the north. Considering the expedition a success, Ives reported he had found "a practicable line of communications between the river and the Mormon Road."[20] Some work would be required to make it passable for wagons, but it was possible. The southern invasion route had been established.[21]

Mormons in southern Utah became convinced that the threat from the south was real. Their suspicions were confirmed when Hamblin returned to the settlements in March, having reconnoitered the Ives expedition as it lay in Cottonwood Valley. Alarmed by the steamers and soldiers ascending the river, the Mojaves had invited Hamblin and his missionaries to return to the Colorado. Fearing the government soldiers would drive them from their land, they now decided to make peace with the Mormons. Thales Haskell, one of Hamblin's party, actually succeeded in boarding *Explorer*, disguised as a California-bound emigrant, where he heard from Ives's own lips that he was "exploring the river to see if supplies might not be brought into Utah cheaper than they could be brought over the plains."[22] In addition, two of Hamblin's men discovered Ives's reconnaissance as it was linking up with the California road.[23]

Lieutenant Ives and Captain Johnson were both aware of the difficulties between the Mormons and the federal government before their expeditions got under way.[24] Johnson suggested this was the primary reason for the Colorado navigation. And Lieutenant White, who accompanied Johnson upstream, included details of the proximity of the Salt Lake road to their navigations;[25] although it was Ives who actually made this connection. The press was also of the opinion that the Ives expedition was, in part, a military expedition against the Mormons. It was not long before several such articles found their way into Salt Lake City.[26] In the final analysis, the true purpose of the Colorado expeditions was unimportant. The only significant information was that which reached the ears of Brigham Young, and in the winter of 1857–58 correct information was scarce in Utah.

On January 19 a group of Mormon missionaries arrived in Salt Lake City from the west coast. Included in this group were Apostles Ezra Taft Benson and Orson Pratt, who were returning from their missions in England. These men asserted that Utah was in immediate peril from the south or west. Gen Winfield Scott, himself, was said to be en route to California to direct the war movement from that point. They also brought word that the army had issued orders "for all the disposable force of the army to start early in the spring to reinforce Colonel Johnston's command," and that Missouri was offering volunteers to fight the Mormons.[27] The apostles, it was said, had to travel incognito to "keep from being taken up."[28] On January 24 these men spoke before the congregation in the Tabernacle. One Salt Lake City man wrote after attending services: "This morning I went to the tabernacle & heard E. T. Benson giveing a Journal discourse of his Mission. . . . the United States are now Shipping Troops of Soldiers round to Callaforia trying to come in on us from every side."[29] It was a dismal message.

The day following Benson's speech, Brigham Young wrote to Joseph Horne giving him instructions to proceed to southern Utah with a company of men to "find a location for a cotton farm at the junction of the Santa Clara and Rio Virgin Rivers."[30] Upon his arrival at Harmony, Horne was to consult with John D. Lee, who was to point out the location selected by Brigham Young. The cotton farm, like the Ives expedition, started out innocently enough. Young had spoken to Wilford Woodruff about getting up a company for the cotton country on December 31 with no apparent purpose in mind other than to grow cotton.[31] Nor is any other significance to this mission apparent from Horne's diary or Young's letter of instructions, with the possible exception that Young did "not want any others to settle where you do unless they are sent from this place for that purpose."[32] Future events, however, indicate Brigham Young may have been preparing for his abandonment of church headquarters in Salt Lake. It appears that John D. Lee was privy to some hidden motive Young had in founding the cotton farm at this time. After meeting with Horne early in February at Harmony, Lee recorded in his diary: "I started south according to my appointment to locate or Point out the location intended to be made by Pres. B. Young for a resting place for his famely & that of the 1st Presidency."[33] Apparently there was more to the "cotton farm" than meets the eye. The term "resting place," as used by Lee, had in the past been used by Brigham Young and other church leaders to describe a settlement place. Utah was often so denominated at the time of the exodus from Nauvoo.[34] Possibly during the January session of the legislature, while Lee was in Salt Lake, Young spoke to him about the possibility of the First Presidency going underground. Lee had been in conference with Young on the evening of January 4, the day after the ominous California mail was delivered to Salt Lake.[35] It seems probable that during his conference with Lee, Young confided his plans for a "resting place" and suggested the location, which is near the present city of St. George, Utah.

Lee's cryptic diary entry raises as many questions as it answers, however. Why, for instance, was Brigham Young considering the establishment of a "resting place" so near the supposed invasion route of the U.S. forces thought to be penetrating the territory from the Colorado? Or was the location merely to be a winter home for Young and his associates in the milder climate of the south? Brigham Young's actions at this time suggest a curious interest in the uninhabited regions of the territory lying adjacent to the established settlements. At a time when the Mormon kingdom's far-flung settlements were being abandoned and the settlers recalled to the Wasatch Front settlements, Young also began taking a serious look at Ibapah Valley in extreme western Tooele County near the present Utah-Nevada border. During the January session of the legislature Young was granted the sole rights to Ibapah on the western fringes of the Great Salt Lake Desert.[36] Shortly thereafter a company was organized to explore and settle the valley under Young's direction.[37] Does the Ibapah venture, undertaken at virtually the same time as the Rio Virgen enterprise, represent an alternative location for a resting place? Or was this the beginning of Young's focus on the southwest deserts as a place of refuge for the Saints? Large-scale exploration of the White Mountain country southwest of Ibapah Valley was ordered by Brigham Young during the following month.

Until now the church had put up a pretty solid front. From this time on, however, the pattern changed. An increasing doubt began mounting in the minds of church leaders, as every arrival and every mail brought more disturbing information for the Saints. One of the first to exhibit signs of doubt was George A. Smith, who declared in the Legislative Council on December 21, "If we carry out these resolutions we may prepare our necks for the Halter if they catch us."[38] Mormon leaders showed signs of receding confidence as the winter rolled on. Tabernacle speeches became less bold, and more emphasis was placed on alternative solutions to end the conflict. The people, however, never seemed to doubt the outcome.

On February 3 the California mail was again received in Salt Lake City. The news was grievous. Included was a copy of President Buchanan's message to Congress of December 8. Governor Young, he declared, had brought his people to the brink of open rebellion, and the hope of avoiding a military confrontation had vanished. As a result, the administration was recommending to Congress the raising of four additional regiments for Utah.[39] This confirmed Benson's report of two weeks before and made the southern invasion all the more plausible.

Comment on this latest turn of events was plentiful. Wilford Woodruff concluded in his diary that "the United States are determined to annihilate we mormons." And in an apparent mood of resignation, he added, "the war is now between God and the Devil."[40] Samuel Pitchforth of Nephi received the news two days before it reached Salt Lake City. On February 1 he wrote:

California mail came in tonight Brought a paper with Pres Buchannans message in it I learned that he recommends a large force to be sent to Utah and that would frighten the Mormons so they would give up without fighting. The news is that California has 10,000 men on hand to come against the saints and that 500 would fit themselves out—when I hear thease things I feel like saying O ye fools! how little do you know that your days are numbered. for Zions sons shall increase.[41]

The day after the news arrived in Salt Lake City, Woodruff met the mail carrier in Captain Hooper's store. Questioning him about conditions in the south and the possibility of an invasion from that quarter, Woodruff was informed that the last steamer to leave California had been given orders to "send 4000 men immediately on the southern route & 4000 men from Oregon and 2000 would start soon from the Missouri River and 2000 now at Fort Bridger would make 12,000 men."[42] Although the mail carrier had almost certainly fallen victim to the gossip that was then running wild up and down the California coast, it was disheartening news for the apostle.

Brigham Young now became aroused. While almost the entire Utah militia was concentrated on the eastern front, the territory seemed to be flanked on every side. Young fired off a letter to Amasa Lyman:

> Our enemies are still anxious to do us all the harm they can and may soon undertake sending in troops by the south route, for which reason you readily see the necessity for your being constantly on the alert. . . .
> You are probably aware, of this, that a Lt. Ives with a surveying party of some 100 men is about to proceed or is proceeding up the Colorado to explore it to its sources.[43]

Brigham Young's frame of mind on February 4 is illustrated by a letter he wrote to Henry W. Bigler and John S. Woodbury of Nephi the same day he wrote to Lyman: "The present administration has openly come out and is following the lead of Missouri and Illinois, determined to crush out 'Mormonism' by killing every man, woman and child that will not renounce it."[44]

Other disturbing letters were also included in the latest mail from the coast. Orson Hyde, the Mormon apostle who had recently returned from the now-defunct Carson Valley settlement, received a letter from one "Lucky Bill," an informant still in the valley. Hyde was warned that a company was then fitting out at Placerville "to come into our settlements for the purpose of robbing and plundering."[45]

The Mormons feared the California threat all the more because they were facing the federal army on the east. It was an uncomfortable situation and contributed greatly to their sense of isolation and encirclement. According to George A. Smith, "Our greatest danger lies in the people of California—a class of reckless miners who are strangers to God and his righteousness. They are likely to come upon us from the south and destroy the small settlements."[46] Perhaps it was this fear that prompted Albert Carrington, editor of the *Deseret News*, to reprint the following lines from the *Sacramento Age* on February 17, the same day he reprinted another article advocating the establishment of a southern invasion route by the Ives expedition:

> Some are saying that, were a call made in California for volunteers to fight the Mormons, a great many thousand could be obtained in a remarkable short time. We do not deny this, still we would ask those who talk so loudly, what they think would be the cost of the equipment and the march.[47]

Paranoia was settling in over Salt Lake City. Their enemies, it seemed, were closing an elaborate set of pincers. Mormon leaders saw themselves rapidly becoming surrounded, and this was not only their own assessment. Some members of the federal army reached the same opinion. Capt. Jesse Gove, of Johnston's command, wrote home on April 9 asking, "Where are they to go? Troops surround them on all sides."[48] There was no ordinary way the Mormons could win a fight against the odds they believed they were set against. Their sole refuge was their trust in God.

Brigham Young decided to take a defensive measure. On February 21 Young proposed to his close advisors "sending some men into the desert to look out habitation for this people and to plant some grain."[49] Young had not, as yet, lost all faith in a military victory, but with every passing day he became increasingly aware of the Saints' vulnerability. The searching out of the deserts, as proposed on February 21, was only a precautionary measure, like the caching of the grain and securing "hiding places" in the mountains the previous fall. But unlike these early safeguards, Young was now turning his attention toward the deserts rather than the mountains, and grain was to be sown, not cached.

Although military plans were being de-emphasized, the troops were still kept in readiness. Brigham Young was not one to burn any bridges behind him. He preferred to keep all his options open while he emphasized the various facets of his strategy. From this time forward, however, the secondary plans received increasing attention. The prophet was still convinced that the kingdom was on the ascendancy. In fact, he said privately on March 13 "that within 12 years he would say who shall be president of the United States."[50] But perhaps for the immediate future a re-evaluation was in order. God would certainly deliver his people, but how and when? Brigham Young felt he was the instrument through whom God would work his plans, but in the late winter of 1858 it was a heavy burden to carry.

From a position of security, if not outright jubilation, a few weeks before, church leaders had grown increasingly cautious. The mood in Salt Lake City was somber. Gone were the fiery speeches of last fall. It was a time to prepare to meet the enemy. But as the crisis peaked, it appeared the promises of fall would stand hollow and unfulfilled. Brigham Young was turning his attention away from a fight. Mormon strategy was in a transition stage. The salvation of the kingdom might not lie in a military victory after all.

As Brigham Young was proposing an investigation of the deserts to his close associates on February 21, George A. Smith began to prepare the people for the change. On the same day, Smith told the congregation in the Tabernacle "to be ready for all requirements that are made from the prophet of God."[51] His listeners had little idea what they were being prepared for; but the rain falling gently outside was a subtle reminder that spring would soon be upon them, and the federal troops would be on the march.

# IV

# SEBASTOPOL

The wheels of the White Mountain Expedition were beginning to roll. Two days after proposing the investigation of the deserts, Brigham Young sent letters of instruction to several of the ecclesiastical heads of southern Utah. These letters, dispatched simultaneously to Lewis Brunson, Bishop of Fillmore; Philo T. Farnsworth, Bishop of Beaver; Isaac C. Haight, Stake President of Cedar City; and Tarleton Lewis, Bishop of Parowan, were clearly written by the president of the church, not the governor, not the military—an indication that the church itself was assuming direct responsibility for the defense of Utah. Young wrote to Brunson,

Great Salt Lake City
Feby 23rd 1858

Bishop Lewis Brunson,
  Fillmore City,
    Dear Brother;
      It is our intention to send out some old men and boys to the white and last mountains to the west of the settlements and find places where we can raise grain and hide up our families and stock in case of necessity. It is our wish to have the brethren go prepared with teams, seeds of various kinds and farming utensils so as to have grain raised at these places the present season. You will therefore select a few men of the kind above suggested and in connection with Bishop Farnsworth who will do likewise send out a party of fifteen or twenty men to search out and make a selection of and location at such place or places as may be suitable for the purposes above mentioned. You will also select a few young and middle aged to go as explorers to pass about after having made a location to find other suitable places and report back.
    The brethren are particularly instructed to conciliate the Indians and secure their friendship taking pains to learn their language and exercise a salutary influence over them and whenever there shall be found a man who does not pursue this course towards the Indians he must be dismissed from the mission and sent back.

I remain Your Brother
in the Gospel of Christ
Brigham Young[1]

It was undoubtedly Young's intention to keep his most effective
men in the ranks of the Legion when he asked that "old men and
boys" be the principals of this expedition to the desert. In a letter
dated March 10 to Bishop W. G. Young of Big Cottonwood, Brigham Young made this policy clear. The bishop, who was then
organizing the company for settlement of Ibapah Valley, was advised to "let old men and boys be principally selected for this mission. . . . No one that is called to go in the standing army must be
selected. . . . "[2] This is a clear indication that Brigham Young's
designs for the White Mountain country did not, at this stage, su-
persede the military option. Nevertheless, Young's instructions to
the southern bishops foreshadowed a trend toward implementation
of the alternative strategy to "burn up and flee." Despite his assertion that the expedition to the White Mountains was only "in case of
necessity," Young wanted the grain planted in the desert oases in
time that a crop could be harvested "the present season." It was the
prophet's dual defensive strategy seen throughout the war but with a
new and pronounced emphasis on the alternative plan.

On February 25 Lyman and Kane arrived from the south and
went into conference with Brigham Young. Certainly Apostle Lyman informed Young of the gloomy picture in the south as painted
by Major Blake. Lyman's revelation no doubt served to darken the
already dismal scene and confirm earlier rumors and reports that
had found their way to Salt Lake City. The apostle returned to the
south in early March under orders to reconnoiter the enemy's advance up the Colorado and locate a defensive site where an effective
stand could be made.[3]

Brigham Young's discussions with Colonel Kane had a far more
serious impact on the outcome of the Utah War. Kane was no
stranger to the Saints. Since the Mormons had nursed the ailing
Pennsylvanian back to life at Council Bluffs, Iowa, in 1846, the colonel had become an outspoken advocate of Mormon causes in the
East. On numerous occasions throughout the 1850s, Kane used his
substantial political influence to come to the Mormons' rescue in
Washington. Besides persuading President Fillmore to appoint
Brigham Young to the Utah governorship in 1850, this unofficial
ambassador of the Mormons defended the Saints against the charges
of the "runaway officials" (that is, Brandebury, Brocchus, and Harris) two years later, and even took to the lecture circuit on their behalf. Early in 1857 Brigham Young wrote to Kane asking for his

assistance in countering the charges of Judge Drummond and to urge the cause of Utah statehood. Young's thorough attention to defense of the Mormon kingdom did not conclude with military preparations. The churchman was not about to assign the present conflict to providence until he had played every card in his hand, including his political ace—Colonel Kane. In mid-August Young dispatched Samuel W. Richards of Philadelphia to again enlist the aid of Kane. The colonel, however, found the administration in Washington in no mood to compromise on the Mormon issue. When December found the federal army in its embarrassing predicament at Camp Scott, Kane secured an interview with President Buchanan. Although Buchanan refused to modify his position, he did give the colonel a letter of introduction and permitted him to go to Salt Lake City to dissuade Young from resisting the army. The letter was not a license to negotiate with the Mormons; the president felt, under the circumstances, it was improper to negotiate with "rebels." Buchanan made it clear that Kane was not his spokesman —officially or unofficially.[4]

On the night of Kane's arrival in Salt Lake City, a meeting was called with the church's First Presidency and several of the apostles. Kane attempted to appeal to the Mormons' pride, asking them to "enlist your sympathies in behalf of the poor soldiers who are now suffering in the cold & snows of the mountains."[5] He requested and received a private interview with President Young. Although the exact content of the discussion is unknown, Kane apparently tried to persuade Young to make some conciliatory gesture toward Colonel Johnston. Roberts contends that Brigham Young flatly rejected Kane's proposals, telling the colonel he would take the counsel of no man "only as God dictated," and that since "he had been inspired to come here, he should go to the army and do as the Spirit of the Lord led him, and all would be right."[6] Other historians have felt that Kane went to Camp Scott with specific proposals from Young to end the conflict peacefully. Eventually, Young did concede to offer some flour and beef to the army.[7] Before leaving for Camp Scott on March 8, Kane spent his time holding numerous interviews with church authorities.

On the morning of Kane's arrival in Salt Lake, George A. Smith took the stage to Provo, forty miles south of the Mormon capital, and returned the day following. Although Smith's purpose in going to Provo is unknown, events indicate he may have been sent to inform the local authorities of the plans for the White Mountain district and to begin organizing a company from Utah County to participate in the expedition. Brigham Young's letters of instruction on this matter had only been forwarded to authorities in the south; yet the final composition of the expedition contained substantial numbers from Utah and Salt Lake counties. Instructions to these communities must have been delivered in person. George W. Bean, of Provo, wrote in his journal that it was about March 1 that President Young called him "to make up a small company & proceed to explore the Desert regions west of Fillmore and Beaver to find hiding places for the people to flee to."[8]

Smith's unusually quick return may have been prompted by the arrival of Lyman and Kane in Salt Lake City. As the pair had to pass through Provo on their journey north, Smith would likely have been aware of them. Shortly before Kane's departure for Camp Scott, the apostle returned to Provo where he spent six days meeting with local authorities. On the evening of March 6, Smith attended a council meeting of the principal authorities of the Utah Stake, where all the settlements of Utah County were represented.[9] From events that followed it seems likely that Smith revealed more of the plan to explore the White Mountains and to organize a company from the local settlements. The following day was Sunday. In the 6 P.M. meeting in the American Fork chapel the subject of the White Mountain Expedition was presented to the congregation by Bishop Harrington. Harrington had almost certainly been present at the council meeting with Apostle Smith the previous evening. Two men, David Wood and John Shelley, were called upon to represent American Fork on the desert mission. Contributions were then called for to support the undertaking. Ward members donated sixty-two pounds of pork, five pounds of beef, ten pounds of butter, and two shirts. The bishop's counselors, Mercer and Bournes, were assigned to see that the two would-be explorers were properly fitted out for the expedition.[10]

The American Fork pattern was probably repeated in each of the other half dozen major settlements in Utah County on or near the Sunday after the council meeting, according to the apostle's instructions. There were some who were called to the mission during the days that followed Sunday, March 7. Edson Barney, for instance, wrote that he received his call on March 10.[11]

The American Fork record is consistent with Brigham Young's

letters to the southern bishops in that the expedition was a church affair. Members of the expedition were called by their bishops, not by
their commanding officers as in previous defense strategies. Brigham
Young was moving to take direct command of the kingdom's
defense. In this time of emergency all resources were under the control of the prophet, and lines of separation of powers, usually hazy,
were becoming nonexistent.

On the evening of the big council meeting in Provo, a concurrent
event in Salt Lake City likely contributed to a change in the status of
the White Mountain Expedition. During the evening prayer circle
with the apostles on March 7, Brigham Young announced that he
had received a dream the night before which was described as
follows in the church annals: "Prest. Young said he saw this city last
night, in a dream placed upon high rocks, thousands of feet high,
men, women and children, with a river at the bottom full of brigs
and boats with our enemies in them, but they could not get to us."[12]
It is not stated whether this dream was considered to be a divine
revelation; dreams were often so regarded by church members. But
the fact that Young mentioned it and the historian recorded it in the
church records testifies to the significance attached to the remark. It
was at least an indication of where Brigham Young's thoughts were
leading him in the late winter of 1858. Less than two weeks after this
dream the plan to remove Israel to the desert sanctuary—the "high
rocks" beyond the enemy's grasp—became the primary defensive
strategy of the Saints.

As Lyman and Kane departed on their separate missions of pre-
serving Zion the following day, more gloomy news reached the city
—this time from the north. The Mormon mission at Fort Limhi,
near the Salmon River in present-day Idaho, was under siege by
hostile Indians. Two of the missionaries had been killed and others
wounded in the February 25 assault. It was reported that elements of
Johnston's command had been in the region inciting the Indians to
attack the mission. The church placed the blame squarely on the
government. When it was learned in Salt Lake City on April 3 that
another missionary from Fort Limhi had been killed, the church historian lashed out against the government calling the killing "another
result of American bribery among the Indians, who like congressmen have their price. A degrading move for a great nation to
hire the savage to murder because of their religion."[13] This was
grievous news indeed. If the army were really operating in the north

the enemies of Zion had actually succeeded in surrounding them, according to intelligence received in Salt Lake City. It may be significant that Brigham Young's tender of supplies for the Utah expedition was made within hours of receiving word of the Fort Limhi attack. Colonel Kane, having left the city for Camp Scott on March 8, the same day the dispatch arrived from the Salmon River, had to be overtaken by special express the following day.[14]

While Salt Lake was still reeling from the news of the Salmon River attack, another report of government bribery among the Indians reached the city. On March 10 a report came through that the Indians were preparing to take Echo Canyon, the key to the Salt Lake defense, and were holding it for Johnston's army.[15] A company of militia was immediately dispatched to the canyon. The rumor proved to be unfounded, but the incident serves to point out how vulnerable the Mormons were to such hearsay. Church leaders seemed at the mercy of such reports. Unfortunately, decisions had to be made before most of these rumors could be verified. In their zeal, the Mormons were overreacting to the threats they saw surrounding them on every side.

Throughout the campaign, charges of Indian alliances were hurled back and forth between the Mormons and the government. Although both sides officially prohibited such practices,[16] there is evidence that each party was to some degree guilty. Letters from Nauvoo Legion headquarters to district military commanders in August contained orders to "instruct the Indians that our enemies are also their enemies. . . . "[17] As we have seen, Hamblin, too, was attempting to form alliances with the Mojaves to aid in the defense of the Colorado country.

As for the government's involvement with Indian alliances, it is known that the day before the Fort Limhi attack B. F. Ficklin, a quartermaster agent for the army, had been in the region attempting to buy cattle for the U.S. troops.[18] Most of the Mormon cattle at Limhi were lost to the Indians and never recovered. Friendly Indians had also reported to the Mormons that the soldiers had offered to pay them $150 for every Mormon they could bring in and $1,000 for Lot Smith.[19] Whether true or false, these reports were the basis for Mormon opinion and they influenced the decisions of the Mormons. Blood had been spilled—Mormon blood—to them, confirmation of the army's evil intent.

One of the ironies of the Utah War is that, while the two opposing

armies faced each other across Echo Canyon, the only blood of the
war was shed by noncombatants on the periphery of the war zone.
No blood was spilled within hundreds of miles of Johnston's forces;
instead, the toll of war was paid by innocent bystanders at Mountain
Meadows and Salmon River.

March 18 was a cold and stormy day in Salt Lake City. At 2 P.M.
a "council of war" was held in the church historian's office. Present
were the First Presidency of the church, eight of the twelve apostles,
and thirty officers of the Nauvoo Legion.[20] The purpose of the council was to discuss defense strategy in light of the latest developments
and the alternatives and options available to them. Hosea Stout, a
member of the council, recorded the discussion in his diary:

> . . . The object . . . was to take into consideration the best plan of operations
> to be adopted to counter act the purposes of our enemies, whether to attack them
> before they come near us or wait untill they come near, or whether it is best yet to
> fight at all only in unavoidable self defense or in case a large force is sent against
> us this spring whether to fight or burn our houses & destroy everything in and
> around us and flee to the mountains, deserts &c &c &c It appears that the course
> pursued hitherto by Gov Young in baffelling the oppressive purpose of Prest
> Buckhannan had redounded to the honor of Gov Young and the Saints and
> equally to the disgrace of the president and his cabinet  Mormonism is on the
> ascendancy. If we whip out and use up the troops at Bridger will not the excite-
> ment and sympathy which is now raising in the states, be turned against us.
> Whereas if we only anoy and impede their progress while we "Burn up" and
> flee, the folly, the meaness of the President will be more apparent and he and his
> measures more unpopular &c. This is about a fair statement of the subject matter
> in council  There was no definite measure adopted.[21]

Although Stout admitted that no plan was definitely decided upon,
he was clearly infatuated with the plan to "burn up and flee. Apostle
George A. Smith, who attended the council, wrote on the same
date that it had been Brigham Young's plan "to go into the desert
and not war with the people, but let them destroy themselves."[22]
Young obviously had a change of heart since the stormy days of fall
when the prophet condemned the U.S. forces. Now he was trying to
persuade the church and military leadership that the future of the
kingdom lay in passive removal to the deserts.

The "council of war" was more of a formality than a strategy session. Young no doubt hoped to sell his plans at the March 18
meeting, but his mind was already made up. Three days before the
council, President Young had written to Bishop W. G. Young of Big
Cottonwood instructing him to defer settlement of Ibapah Valley for
the valleys west of Fillmore. Although Young cited Indian disturb-

ances in Ruby Valley as the reason for the change, the company from Big Cottonwood was now being directed to settle in the same region that the White Mountain Expedition had been instructed to explore.[23] By mid-March Brigham Young had already decided to begin settling the White Mountain country.

By the following Sunday, March 21, the prophet was ready to unveil his new defense plans and announce to the Saints his scheme of removal to the southwest deserts. The military option appeared futile, and Kane's mission seemed doomed. Kane himself believed that Young's decision to desolate the territory was made in anticipation of receiving more negative intelligence from him, noting that "the escort which accompanied me within 40 miles of Bridger having returned without favorable intelligence, or the mails which he [Young] expected."[24] Time, too, was becoming a critical factor. The snow had cleared up in Salt Lake City, and the morning sun was streaming through hazy skies as the Tabernacle filled for ten o'clock services. It was soon understood this was no ordinary meeting. At 10:15 Heber C. Kimball made a motion that the meeting be resolved into a "special conference" to transact business. The vote was unanimous, and Brigham Young rose to address the congregation. It was a remarkable speech, rich in insight into the mind of the prophet during this troubled period. Young began by carefully preparing the Saints for the reversal in strategy:[25]

> . . . The people now and for some years past have acknowledged the First Presidency to be their leaders, and yet there is not a man or woman in this kingdom, who has the Spirit of it, but what fully understands that it is not man that leads them, but it is the Lord Almighty who directs their movements through his servants. . . .
>
> We acknowledge that we are led by the hand of the Lord, and if he does not lead us we may expect to fall into the ditch. Now the question arises, what is the best policy for this people to adopt? We exclaim at once, it is policy to follow the Lord and his dictations. We acknowledge that, and that is what we wish to do; consequently, according to the best light and knowledge we are in possession of, we will tell you what we think the Lord wishes of us and his policy concerning this people. . . .
>
> The policy that I believe the Lord designs concerning this people we can learn by referring to several passages that are written and given to us for our instruction concerning the last days. The word of the Lord to us is, "I will fight your battles, said the Lord." He has done so, thus far; and he will do so, if we take his counsel. Although we have had to leave our homes several times, and a great many lives have been lost in consequence of the sufferings, yet the Lord has fought our battles. . . .
>
> I want you to understand that I am your earthly shepherd you must follow me, or else we shall be separated. . . .

Our enemies are determined to blot us out of existence if they can. . . . And as the kingdom of God grows, the enmity of the wicked will increase and extend broader and broader until we shall see the day when the whole wicked portion of mankind is as much opposed to us as any portion of them is now. "We are to be killed," is the constant feeling and cry of our enemies. "You 'Mormons' must be used up, or else you must bow down to the Christianity of the 19th century," say the world. . . .

## President Young then spoke of the futility of violent resistance:

Should I take a course to waste life? We are in duty bound to preserve life—to preserve ourselves on the earth—consequently we must use policy and follow in the counsel given us, in order to preserve our lives. Shall we take a course to whip our enemies? or one to let them whip themselves? or shall we go out and slay them now? We have been preparing to use up our enemies by fighting them, and if we take that course and shed the blood of our enemies, we will see the time, and that too not far from this morning, when we will have to flee from our homes and leave the spoil to them. That is as sure as we commence the game. If we open the ball upon them by slaying the United States soldiery, just so sure they would be fired with anger to lavishly expend their means to compass our destruction, and thousands, and millions if necessary, would furnish means, if the Government was not able, and turn out and drive us from our homes, and kill us if they could. . . .

. . . But let us begin a fight with the Government troops, and we shall have to leave our buildings and they will possess them, and I am in favor of leaving them before I am obliged to. . . .

Young's admission on this point is in extreme contrast to the extravagant claims of just six months before. Now Young was ready to drop the bombshell:

Where are you going? To the deserts and the mountains. There is a desert region in this Territory larger than any of the Eastern States, that no white man knows anything about. Can you realize that? What is the reason you do not know anything about that region? It is a desert country with long distances from water to water, with wide sandy and alkali places entirely destitute of vegetation and miry when wet, and small, scattering patches of greasewood, and it is a region that the whites have not explored, and where there are but few Indians. There are places here and there in it where a few families could live.

Four [three] years ago this spring we sent Bishop David Evans and a company to go to that desert, for we then had too long neglected to explore it. We wanted to plant settlements there in preparation for this day, for we have had foreshadowings and a promise of the scenery now before us. That company did not accomplish the object of their mission; they were absent a few weeks and went to the first mountain, but they did not go to the mountain where they were sent, and made no settlement. Now we are going to try it again.

Probably there is room in that region for 500,000 persons to live scattered about where there is good grass and water. I am going there where we should have gone six or seven years ago.

Brigham Young seemed to have great confidence in the region he was speaking about despite the fact that it was admittedly unexplored.

The transplanting of the gathering was no small task. The logistics of moving thousands of people into an unexplored wilderness hundreds of miles from the settlements would be enormous under normal circumstances, but the Saints now had to attempt it with an army at their heels. President Young continued his lengthy speech, giving the people some of the rudimentary details as he had worked them out:

> "When are you going to start?" As soon as this snow is off I am going to start part of my family. I am going to a place that I can say to our enemies, "whither I go you cannot come." . . .
> "How many are you going to call?" Only five hundred families to leave this city immediately, though more may go now, if they wish to. . . . "How can we go without provision?" We are going to send that. . . . We have enough [wheat] to load 1,200 teams, 40,000 bushels of wheat. . . .
> We want five hundred families to go south forthwith, and be ready to raise corn, potatoes, squashes, beans, etc., etc., this season. In these valleys we now have more grain in the ground than we know what to do with. Instead of planting the sugar cane seed here, plant it there, and you can make your sweet unmolested.
> I would cache window and door frames and casings, etc., and thus save all that we can; we may come back here. . . .

Brigham Young's decision to remove to the desert was coupled with the earlier threats of laying waste to all they left behind. No doubt, Young had been influenced in this decision by the siege of Sebastopol during the Crimean War in 1855. More than one reference was made to Sebastopol in this speech. In this famous battle, Lord Raglan had laid seige to the city of Sebastopol for more than a year. When its beleaguered Russian defenders realized the hopelessness of their situation, they burned the city and left it for the British. The Russian general who commanded the city recalled: "It is not Sebastopol which we have left them, but the burning ruins of the town . . . having maintained the honor of defense in such a manner that our grandchildren may recall with pride the remembrance of it."[26] Now Brigham Young was about to turn Salt Lake into another Sebastopol. Buchanan "has given orders to the soldiery to build a station 'at or near Salt Lake City' in Utah Territory," declared Young;

> those orders must be fulfilled, or both political parties of the nation are disgraced, so I am for letting them come and take 'Sebastopol.' . . .

No doubt some of the brethren will be a little surprised at this move, and think it hard. . . . You may ask whether I am willing to burn up my houses? Yes, and to be the first man that will put the torch to my own dwellings. . . .

The perplexing problem of dealing with a hostile army now encamped on their borders was also addressed:

Some of you may think I am imprudent in making these statements here, lest our enemies hear of them and start to come here before we are ready for them. If they do that, while we are doing all we can to get away, we shall kill the infernal scoundrels. They may have 'Sebastopol' after it is vacated, but they cannot have it before, according to my present feelings. . . .

If anyone sends out word that the army may come in, and that we are not going to fight them, send word at the same time that if they come in to annoy us while we are hastening away, we will send them to hell, God being our helper. . . .

Our Elders are willing and many are over-anxious to fight, and I also would be for killing, if I was crowded into a corner and could not back out. But I would sooner see this city laid in ashes, than to lose one good Elder.

The exodus to the desert was very possibly to have been of indefinite duration. While it is true, Young stated, "we may come back here," the implication was that we may also *not* come back. The proposed destruction of Salt Lake City and other settlements indicates the Mormons were serious about leaving the Wasatch Front permanently. Brigham Young told the people that they would soon have better homes and gardens than the ones they destroy. "The buildings I now have do not begin to satisfy me," he claimed. He also asserted that a trek in the wilderness would be good for the health of the Saints. Young then attacked those who would accuse him of misleading the people:

Many may say, "br Brigham, perhaps you are mistaken; you are liable to err, and if the mob should not come, after all, and we should burn up our houses and learn that the Government had actually countermanded their orders and that no armies are coming to Utah, it would be a needless destruction. . . . How easy it is for men to be mistaken, and we think a Prophet may be mistaken once in a while." I am just as willing as the Lord, if he is disposed to make me make mistakes, and it is none of the business of any other person. If a people do the best they know how, they have the power to ask and receive, and no power can prevent it. And if the Lord wants me to make a mistake, I would as soon be mistaken as anything else, if that will save the lives of the people and give us the victory. If you get such feelings in your hearts, think of what my conclusion on the subject is, and do not come to my office to ask me whether I am mistaken, for I want to tell you now, perhaps I am.

This fascinating policy speech was closed by saying, "I have opened the subject and will now sit down and let others unfold a little more.

My mind is too full this morning to come to close points. May God bless you. Amen."

The meeting was a long one. Heber C. Kimball, Daniel H. Wells, John Young, and Wilford Woodruff all took to the pulpit. Kimball said that in "ten days or two weeks he and his brethren would start a company for the desert, and told the brethren what course he intended to pursue."[27] Apostle Woodruff chided the Saints for their lack of faith and obedience, blaming them for the reversal in policy:

> How often have we been told by those men who lead us that if we would live so as to see eye to eye, we should never be moved out of our inheritances. If this people had the light of Christ in them, and could see and understand, I know there would be faith enough to hold that army at bay. Just as long as our hearts are on our gold and silver, our farms and our possessions, just so long will the Almighty scourge us, until we learn the important lesson that our religion is supreme over all things. . . .
>
> What is the value of our houses and lands compared to the Holy Priesthood and the Gospel of Jesus Christ? We are placed here, to maintain and establish the Kingdom of God, and with us it is that kingdom or nothing. This is the way I feel this morning.[28]

Brigham Young then rose a second time to address the congregation, presenting a few more items to the people. The Mormon prophet requested all those in the congregation who had never been driven from their homes to stand. Three-fifths of those assembled in the Tabernacle rose to their feet. "Now who will go first? Shall we call upon those who have been driven, or those who have not?" asked Young. "Shall I leave it to the congregation to decide, or shall I decide for you?"

"You decide!" came the voice of the people.

"I should decide that those who have never been pioneers shall be pioneers this time. . . ." That evening the bishops were to select about five hundred families from the class indicated to spearhead the new gathering. Brigham Young closed his speech with this timely warning: "Bishops and military officers, take due notice and govern yourselves accordingly; it is clear in the south."[29]

The course of action was now set. Unless Kane could perform a miracle soon, a tactical retreat into the desert wilderness was no longer a contingency plan—it was THE PLAN. The military would fight only a rear-guard action if required and possibly a guerrilla war for the preservation of the gathering; but no longer was active resistance a policy. If God would not give them a decisive military victory, he would at least overrule the situation for good.

Reactions to the change in policy were generally positive. Bishop Charles B. Hancock of Payson wrote to Young that there were several from his settlement who wished "to go as pioneers to the Desert should you deem it wisdom for them to go."[30] William Luck of Mill Creek seemed to have no reservations when he wrote, "I am engaged in making flour boxes and filling them and getting ready to leave for the desert according to counsel."[31] And Mary Ann Young, a wife of Brigham Young, philosophically declared on March 23: "I am in favor of leaving here without fighting. I am very comfortably situated, but I would be sorry to think that one good brother's life was lost in defending my home. I would rather leave peaceably. We shall be innocent & God will bless us with his holy spirit & we shall be happy on the desert."[32]

There were, however, a few who grumbled. Roberts noted that "it is evident from the amount of urging and defense that was made respecting the proposition that it did not at first meet with universal approval."[33] It appears that Apostle Smith, the outspoken church historian, was himself disappointed when he wrote on March 22: "The standing army of 1000 men has been fitted up with a riding horse and pack animal to each man with revolvers and rifles, all rigged for active service; when the Prests. counsel to evacuate Sebastopol without the consent of Lord Raglan appears in tomorrow's news."[34] But Smith had long ago resigned himself to do whatever he was called to do to preserve the kingdom. On April 5, just two weeks after writing the above statement in the church records, he penned this touching sentiment to Thomas B. H. Stenhouse:

> I have been driven from Missouri, where I left a good property and planted fruit trees for somebody else to eat. I passed through the same ordeal in Illinois. I preferred leaving my homes to renouncing my religion. The Government expelled me from Nebraska, although they were well aware of my intention to leave in a few months for the mountains; and I can go again and again, until death shall furnish me a quiet resting place, should our insane countrymen continue to trample the sacred rights of free men, guaranteed by the institutions and blood of their fathers, under their feet with impunity.[35]

Preparations for the abandonment of Salt Lake were immediate. Within twenty-four hours the church historian's records were being crated for the move south. The cut stone for the temple, then under construction, was cached, and the temple grounds were plowed up to cover the foundations with earth. As much as 20,000 bushels of wheat were hauled south. Even the press and type of the *Deseret News* was being made ready for the move, and by the time of General Conference on April 6, the Tabernacle was without its organ. So complete was the desolation of Salt Lake City to be that Brigham Young offered to purchase the buildings of nonmembers of the church, so they could be fired with a clear conscience.[36]

President Young's "Sebastopol" speech of March 21 went to the press immediately. By March 24 two copies of this speech were on their way to all the ecclesiastical authorities outside of Salt Lake City, and by the 31st the circulars were in the hands of nearly every authority from Cache Valley to the Rio Virgin.[37] A cover letter was included with the circulars with specific instructions, which varied depending on the locality. All orders were aimed at completing the exodus from the northern counties into the south as the first step towards resettlement on the deserts. The logistics of the evacuation would be tremendous, and Young knew everyone and every settlement would have to contribute heavily to bring it off successfully. President Young's letter to John D. Lee of Harmony is given in full:

> G.S.L.c.    March 24, 1858
>
> Elder John D. Lee
>
> Dear Bro. You will learn by the circular two copies of which are now forwarded to you, that the policy has varied somewhat from the past. Please loan the circulars to none except those who will faithfully return to you again & keep the policy at home. You will understand that we shall need many teams for the present movement, and we expect Washington county to assist us as much as they can conveniently, and to furnish covers & bows to the wagons they send to our aid, so far as they have them. You can begin to send teams here for families &c., as soon as the weather or roads are sufficiently settled. As we shall not plant or sow any more north of Utah county this season, you will also see the propriety of raising all the flax, sugarcane, California barley, corn, potatoes & other vegetable &c. that you are able to. It is at present expected to make Headquarters at Parowan for a time, when we arrive there.
>
> Your Brother in the Gospel,
> Brigham Young[38]

In other letters that went out that day, Bishop Brunson of Fillmore was told to expect families to stop "for a season" in Millard County. Young suggested they be settled at Cedar Springs (present-day Holden), the sink of Chalk Meadows, and Corn Creek (if Kanosh, the Ute chief, did not mind). Brunson was also instructed to plant an assortment of specific crops from the sink of the Beaver River to the mouth of the canyon.

Bishop Blackburn of Provo was informed that President Young's family would be located in his city, and two "large halls" would be required for them.[39]

The Saints north of Salt Lake were not required to move, as yet, unless they so desired. Chauncy West was sent north to ascertain the feelings of the "ecclesiastical, civil, and military" officers of that region. Although Young told them they were at liberty to stay if they wanted to do so, he suggested that it would be wise to move "towards the desert," since the army would be "between you and us" when they came in and occupied Salt Lake.[40]

In all the letters that went out on March 24, Young requested that the circulars be kept secret. Apparently, he was trying to keep the army from knowing his intentions. The move south could not be kept a secret, but perhaps the ultimate destination and other particulars could be hid for a time. It is worthy of note that while the prophet was speaking on the 21st, he declared his intention to prohibit anyone from going to the army. This, he said, included the teamsters who had left the army and come into the city during the fall. While they had professed a desire to go on to California, some were now desirous of returning to the army, and Young suspected they might be spies. "They have the privilege to go from the Territory, but not to go back to the army," was the prophet's declaration. Until now, families who wanted to go over to the army had been at liberty to go, and had even been helped. "That has been the word all the time, until now," affirmed Young; "but now it is, they can not go."[41] Clearly, an attempt was being made to keep the army ignorant of various particulars of the big move. Even the *Deseret News* carried only a few lines about the policy change, and they were veiled in the Sebastopol symbolism. The article was captioned "Uncivilized Mode of Warfare."

> At a special conference held in the Tabernacle in this city, on the 21st inst., it was unanimously agreed to abandon "Sebastopol" to our enemies without the consent of Lord Raglan, if they persist in carrying out the unconstitutional policy adopted by the present administration.[42]

It seems preposterous that President Young would announce his plans to a packed assembly in the Tabernacle, and then attempt to keep his remarks a secret. From what was actually said in the speech, the exact location of the desert oasis was still a mystery. Brigham Young himself did not know the precise location. It was only to the southwestern desert regions that reference was made. To the listener in the know, the best clue to the ultimate destination of the Saints was the reference to Bishop David Evans's expedition of 1855 which was sent to the White Mountains. One familiar with

Evans's explorations would have a good idea of the country Young was now considering for settlement. As will be seen, this clue was lost to most people both inside and outside of Utah.[43]

The circulars did not stay confidential for long. A party of Mormons arrived in San Bernardino on April 20 who had seen the document, and the story was picked up by a San Francisco correspondent to the *New York Herald* and published by that paper on May 31.[44] Even the week before, the *Herald* was printing articles written by correspondents with Johnston's army at Camp Scott proclaiming the Mormons were abandoning their homes for the "White River Mountains" or the "White Mountains, near the borders of New Mexico."[45] It appears that first intelligence of the new Mormon policy reached the army by way of William Gilbert of the firm of Gilbert & Gerrish, gentile merchants from Salt Lake City. Gilbert had witnessed the exodus going south as he was coming up from California. When he reached the army on April 9, he reported that he had left Salt Lake City on the last of the month and it was then being evacuated at a rate of one hundred wagons per day. "The Mormons," he explained, "are leaving the valley and going to the White Mountains."[46] Although the term "White Mountains" was not used in Young's "Sebastopol" speech, Gilbert had apparently received the correct information. It was a luxury not shared by many.

The prophet's efforts to mask his intentions worked for only nineteen days. After the news reached the army, a flurry of letters was sent east by newspaper correspondents traveling with the Utah expedition. The result was a corresponding profusion of articles about the new Mormon policy in the national press. Most of these reporters were ignorant of the Great Basin geography and the location of the White Mountains, but occasionally a correspondent would accurately identify the destination of the Mormons. A writer employed by the *Washington Union*, who claimed to have "lived among the Mormons for a year, and knows the habits of the people," described the White Mountain region with fair accuracy:

> This district of country is situated in the southwestern portion of the Territory of Utah, bounded on the west by the Sierra Nevada Mountains, on the north by the Humboldt River Mountains, on the east by the Desert and the southern spurs of the Goose Creek Mountains, on the south by the Sierra Nevada and the intervening spurs of the great Sierra Madre Mountains. This throws them about six hundred miles further into the mountain fastenings of the continent, in the midst of the richest gold district on the pacific coast. By this movement they hope to allay the apprehensions of the Government and public at large, while they will

push forward with redoubled force and energy their schemes of immigration, colonization, and accumulation of native wealth and munitions of war.[47]

Despite the article's generally correct assessment of the White Mountain geography, it was only one of a flood of speculative articles which had the Mormons leaving their homes for sanctuaries from Sonora to Alaska.

Brigham Young's attempt at secrecy was doomed almost from the beginning. It was all but impossible to keep such a massive plan contained. The White Mountain Expedition itself remained obscure, however. The trails of the explorers were never publicly revealed, and later journalists could only guess at where the Mormons had been. In 1859 an article appeared in the *Atlantic Monthly* which illustrates this point.

> Long wagon-trains were sweeping through the city every day, accompanied by hundreds of families, and droves of horses and cattle. . . . What was its object and what its destination are still mysteries; but it was probably directed toward the mountain-ranges in the southwestern portion of the Great Basin, of the topography of which region—hitherto unvisited by Federal explorers—the Mormons undoubtedly possess accurate information.[48]

Shortly after Brigham Young's circulars were received, teams began to roll into Salt Lake City from all the outlying settlements ready to take the residents south. Within a week, the exodus was well under way. On April 1, Brigham Young and his family abandoned Salt Lake City.

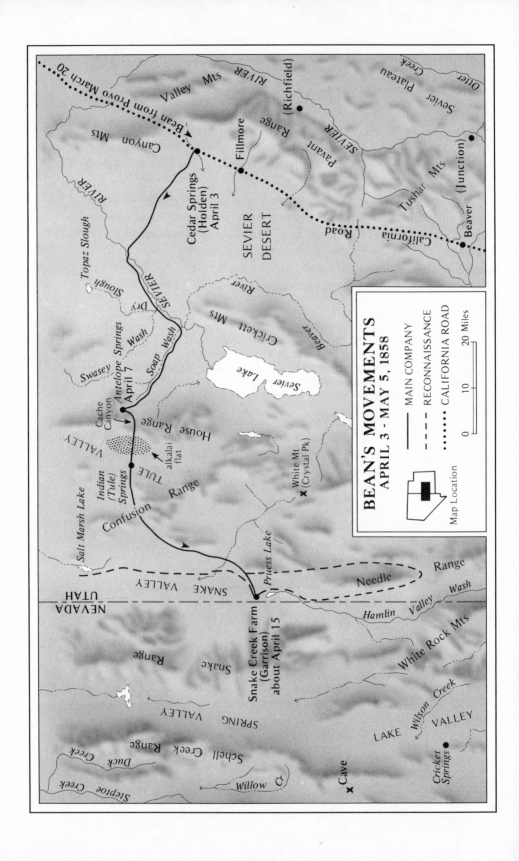

BEAN'S MOVEMENTS
APRIL 3 - MAY 5, 1858

MAIN COMPANY
RECONNAISSANCE
CALIFORNIA ROAD

0    10    20 Miles

Map Location

# V

# TO THE WHITE MOUNTAINS

There was only one preparation that had not been made. The Saints who were rapidly emptying Salt Lake City had no place to settle! The desert oases had not yet been discovered. Brigham Young was painfully aware of the problem, and on the day of his famous "Sebastopol" speech, he fired off a letter to George W. Bean whose party had just begun to march south from Provo. Bean's previous instructions had been to find suitable places for settlement "in case of necessity," but the tenor of this latest communication was decidedly more urgent. In this letter he told Bean:

> As soon as you get on to the Desert, to a place suitable to stop for a season, I want you to send word immediately to the [Cedar] springs or to Fillmore [illegible] how many more can go besides those who have already started. We are about starting onto five hundred families from this city who will leave in a few days also bound for the Deserts as soon as the present storm is over.[1]

For the next few weeks, at least, George W. Bean and the White Mountain Expedition carried the hope of salvation for the Mormon kingdom.

Brigham Young seemed to think that the desert sanctuary could be found very quickly. This thought was also reflected in Heber C. Kimball's March 21 speech in which he stated, "in ten days or two weeks he . . . would start a company for the desert." In this, the church leaders were greatly disappointed, for they had considerably underestimated the time necessary to locate the place of refuge. The Saints were crowding into the settlements of Utah County and southward waiting for instructions, but there was nothing to tell.

According to Bean, he had been chosen to lead the expedition by Brigham Young himself.[2] The choice of George W. Bean was an excellent one, as he was extremely qualified for the task. Although Bean was just twenty-six at the time of this call, he was already a proven veteran and an accomplished Indian interpreter, explorer, and guide. Born on the western Illinois frontier in 1831, he came to Utah at the age of sixteen with the pioneers of 1847. Two years later

he settled at Fort Utah (later Provo). Bean was strong and ambitious. His six-foot four-inch frame offered a commanding appearance. But at the age of eighteen, a near fatal accident changed
his life forever.

During a military exercise at the fort, a cannon exploded sending
hundreds of wood and iron fragments into his body. His left arm was
shattered and had to be amputated 3½ inches below the elbow
which, according to Bean, "left a useful stub." Although he was now
handicapped, he proved to be no invalid. He soon realized he would
probably never be able to compete as a farmer, and he accepted the
situation. During his long convalescences, therefore, he spent much
of his time studying the Indian languages, the Utes who hung
around the fort being his teachers. Although he had little formal
education, he could soon speak the Ute dialects with fluency. In a
short time, he gained a reputation as an interpreter and scout and
was frequently employed by the federal government, the territory,
and the church. He was a member of an expedition to the Uintah
Basin in 1852, and his services as an interpreter were used extensively during the Walker Indian War of 1853–54. In 1855 he was the
chief interpreter at the Gunnison massacre trial. Later in 1855,
Bean, along with Orrin Porter Rockwell and others, was employed
by Col. E. J. Steptoe to explore the Great Salt Lake Desert to locate
a more direct wagon route to California. Upon his return, he was
called by Brigham Young to the Las Vegas Indian Mission as a missionary to the Southern Paiutes. With the abandonment of the mission in 1857 and the outbreak of the Utah War, Bean was assigned,
with Oliver B. Huntington and Peter W. Conover, to bring in the
Carson Valley Saints, crossing the desert on Huntington's trail of
1854. George W. Bean was the logical choice to lead the expedition
to the White Mountains country. He knew the desert, he knew the
Indians, and he was fiercely dedicated to his religion.[3]

Another prominent member of the expedition from Provo was Edson Barney. Barney was fifty-one years old when he was called to the
expedition. The upstate New York native had joined the church in
1831 and was a survivor of the Missouri and Illinois persecutions.
Barney came to Provo in 1852 where he had recently served as a captain in the Nauvoo Legion. Like Bean, he was also a veteran of the
Las Vegas Indian Mission and was well qualified for his latest
assignment.[4]

Other prominent men to go from Provo were David E. Bunnell, a

Fig. 2. George W. Bean. *From Autobiography of George W. Bean.*

forty-nine-year-old New Jersey native, and Dr. John Riggs. Riggs was originally from Connecticut, coming to Utah in 1851. During the Walker War, he served as a captain and surgeon in the militia. For the past five years, he was the president of the Sixth Quorum of Seventies, a Mormon priesthood group, in Provo.

The Utah County men were augmented by a small company from Salt Lake City who had left the city on March 10.[5] The entire force, estimated to be about forty-three men, departed Provo under clear skies on March 20.[6] Their immediate destination was Cedar Springs (the present site of Holden, Utah), where they were to rendezvous with contingents of the expedition from the southern settlements before pushing across the western deserts.

It was on the following day, as they were camped on Summit Creek (Santaquin), that President Young's urgent message reached them. Bean now realized the gravity of the situation, and he hurried his men off toward their rendezvous in the south. Cedar Springs was one hundred miles below Provo, and the roads were in poor condition from recent heavy storms. Three feet of snow had fallen in the south during the previous week,[7] and three more inches had been laid down the day before leaving Provo. Notwithstanding the deep snow and mud, Bean kept his men sloshing through the quagmire toward their rendezvous. It took the party one full week to reach Chicken Creek (present-day Levan) with their heavy wagons, a distance of only sixty miles. Here they found dry ground and feed for the tired animals.[8]

Brigham Young, thinking the company was still standing by at Summit Creek, dispatched another letter to Bean on the 24th. In light of his urgent plea of just three days before, this letter seems somewhat difficult to justify. Young wrote: "Owing to the state of the weather and the condition of the roads, and other plans of which you will soon learn, it is deemed best for all to return to your several homes and get your families and move them up to where you now are, and let those who may have no families also return and assist those who have families, if any such assistance is necessary."[9] Perhaps Young felt the evacuation of the city was more important than finding the sanctuary at the present time, or that the time could be better spent in helping with the exodus than floundering over useless roads. Perhaps, too, there was an emergency brewing in Salt Lake. Rumor was spreading that Johnston might attempt to force Echo Canyon earlier than had been anticipated. It was this fear that prompted the officers of the Nauvoo Legion to hold a council in Salt Lake on March 29.[10] Maybe the evacuation of Salt Lake City could wait no longer. On April 5, two thousand Mormon militiamen were ordered to march east in the morning to meet the imagined threat.[11]

It is only speculation that the "other plans" mentioned in Young's letter to Bean were the same as those described above; yet it would seem likely that if Johnston's force appeared threatening, Young would hasten the exodus in every way possible—perhaps at the sacrifice of the White Mountain Expedition. As Brigham Young declared on April 3, he was "determined to place the women and children of this people in a position that the men can defend them."[12]

When Young's letter finally caught up to the expeditionary force on Chicken Creek, it caused a division in the camp. Bean knew that they had proceeded much further than Brigham Young was aware of. They had struggled through deep snow and mud and were now camped within forty miles of their rendezvous with the southern half of the force. He considered it best to go on to Cedar Springs as planned and thought that if President Young had been informed of their whereabouts he would certainly approve. As he explained to the prophet in a return letter on March 27: "The way that I feel on the matter is that you think we are yet lying by at Summit but knowing the anxiety that you have in relation to this exploration going on we pushed out in deep snow through Juab Valley."[13] But others in the camp saw it differently, and about half of them refused to go on, making preparations to return to Salt Lake City.[14] The aura of the prophet weighed heavily upon them, and they could not consciously disobey his orders. Because of this, the company remained at Chicken Creek until the express rider returned with official clarification, which was, as Bean knew, to proceed. This delay cost the expedition several days of valuable time.

The company finally arrived at the rendezvous point on March 31. Cedar Springs was actually a tiny settlement consisting of a small fort, fifty yards square, and a few families.[15] Upon his arrival, Bean wrote a report to President Young explaining their location and the organization of the company. He also related that an evil influence seemed to be upon them: "Many small accidents have happened unto us since we started," Bean explained, "& I have sometimes thought that the Evil one was laying every obstacle in our way for to prevent the accomplishment of our mission."[16] Such was the importance attached to the expedition, that the devil would attempt to stop it in every way possible. Little did Bean know that his severest trials were yet to come. Bean also asserted in this communication that he believed he would be able to report the discovery of the desired sanctuary within two weeks, a gross underestimate of the desert country they were about to penetrate.

Soon after reaching Cedar Springs, two companies from Iron County joined forces with Bean, who was somewhat surprised to see the men from settlements so far south. The Parowan company consisted of twelve men under the leadership of Orson B. Adams. The New York State native was forty-three years old at the time of this call. He had been through the persecutions in Nauvoo, and was a veteran of the famed Mormon Battalion during the War with Mexico. Adams was an original pioneer of Parowan in 1851, and had served there as an officer in the legion. Currently, he was serving as first counselor to Bishop Tarleton Lewis. Also conspicuous among the twelve Parowan men was Urban Van Stewart, a pioneer of 1847, formerly of Tennessee. Stewart was also a member of the Nauvoo Legion. The company departed Parowan on March 26.[17]

The sixteen-man Cedar City contingent arrived at the Springs on April 1 with eight wagons (four with ox teams and four with horses), twenty head of oxen, and eighteen head of work horses and mules.[18] The company was commanded by Charles C. Hopkins who, like Adams, was a veteran of the Mormon Battalion. He was presently serving in one of the Cedar companies of the legion and was alleged to have had a hand in the Mountain Meadows Massacre during the fall.[19] Also among the Cedar brethren was John Woodhouse who had recently been involved with the "Saltpetre Mission" to produce gunpowder for the Mormon troops.[20] Young's letter of February 23, in which he ordered the exploration of the White Mountains, did not reach Haight at Cedar City until March 10, having gone out in the Deseret mail rather than by express.[21] On the 24th Haight was able to report to Young that the company was fully organized and on its way. The men had started for the rendezvous on March 21. Haight mentioned that four members of the party were men returning from San Bernardino who were on their way to Lehi. Unfortunately for them, their stopover in Cedar City won them a trip to the White Mountains. Haight also reported that Lyman had arrived in Cedar City and intended to start for the Colorado River on March 29.[22]

Bean waited three days at the Springs for the Fillmore and Beaver companies to arrive, but the Iron County men had brought word that these companies were still a few days back. It was therefore decided to pull out on the morning of April 3, whether they had arrived or not. The lagging companies could catch up later. Bean explained the move to Young in a letter written on April 2: "I knew that you wanted to hear from there immediately and our guides thought we could gain a few days & also it would make it more convenient about camping at the small springs on the route."[23]

The guides spoken of by Bean were two Pauvan Utes from Kanosh's band. One was Mashoquab, the Pauvan war chief;[24] the other is unknown. Although Mashoquab has carved out a niche in history for himself by wreaking vengeance at the Gunnison massacre, he was a valuable guide. As recently as 1857 he had guided the Webb party to Snake Valley, where, through an act of bravery, he preserved the lives of Webb and his companions from a band of hostile Snake Indians who sought to kill them.[25]

Bean knew that his combined force would total over one hundred men. Consequently, he organized the expedition into two companies. The first company consisted of the horse and mule teams, while the ox teams would follow in the second.[26] This would make traveling easier and allow the Fillmore and Beaver companies to overtake the rear elements of the force with less difficulty. The second company was placed under the command of Edson Barney, but command of the first is in question. It would seem logical that Bean would command the advance elements of his own expedition, and this is the inference in his April 2 report to Brigham Young. Orson B. Adams wrote, however, that his company was commanded by Captain Miller of Nephi.[27] Unless Miller was in charge of the first company, his inclusion in the expedition leadership is unclear. He is not referred to in any of the other known accounts of the expedition, nor was there a company from Nephi present. Miller may have joined the Provo–Salt Lake company as it marched south through Juab County. Perhaps Adams simply confused Miller with Bean. Miles Miller of Nephi was an old Mormon Battalion comrade of Adams's and Hopkins's from Mexican War days.

The expedition was as well equipped as it was officered. With all its combined elements, the company possessed fourteen horse and mule teams, about thirty ox teams, and a large number of heavy wagons.[28] They also carried farming implements and seeds of every kind. Believing they would soon have to accommodate the people of

Salt Lake City, they were well aware that these seeds would have to be in the ground at the earliest opportunity.

At last the expedition was underway. Bean pulled his force out of Cedar Springs on the morning of April 3, and commenced a north-west march across Pavant Valley toward the Sevier River, twenty-five miles distant. Skirting to the north of Clear Lake, the companies penetrated the Sevier Desert and reached the river late on the second day. A camp was struck on the south bank near the present site of Deseret, Utah. Swollen by recent heavy storms in southern Utah, and with treacherous beds of quicksand straddling its banks, the Sevier proved difficult to cross. On April 5 a ford was located and the crossing effected. While the horse and mule teams continued down-stream in the direction of Sevier Lake, Barney's ox teams made a temporary camp on the north bank, allowing the former company to gain nearly a day's march on them. Some of the men used the respite to catch up on their washing.[29] Near the river, two horses were discovered roaming freely on the range with bells tied to their necks. Their owners, for the time being, remained a mystery.[30]

From the crossing of the Sevier, the two companies continued downstream about fifteen miles to where the river makes its southern bend to enter Sevier Lake. The expedition was now in the vicinity of Soap Wash, normally a dry streambed, but with the recent heavy storms, it was probably wet, perhaps even flowing. Soap Wash offers drainage to the eastern slope of the House Range, twenty-five miles to the northwest, as it descends a gentle decline across the desert to the Sevier River. After camping near the confluence of the two water-courses, Bean turned his expedition up Soap Wash toward a pass in the House Range. These mountains, known to the explorers as West Mountain Range,[31] were a formidable barrier at first view. The near perpendicular cliffs could be traversed in only a few places. Bean chose to make the ascent at Dome Canyon Pass, which had also been Evans's choice in 1855.[32]

The land that lay between them and the pass was a most desolate stretch of desert waste. Vegetation was extremely sparse in this region and consisted mainly of scrubby sagebrush. In places there was no vegetation at all for considerable distances. The soil was sandy with alkali patches scattered across the surface. James W. Bay of the Cedar City company recorded in his journal that for miles in this vicinity there was "no[t] a spear of grass to be seen."[33]

Up the long incline from the Sevier River the two companies

Fig. 3. The Sevier Desert near Antelope Springs, Millard County, Utah. *By author, June 1979.*

Fig. 4. The alkali flats of Tule Valley, Millard County, Utah, looking east toward House Range. George W. Bean's company crossed the valley at this point. *By author, June 1979.*

made their way to the base of the mountains. Two days behind them, the Fillmore and Beaver companies were following in their tracks. At the foot of 9,678-foot Swasey Peak, Bean's force discovered the refreshing Antelope Springs, finding good grass and water "for small companies." Here among the foothills of the imposing House Range, the advance company established a camp for the night of April 7. This place offered a commanding view of the desert they had just crossed. Almost due south the Sevier Lake was plainly visible, the sun glinting off its pure white alkali beds and thin sheet of water. To the southeast the shiny, snow-covered peaks of the Wasatch Range dominated the view.

On the morning of the 8th the advance company began its long, winding ascent up the slopes of the House Range to Dome Canyon Pass, while the ox teams commenced moving up to Antelope Springs. Bean called the pass Cache Canyon, probably because the company cached some provisions there, although his letters and reports are silent on the matter.[34] It was here in the canyon, according to one contemporary account, that the owners of the horses picked up on the Sevier were located. As they marched across the valley the previous day, it had become evident to the explorers that a great storm had swept through the region. Wagon tracks, too, were discovered wandering aimlessly across the desert. On the slopes of Dome Canyon Pass the tracks dead-ended at a grisly scene, as the explorers happened upon the burnt-out ruins of the wagon with four human skeletons lying nearby. The men theorized that the four travelers, whoever they were, were caught in a blizzard, burning their wagon in a desperate but unsuccessful attempt to withstand the storm's fury.[35] The scene now confronting our White Mountain explorers appears to have been a harbinger of approaching evil, for within hours the expedition itself encountered a deadly blizzard.

With Bean and the advance company on the summit and Barney's ox teams at the springs below, the expedition was assailed by what Bean called, "the roughest snowstorm it was ever my lot to meet." And again alluding to the Evil One, he asserted: "It seemed that an opposing power had got into our path trying to prevent our further progress." Caught in the open, the men "got into any shelter possible" and waited out the storm, which lasted twenty-seven hours. Some of the men dug holes in the ground "to shelter and save themselves." Raging winds tore the wagon covers to strips, and cattle were driven forty miles before the storm. Six horses and a cow were lost, some of which had been driven to the edge of a high cliff where they fell to their deaths.[36]

Barney's company at Antelope Springs fared little better. Bay noted that twice during the night he had to drive his cattle back from the desert until he finally chained his three yoke of oxen down. In the morning the snow had drifted as high as their backs, but he did not have to hunt them down. He did have the misfortune of sleeping in cold, wet clothing, however.[37]

Two or three days were required to reassemble the expedition. During this time, the Fillmore and Beaver companies overtook them.[38] They also had a rough time of it, being caught on Soap Wash with no shelter. The tempest hit them with such fury that "many were fearful of losing their lives."[39] It was then that Orange Warner, the captain of the Fillmore company, proved his worth. By his strength of character and his courageous efforts he was able to maintain order in the hapless camp despite becoming lost in the storm himself. According to one Millard County man:

> He rustled the wood, made fires & got them warmed up & to bed, then went in quest of the cattle that were drivin by the storm wind & slete of snow & when he could no longer keep the cattle from going a stray with the storm he tried to get back to camp but the darkness & storm prevented & he had to keep warm as best he could, holding to his horse all night, whiping stomping beating, anything to keep up the heat of the body but morning came at last . . . had he not been a strong courageous man he would never have ben able to wethered it through.[40]

Orange Warner, like a number of other expedition leaders, was an upstate New York man. He was in his early fifties at the time he was called to the White Mountain Expedition. Warner had been an original pioneer of Fillmore in 1851. He was a member of the Nauvoo Legion and was an Indian war veteran. The Fillmore company was composed of about sixteen men and boys.[41] One of the explorers was Warner's young son Mortimer, who was so eager to go on the expedition, he ran away from home and overtook the company.[42]

The first to link up with the main group was the Beaver company on April 11. This company was commanded by a thirty-year-old Scottish immigrant named James Low.[43] Low was a lieutenant in the Beaver company of the legion. His company consisted of "17 men provided with 6 wagons; 30 animals (horses and mules) a plough to each wagon, 2 bushels seeds—wheat; ½ bushel of potatoes & garden seeds in proportions."[44] The company had been impeded by the heavy snow and had not departed Beaver until April

1.[45] It was seventy miles through deep snow and mud to Cedar Springs for the rendezvous with Bean. This put them two days behind him. The Fillmore company came in right behind Low's men.

The combined companies formed an expeditionary force of 104 men with over forty teams and wagons. A survey of the expedition's personnel shows the ages of the men varied greatly. In the face of necessity, it seems that Brigham Young's counsel to use "old men and boys" with a few "young and middle aged to go as explorers" was largely disregarded. Of course the very young and the very old were represented. Mortimer W. Warner was barely sixteen when the expedition began, while others, like one Rhodes of Salt Lake City, was old enough to be called "Father Rhodes" by the members of the expedition. Many of these men, however, were directly from the ranks of the Nauvoo Legion. Of course the White Mountain Expedition was significantly more important now than it was in February, when the idea was first broached. But the expedition was largely organized before the change in policy and Brigham Young's "Sebastopol" speech. The small settlements in the south, which made up the majority of the expedition, were severely pressed for manpower. Many of the men were absent in Salt Lake City forwarding wagons and teams to aid in the exodus; others were helping with the evacuation of San Bernardino; and still others were being enlisted by Amasa Lyman for his reconnaissance of the Colorado River. The White Mountain Expedition had to take what it could get. The northern settlements were bearing the brunt of the military manpower need, and the men evacuating Salt Lake City were needed to help settle their families in Utah County and elsewhere. There was no room for any man to neglect his duty in southern Utah in the spring of 1858.

Finally ready to press onward, the Bean company began its descent of Cache (Dome) Canyon. The view to the west was magnificent. Looking down the canyon like the sights on a rifle, they saw a vast alkali plain before them stretching for miles across the desert floor. Because of this, Bean called it Saleratus Valley.

The descent was steep. Bean later reported the canyon was "a complete wall of rocks on each side. . . . about five miles long and from fifty to two hundred yards wide."[46] In this account, made after he returned from the expedition, Bean somewhat underestimated the width of the canyon.[47] The company rolled across alkali for more than three miles before re-entering the sage and greasewood so typical of these valleys. The alkali flat was a perfect white sheet, void of all vegetation. The valley was twenty-five miles wide, flat, and very dry. Only one spring was discovered in this desert. The oasis, called Indian Spring by the explorers, was a small pond surrounded by rushes standing in the center of the valley due west of Cache Canyon Pass. Tule Spring, as it is now called, offered a welcome respite to the explorers.

Proceeding west, they crossed a low divide (Cowboy Pass) and entered Snake Valley, which Bean called Long Valley. From Cowboy Pass in the Confusion Range they got their first good look at the majestic Snake Range with 13,063-foot Wheeler Peak towering over the valley. To the north a large alkali bed was visible, and many small patches were scattered through the valley. Bean brought his force down the divide and then turned south to explore for water along the western foothills of the Confusion Range. Here they discovered a fair-size creek coming up from the south, which they called Meadow Creek, probably because of the willows and rushes which grew along its banks. This was the stream presently known as Baker Creek, which sinks not far away.

From this point they were almost directly east of some of the higher peaks in the Snake Range. Bean called this snow-capped range the White Mountains. Marching fifteen miles southwest across the valley floor, the Mormons discovered Snake Creek at the foot of the massive Wheeler Peak. The expedition had now reached the present Utah-Nevada border. Bean estimated they had traveled 150 miles since leaving Cedar Springs. Upon further examination of the valley, another stream was found flowing up from the south which emptied into a small lake just below Snake Creek. Pruess Lake, as it is known today, was estimated by the explorers to be one-quarter mile wide by one-and-one-half miles long. The stream itself was fed by large springs twenty-five miles to the south, and attained a width of five feet and a depth of three feet before terminating at the lake. Lush meadows capable of supporting large numbers of cattle flanked the creek in the south end of the valley.

Snake Creek was the best, if not the only, prospect for a settlement yet found. Bean reported: "Here we found pretty good land and sufficient water to justify making a small settlement. The best of pine timbers within a few miles, grass not very convenient."[48] Although this valley was far from being the total answer sought by

Brigham Young, it was a start. Here, on the site of present-day Garrison, Utah, the White Mountain Expedition planted its first seeds.

To facilitate the founding of the new settlement, Barney was elected president of the mission. Meanwhile, the one-armed George W. Bean took a fast horse to Provo to confer with Brigham Young. It was April 22 when Bean rode into Provo, more than a month since he had forced his way south through deep snow.

Back in Salt Lake City, the exodus was in full swing, as was evident to Bean by the thousands of families camped along the river bottoms west of Provo. Brigham Young was continuing to rally the Saints with his speeches and trying to sell them on abandoning their homes. His March 28 Tabernacle speech, his first since the "Sebastopol" speech of the week before, attempted to further justify and rationalize the new policy while making it appear more attractive:

> The prospect of ancient "Mormonism," of again leaving our homes, probably gives a spring to our feelings, especially since we, for the first time, have the privilege of laying waste our improvements, and are not obliged to leave our inheritances to strangers to enjoy and revel in the fruits of our labors. It is a consolation to me that I have the privilege of laying in ashes and in the dust the improvements I have made, rather than those who would cut my throat, solely for my faith, shall inhabit my buildings and enjoy my fields and fruits. Heretofore I have often left my home and the fruits of my labours for others to enjoy. . . .
>
> There is a great deal of inquiry as to whether we shall be under the necessity of burning. We are now under the necessity of preparing for it, and that is enough for the present. . . .
>
> The Lord is leading this people as he designs for the building up of his kingdom, and we need not worry about it. . . .
>
> We are able to defend this city and keep out our enemies; but if we prove to our Father in heaven and to one another that we are willing to hand back to him that which he has given us, (which is not a sacrifice,) and that we love not the world nor the things of the world, he will preserve the people until they can become righteous.
>
> You never heard me say that we would stick to this city; but we will defend ourselves against the floods of iniquity which our enemies wish to overwhelm us with by the introduction of a licentious and corrupted soldiery. . . .
>
> Some may marvel why the Lord says, "Rather than fight your enemies, go away." It is because many of the people are so grossly wicked, that, were we to go out to fight, thousands of the Elders would go into eternity, and women and children would perish.
>
> Is every man and woman wicked? No: the majority of this people are doing the best they can; . . .
>
> We have talked about redeeming Zion [Jackson County], but the people are not yet righteous enough to receive and build up Zion in its purity, though they are growing to it. . . .
>
> . . . God is not willing that unholy hands shall carry out his judgements in the latter days.

When men go out to fight, I want them to go so full of the power of God that
balls cannot hit them. . . .

I am willing to leave this place, if I am called upon, and to take joyfully the
spoiling of my goods. . . . Perhaps we may come back here, and perhaps not. I
would as soon be here as anywhere, and anywhere as here, wherever the Lord
may require me.[49]

It was four days after this speech that Brigham Young and his
family abandoned the city. Accompanying him were Heber C. Kimball, Daniel H. Wells, Apostles Smith, Benson and Taylor, and a
few other church authorities. The weather was cold and windy. At
times the horses pulling the wagons were obscured from view by the
blowing dust. President Young was not well. The strain of leading
the people through the crisis was wearing on him. William Gilbert,
who met him on the road April 2, recalled that "both the prophet
and his chief familiar, Kimball, had a worn and jaded look, as if
under the pressure of much care and responsibility."[50]

Arriving at American Fork the first evening, the group lodged at
the home of Bishop Harrington. President Young took the opportunity to address the citizens of the town. In this sermon, the president
admitted the strain of his calling. "The President compared himself
and his situation," wrote the church historian, "to a man who has a
family of fifty blind persons to lead over rough bad roads, bridged
along and planks out of the bridges, and had to cross on the string
pieces. He exclaimed, 'O how thankful I would be if the people
could all see better than I.' "[51] Brigham Young was walking a
tightrope, and he knew it. It was April, and the federal army would
soon have to be brought to terms, one way or another.

On the 2d Young deposited his family in Provo and headed back
to Salt Lake to direct the evacuation and prepare for the church's
annual General Conference on April 6. On Sunday the 4th Brigham
Young admitted to his followers that perhaps the promised hour of
deliverance was not as near as had been thought. He "alluded to the
ancient prophets being mistaken about the second avent of the Mes-
siah, and to the possibility of this people being mistaken also."[52]
Clearly, the prophet's confidence was fading. The boldness of his
earlier war sermons was nowhere to be found.

Tuesday, the day of General Conference, found the Tabernacle
only partially full, as hundreds of families had now evacuated the
city. Wilford Woodruff wrote on April 6 that "the rodes [sic] are
lined with men women and children and waggons all moving

south."[53] Conference speeches dealt largely with the necessity of moving south and instructions on how this was to be accomplished. The people of Ogden were advised to move into Salt Lake City, and the citizens north of Ogden were to locate in Ogden. In such stages all the people north of Utah County, well over half (perhaps two-thirds) of Utah's population, were to be evacuated into the south. A small army was to be left behind to begin the destruction of property when the time came, or fight a rear guard action if necessary.[54]

There was more than defense involved in the move south. President Young was also waging an intensive public relations campaign aimed at the American people. The prophet was very conscious of the impact the policy might have on public opinion. He felt that, despite strong anti-Mormon sympathies in the nation, the people had no taste for the blood of innocent women and children. While Young tried to keep the objective point of the expedition a mystery, the move south itself became a well-publicized public relations tool. Brigham Young's move south had been carefully orchestrated to create the image of a poor and persecuted people being driven ever southward by a relentless, bloodthirsty army. As he recorded the discussion of the March 18 council of war, Stout noted that "the folly, the meaness of the President will be more apparent and he and his measures more unpopular" if the policy of desolation was to be adopted. And Brigham Young remarked to George A. Smith on April 12, "I think the movement we are now making will cause a reaction in the Gov't policy."[55] Even from the beginning, Young was well aware of the importance of public opinion. In a letter to David Evans on September 16, 1857, while discussing the policy of avoiding bloodshed, Young claimed: "This course will give us great influence abroad."[56] The Mormons were already encouraged by what they saw as signs that public opinion was turning in their favor. When it was learned in Salt Lake on April 2 that President Buchanan's recommendation to increase the army by four additional regiments was rejected by a vote of four to one, it was considered to be a positive sign that the public was abandoning it's hostility.[57] Encouraged, perhaps, by his seeming success on the public relations front, Brigham Young ordered the press of the *Deseret News* removed to Fillmore on April 6. The next California mail was to take a paper dated from that place to the States. The second press was to go directly to Parowan, with the succeeding California mail carrying a newspaper from that point.[58] The illusion would thus be enhanced of an innocent people being pushed ever southward by a heartless army. The first number of the *News* rolled off the press at Fillmore on May 5, according to schedule.

Whether Young would have actually led his people on an ill-planned, last-minute hegira into the central Great Basin has been debated by scholars and students of history. Pointing to Young's close attention to public relations, some have argued that the entire move south was no more than a political ploy designed to gain sympathy or at best a safety precaution, and that Young had no real intention of abandoning the Salt Lake Basin.[59] But the organization of the White Mountain Expedition disputes this view. Why expend much-needed manpower and resources on a mission to the southwest deserts if Young never intended to use its findings? Young's urgent appeal to Bean on March 21 was to send back word "immediately," as 500 families (perhaps several thousand individuals) were about to start for the desert. Certainly Bean's actions and reports indicate that he was convinced of Brigham Young's sincerity on the matter, as were many others. The Mormon prophet declared his intentions publicly in his "Sebastopol" speech of March 21, and privately he confided to George A. Smith on April 12 that he did "not feel the least gloom over this city . . . and if this storm works off we must make permanent calculations to store our grain & prepare our huts in the Desert."[60] Brigham Young's actions squared precisely with these remarks. Furniss points to the failure of the church to order the destruction of Salt Lake City as they left the valley as proof of Young's irresolution on the matter.[61] Certainly the move south was not irrevocable. Until the army had shown its intentions there was no need for the Saints to destroy their improvements, only to prepare for it. Young did leave men behind to accomplish the destruction should it become necessary. Brigham Young was not about to close any avenue open to him until he was forced to, and, as yet, he was still awaiting a favorable report from the White Mountain country.

In a letter to his father dated April 4 Colonel Kane, who enjoyed Brigham Young's confidence, asserted that Young would totally destroy Salt Lake City if the army could not be stopped. Kane further claimed that Young had written to him in late March begging a confidential opinion from him in respect to the policy of desolation and removal. William H. Kimball, the letter carrier, even "confessed . . . that a number of families had already removed from Salt

Lake 'into the mtains' S West." Kimball's reference was no doubt to the Bean expedition already underway. Curiously, Kimball would not allow Kane to retain the letter in his possession.[62] If Brigham Young was afraid the letter might fall into the wrong hands (Kane then being at Camp Scott), it doesn't say much for the public relations aspects of the policy. A sympathy campaign, as some have labelled Young's policy of removal and desolation, could not be carried out in secret.

The evidence suggests, then, that the Mormon leader was indeed preparing for removal to the deserts during the desperate early days of spring 1858, conditional upon three factors: first, all diplomatic efforts to resolve the crisis had failed; second, the army proved to be hostile and corrupt as had been anticipated; and third, the White Mountain Expedition was successful in locating a reasonable alternative. Believing all these conditions were imminent, Brigham Young proceeded with his plans for removal. Coexistence with a "brutal soldiery" never seems to have been considered at this time.

Brigham Young undoubtedly looked upon removal to the White Mountain country with reluctance. He did not know whether the region had the resources to sustain the total concept of the "Gathering of Israel," as he and other church leaders had envisoned it, or whether the interior deserts were to provide only a temporary refuge in the quest for a kingdom of God. Such a determination awaited the results of the White Mountain Expedition.

# VI

# THE SOUTHERN EXPLORING COMPANY

By General Conference, it had been hoped the desert refuge would have been found. Brigham Young was getting anxious. He had not heard from Lyman on the Colorado, Kane's mission appeared doomed, and it looked as if Bean would be delayed. Three hundred families had left the city in the last week alone, and the exodus was growing daily.[1] Many of the first to leave were arriving in the southern settlements. John R. Young, who witnessed these refugees in southern Utah, recalled:

> At Parowan, two hundred miles south of Salt Lake City, we encountered a scene that I shall never forget. I remember distinctly, the "Exodus," as it was called, from Nauvoo, when sixteen thousand souls left their homes and commenced that marvelous journey of fourteen hundred miles to the unknown valley of the Salt Lake. But that exodus was like a small rivulet by the side of a mighty river when compared with the seventy-five thousand [perhaps 25,000] men, women, and children that we now met in one continuous line of travel.
>
> Horses, oxen, and cows were harnessed or yoked to wagons and carts; . . . Mothers and children walked along as merrily as if going to a corn husking; each family moving its little bunch of cows and flock of sheep, and all starting on the journey (that was never completed) to Sonora, in Mexico, or some other place.[2]

Although many had reached southern Utah, it was now determined that Utah County would be the rallying point at present.[3] Before the exodus was complete, every city from Lehi to Payson was inundated with refugees living in uncertainty and poverty. The population of the county, normally about twelve thousand, tripled in two months. It was probably this concern that led Brigham Young to call on William H. Dame to head up a second expedition to the White Mountains.

Dame, a Parowan resident, was in Salt Lake City to receive instruction at the General Conference when he got his orders. He was an old acquaintance of Young from Nauvoo days. Like Young, Dame was a native New Englander, having been born in New Hampshire. He joined the Latter-day Saints in 1841 at Nauvoo and went through the persecutions of the Saints incident to that era. In 1851 the prophet had called him to settle Iron County. Now, at age

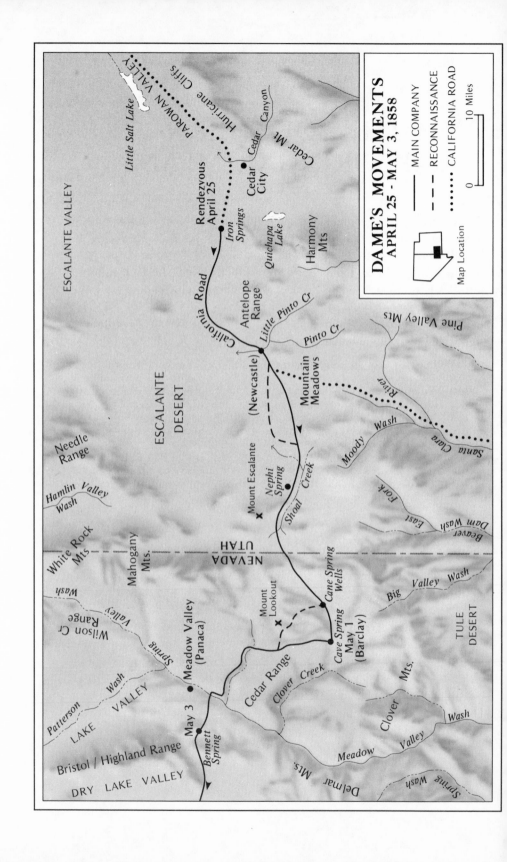

DAME'S MOVEMENTS
APRIL 25 - MAY 3, 1858

——— MAIN COMPANY
– – – RECONNAISSANCE
•••••• CALIFORNIA ROAD

0        10 Miles

Map Location

thirty-eight, he was probably the most powerful man in southern Utah. As a colonel in the Nauvoo Legion, he commanded the Iron regiment, with a military district encompassing the entire southern country from Beaver to the Rio Virgin. Dame was also the president of the Parowan Stake of the church, a position superior to bishop in the church's ecclesiastical structure, and wielded considerable power. Furthermore, Dame had been elected to three successive terms in the Utah Legislature from 1854 through 1856. In 1857 he was a member of Young's entourage on his tour of the Salmon River region. He was a big man, well proportioned, even handsome. His brown wavy hair receded deeply at the temples. According to Brooks, he was "a mild mannered, kindly man."[4] Nevertheless, it is he who is alleged to have given the order to dispose of the Fancher party at Mountain Meadows during the war hysteria of the previous September.[5] In the last few days he had accompanied Brigham Young on his removal from Salt Lake City, and it may have been then that Young first discussed the expedition with Dame. In any event, on April 7, the day following General Conference, Dame was called into the president's office and given his written orders, a copy of which is given below:

G.S.L. April 7, 1858

Col. Wm. H. Dame,

Dear Brother, you are instructed to raise from your Mil. District a company of 60 or 70 men with sufficient horsemen to act as patrolling & exploring purposes; the remainder with wagon, seed grain of all kinds and proceed from painter [Pinto] Creek westerly & North across the desert and seek for & make such locations as may be suitable to raise grain, keep stock, and secret families in case of necessities.

You will be careful to conciliate the Indians and instruct your men to learn their language and seek to gain & exercise a salutary influence over them. If there should be any man with you who will not pursue that course you must dismiss him from the Mission and send him home.

Your Bro. in the Gospel
Brigham Young[6]

In addition, Young instructed Dame to "take loads of water & make deposits along, sending back wagons, as they emptied them," and "if he discovered gold to keep it a secret."[7] He was also told to obtain twenty wagons and a four-mule team for each wagon. Each wagon was to be accompanied by two teamsters and a horseman.[8] Wilford Woodruff, who was apparently present at the meeting, furnished Dame with three pints of sugarcane seed and some King

Fig. 5. William H. Dame. *Courtesy Brigham Young University.*

Philip and white flint corn to be planted when a suitable location was discovered.[9]

Although Young used the phrase "in case of necessities" in his written instructions to Dame, the prophet was apparently convinced that there was a fertile region to the southwest and he was anxious to find it. William H. Dame was to recall in a conversation with John D. Lee a few days after his meeting with Young, that the prophet had warned him: "This is the 4th attempt & if you cant find the Place, I will go myself when I get to Parowan."[10] With these instructions, and the urgency of the moment sufficiently impressed upon him, Colonel Dame took the mail coach back to Parowan to begin the organization of another expedition to the desert. He arrived at his home four days later.[11]

As in the case of George W. Bean, Brigham Young made an excellent choice in the selection of William H. Dame for this assignment. Not only was Dame a proven leader, but he was a man of fierce loyalties to the church. Young had considered sending him to the desert as early as February, remarking to George A. Smith his intention to do so.[12] But for some reason, Dame did not go. When the companies from Iron County started for their rendezvous with Bean in March, Dame had only recently returned from the Mojave with Amasa Lyman, and perhaps other business or responsibilities prevented his leaving again with the first expedition.

Upon his arrival in Parowan, Colonel Dame set out to recruit his expeditionary force from the ranks of the regiment he commanded. It was on the evening of April 13 that John D. Lee lodged at the Dame home. Lee was on a tour of the southern settlements attempting to enlist wagons and teams to be forwarded to Salt Lake City to aid in the evacuation. In his conversations with Dame, he was told of Young's strategy. Lee wrote of his discussion with Dame in his diary:

> Spent the night at Pres. W. H. Dame, who had Just returned from G.S.L.c. with instructions from Pres. B. Young to . . . Penetrate the Desert in search of a resting place for the Saints. Said that he [Brigham Young] hoped that the co. would find a Desert that would take them 8 days to cross, but was affraid that it would take them only 3 days to cross it.[13]

Young's fear again demonstrates his conviction that a fertile region existed in the southwest desert, possibly within a three-day march, which was suitable for habitation. But just as important as locating the oasis was the wide desert buffer, which Young held as an essential component of his defense plan. James H. Martineau, who became a member of Dame's company, wrote that Young wanted to find

> a place of refuge; some valley which should be surrounded by a desert requiring a five-day's march to cross. He reasoned that while small parties might be able to cross such a thirsty waste with comparative safety, an army would find it impassable, and the larger the force the more impracticable it would be; that while a few men might find enough water in a small seep or water-hole to allay their thirst, a thousand men and animals would find it totally inadequate; and that such a desert would be a more formidable barrier than an army of forty thousand men.[14]

Such was the strategy of Brigham Young. Rather than defeat the army by force, he would leave it to the desert. So much rested on the explorations of Bean and Dame.

Colonel Dame asked Lee for his assistance in recruiting the men and animals for the expedition, as Lee was one of Dame's officers in the militia and an influential man in his own right. Lee agreed to hold back some of the best mule teams he had intended to forward to Salt Lake and to give Dame his assistance. While Lee returned home to finish up business, Colonel Dame rode the eighteen miles to Cedar City to confer with President Haight. Haight wrote in his diary that Dame arrived on the 14th, "having orders from Prest. Young to raise another company to go west to explore for a place to hide from the face of our enemies."[15] Cedar City was by far the largest settlement in southern Utah with a population of about two thousand,[16] and Haight had little trouble raising the fifteen men and the animals Dame requested of him. A meeting was called, and the men were enlisted.[17]

Recruiting was not as easy in the smaller settlements. On the 15th, Lee rejoined Dame, and the two proceeded south. At Washington, a 9 A.M. meeting was called on the 16th to lay the matter before the men of the settlement. By ten o'clock, Dame was on his way to Fort Clara, but Lee was asked to stay behind to "Stirr up the Brethren to vigelence & urge the necessity of immediate action."[18] Eventually, fifteen Washington men were enlisted for the expedition. The tiny Fort Clara settlement added three more to the list. All recruits were told to rendezvous on April 23, at Iron Springs, a watering hole on the California road ten miles west of Cedar City.

On the following day, Lee and Dame rode to Harmony, where they assigned Bishop Covington, of Washington, to raise seven teams from Harmony and have them at the rendezvous. On the 18th

Colonel Dame returned to his hometown of Parowan where he addressed the Saints both morning and afternoon.

John D. Lee proved to be of invaluable assistance in getting the expedition onto the desert. Besides his recruiting efforts, he volunteered a wagon and team of his own besides purchasing two mules and two sets of harnesses for the use of the expedition. While Lee was en route to Cedar City with the mules, he was met by an express from President Haight stating that the Cedar company was destitute of meat and wished him to sell them three beeves. Lee cooperated with the request, but he was never compensated for the animals.[19]

The men began to assemble at Iron Springs on the 23d. Colonel Dame and the Parowan company arrived on the following day. In all, sixty-six men had been recruited, although six from Parowan did not arrive in time to go. The list included fifteen men each from Cedar City, Beaver, Parowan, and Washington; and three men each from Harmony and Fort Clara. Dame's entire force was from the southern settlements.

Next to William H. Dame in prominence was James H. Martineau, also of Parowan. He possessed a variety of skills and abilities which were of use to the expedition, and he was unflinchingly loyal to any task given him by the church or community. Martineau was Colonel Dame's adjutant in the Iron military district, and he was also a captain of the Topographical Engineers and the regimental military instructor. One Parowan resident said of him: "Bro. Martineau was what is called a Westpointer a man of education an ability and a man who shone best by the finer side or in private conversation."[20] He was born in Montgomery County, New York, in 1828, the son of a physician. He was well educated and entered the printer's trade when quite young. Martineau's military experience began in the Mexican War when he was eighteen. After the war, he joined the gold rush and struck out for California. In Salt Lake City, while laying over the winter of 1850, Martineau discovered the Mormon Church and was baptized in January of 1850. The remainder of his life was devoted to service in the church. Arriving in Parowan three months after the first settlement there, Martineau became Iron County's first county clerk and the first city recorder of Parowan. At times he was also the Parowan ward clerk, stake clerk, county probate clerk, clerk of the Utah House of Representatives, and Parowan City alderman. In addition, he was a competent surveyor. At the time of the White Mountain Expedition, Martineau was thirty years old and the husband of two devoted wives (both named Susan) and the father of several small children. Men of Martineau's character and experience were rare, and Dame relied on him heavily throughout the expedition. Most of the records of the expedition's southern wing were written and preserved by him.[21]

Another notable individual at Iron Springs was Nephi Johnson. Johnson was born in the Mormon camp at Kirtland, Ohio, in 1833. As a youth, he was an original pioneer of Parowan. In the spring of 1858 he lived at Johnson's Fort (present-day Enoch) near Cedar City. Although only twenty-four, Johnson had been an Indian missionary on the Virgin and Muddy rivers and had the reputation of being the best Southern Paiute interpreter in the country. He was a lieutenant in the legion in one of the Cedar companies, and has unfortunately been linked to the Mountain Meadows Massacre. Johnson was married and was the father of two small children at the time of the expedition. James H. Martineau was his brother-in-law. Nephi Johnson was a fearless explorer and frontiersman, and, like so many others notables of the White Mountain Expedition, he was thoroughly devoted to the Mormon faith.[22]

One of the more unusual characters to enlist for this expedition was Asahel Bennett. Like Martineau, this Wisconsin native had come to Utah with the forty-niners and had been baptized.[23] But Bennett did not stay. He became a member of the infamous Death Valley company which attempted to traverse the Great Basin west of present-day Cedar City in search of the Walker Cutoff. After an unsuccessful stint in the goldfields, he turned to farming near the mouth of the Salinas River. Soon after the death of his wife in 1857, Bennett was persuaded that a small fortune could be made in Utah by returning to the territory with a stock of hard-to-get dry goods. He arrived in Cedar City in the fall and quickly remarried. During the winter it was reported that he would be going into the desert with a company from Cedar to salvage the iron from the wreckage of the wagons abandoned on the trail in 1849.[24] It is believed Bennett was about fifty years old at the time of the expedition. His knowledge of the desert region west of Cedar City was considered to be of significant value to the company organizing at the springs.[25]

Other members of the expeditionary force included Don C. Shirts of Harmony, an Indian interpreter and son-in-law of John D. Lee;

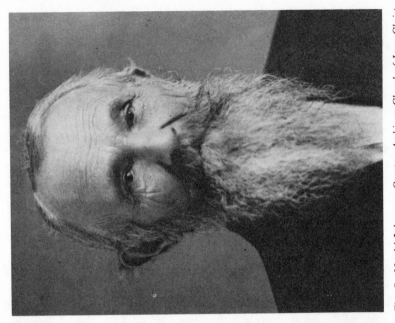

Fig. 7. Nephi Johnson. *Courtesy Archives, Church of Jesus Christ of Latter-day Saints.*

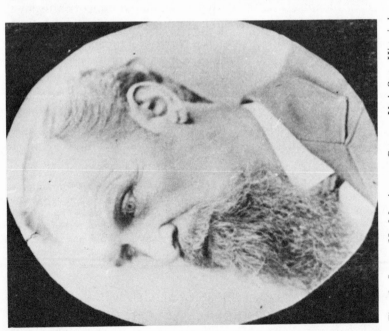

Fig. 6. James H. Martineau. *Courtesy Utah State Historical Society.*

Francis Hamblin of Fort Clara, the brother of the legendary Jacob Hamblin; and Ross R. Rogers, who led the Beaver City contingent to Iron Springs. There was also the elderly Samuel Sheppard of Beaver City, who was affectionately called "Father Sheppard" by the members of the expedition. Sheppard was known for entertaining his friends with tales of his participation in the War of 1812.[26] Thomas Durham, a recent English immigrant, was recruited from Parowan. Durham had received a liberal education in the field of music in England and was known in Iron County as "Professor Durham."[27]

At least two members of Dame's company were not members of the church.[28] These southern Utah men obviously had sympathies or interests in common with their Mormon neighbors. Many of the recruits, especially those from Cedar City, have been implicated in the Mountain Meadows affair, and, undoubtedly, many were involved. Whether this was an incentive to volunteer for the desert mission is unknown. With fury mounting over the massacre, it may have been a consideration.

As the brethren were assembled at Iron Springs, they were visited by some of the local church authorities who wished to send them off with their blessings and their advice. On the evening of Saturday the 24th, President Isaac C. Haight and his two counselors, John M. Higbee and Joel White, came into camp and preached to the men, "exhorting them to be united and sustain our president and prophesied that in so doing we should be blessed."[29]

On the following day, the remainder of the men and wagons arrived in camp with the exception of Samuel Hamilton of Cedar City and six of the Parowan men. It was time to organize the expedition. Martineau recalled in 1890 that he could "not remember a company better organized":

> There were sixty men, twenty wagons each drawn by two horses or mules, and with each wagon an extra horse, saddle and bridle. Two of each mess rode in the wagon, the third riding the odd horse. Thus each driver always had a man to assist in case of need, while the horsemen, twenty in number, served as front or rear guard, explored the passes ahead, hunted water or grass, and performed all kinds of detached service. Each wagon carried a water barrel, pick, shovel, axe, implements and tools necessary for the three men of that mess.[30]

There were in excess of one hundred animals with the company.[31] The wagons carried all kind of seeds to be sown when the refuge was located. Brigham Young himself had sent a large quantity of sugarcane seed with specific instructions as to how and when it was to be planted. An offer to purchase molasses from them in the fall accompanied the seed.[32] Dame received the package only a few days before leaving for Iron Springs.

Unlike the Bean contingent of the expedition, Dame's company did not attempt to retain the original companies from each settlement. Instead, the twenty wagons were divided into two groups of ten with a captain over each ten. The men were not mixed, however, as each wagon mess was composed of men from the same settlement.

By a unanimous vote, William H. Dame was sustained as the president of the expedition. He then proceeded to nominate the following officers: James H. Martineau, historian and topographer; Ross R. Rogers, sergeant of the guard; J. Ward Christian of Beaver, captain of the first ten; George W. Sirrine of Washington, captain of the second ten; Nephi Johnson, chief interpreter; Samuel Sheppard, chaplain; and Thomas Durham, chief of music.[33] All the nominees were sustained by a unanimous vote. The company, now fully organized, was designated the "Southern Exploring Company," as it was beginning its explorations south of George W. Bean's company.

The men spent the remainder of the day making preparations to start in the morning. It was a hot day, and many took the opportunity to dry meat. As it was Sunday, church services were held at eleven in the morning and again in the evening.

There can be little doubt that these men were serious about their role in establishing a sanctuary on the desert. James H. Martineau recalled: "Those who composed Colonel Dame's party fully expected that when they should leave their homes they would never see them again; that their homes would be destroyed during their absence, and their families be brought to them in the desert."[34] With his wife as the only witness, Martineau secretly buried the records of the probate court and the Parowan Ward before starting on his mission. Sealing them in his wife's stoneware churn with melted pine gum, he deposited them under his own corral, believing "the contents of the churn would be safe for many years to come."[35] And although he left his home, "never expecting to see it again," he "did it cheerfully in full faith that God would look after His children."[36]

At 8:20 on the morning of April 26 Colonel William H. Dame's command withdrew from Iron Springs and commenced exploring for Brigham Young's elusive desert refuge. As historian, Martineau kept an accurate log of their daily activities and made other maps and sketches to aid the future settlers of this untamed wilderness.

Fig. 8. James H. Martineau's "Chart Showing the Explorations of the Desert

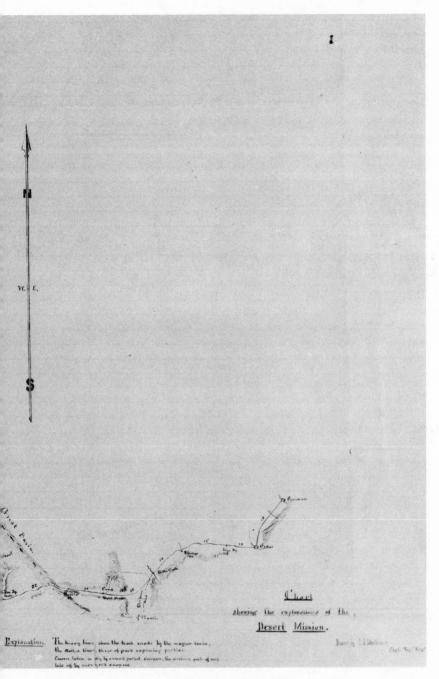

Mission." *Courtesy Archives, Church of Jesus Christ of Latter-day Saints.*

The company marched west along the California road for fifteen miles, arriving at Antelope (Rock) Spring a little after 1 P.M. They stopped to water the stock and then pushed on to Pinto Creek, making camp on the present-day site of Newcastle, Utah, about six o'clock. Dame, Martineau, and Johnson ascended a nearby hill to make observations. During the night Samuel Hamilton caught up with the expedition which had progressed twenty-seven miles from Iron Springs. With the arrival of Hamilton, the Southern Exploring Company was as complete as it would become, now comprising sixty men.

The camp left Pinto Creek in the morning about 8:15. As the California trail veered to the south, nine horsemen were dispatched to explore the country due west along the southern edge of the rugged Escalante Desert in hopes of establishing a direct route west. The attempt proved impractical, however. In a short time, the company reached the point where it was to leave the California road and strike west. It was about three miles from Pinto Creek and eight miles above the Mountain Meadows that the expedition turned off the established route. Less than nine years had passed since Bennett stood at this same juncture and made the fateful decision to proceed to California over an untried route. Now he was about to travel the same road, but for reasons he could never have imagined in 1849. The company called this Bennett's Trail, and for several days they followed in the tracks of the forty-niners. Camp was made on Shoal Creek a few miles west of present-day Enterprise, Utah.

Sometime after midnight, two men rode into camp with an express from Parowan. Samuel Lewis, the son of Bishop Tarleton Lewis of Parowan, and Barnabas Carter were the letter carriers. The fact that Samuel Lewis had guided John C. Frémont over this same ground in 1854 must have aided him in locating Dame's camp in the dark.[37] The riders carried letters from Calvin C. Pendleton and other local church authorities. Pendleton, President Dame's counselor in the stake presidency of Parowan, sent news that Jesse N. Smith, Marius Ensign, Hans Mortenson, and three others from Parowan who were expected to join them would not be coming to aid in the expedition. Some of the men were absent in Salt Lake City forwarding teams for the evacuation, and, for the same reason, the others were unable to raise the necessary animals. A few of the men, including Colonel Dame, used this opportunity to send letters back to the settlements.

Over the next two days, the expedition advanced in a westerly direction up Shoal Creek Canyon, so named by Nephi Johnson because of its shallowness.[38] The canyon began as a wide open bottomland, but it soon necked down to a narrow defile. After three miles of rough going, the canyon opened up again into a beautiful valley of wire grass about one hundred yards wide. The weather was not beautiful, however. The 28th was a bad day for travel. A cold rain drove the explorers into camp at 1 P.M. after covering only eleven miles. Camp was made at Nephi Springs which was named in honor of Nephi Johnson, the interpreter. It seems the spring was set down in a hole, making it difficult to drink from. In an attempt to reach the water, Johnson took hold of a handful of grass to lower himself down. When the grass gave way, the unlucky interpreter fell headlong into the spring and had to be helped out, much to the amusement of his comrades. The spring was known as Nephi's Hole for many years after the incident.[39] Nearby the men found good grass and water and cedar for fuel. But during the night, the rain turned to snow, and water froze in tin cups.

The morning brought an even heavier snowfall as camp got underway at nine o'clock. The snow continued throughout the day, making it cold and dreary for the men. In Shoal Creek Canyon the explorers picked up the first of their native guides. These Indians, unlike their Nevada cousins, were familiar with the white man and were unafraid. As the company pressed further up the canyon, they found themselves in a country thick with cedar and piñon pine. Martineau recorded that it was "here the Indians gather pine nuts."[40] The trail of the forty-niners was found again among the cedars. Here and there the trees had been cut down to make a passage for the gold hunters' wagons.[41]

In the afternoon, the explorers reached the summit of the divide which they called the "Rim of the Basin."[42] They now began their descent in a southwest direction near the present Utah-Nevada border. With an eye out for anything that might be of use to the people of Utah, Martineau carefully noted that strong indications of lead were visible in several red buttes they passed. It was in this area that Bennett proved his worth as a guide by steering the company to the north of Beaver Dam Wash, which had proven such a formidable barrier to the Death Valley company.

Asahel Bennett loved to tell of his experiences as a member of the ill-fated Death Valley party. Martineau wrote many years later:

Mr. Bennett gave us the story around our evening camp fires, and as we followed
the trail of the lost company for more than a hundred miles, and found pieces of
wagons, rusted tools, wagon-tires, and bits of rotton [sic] clothing, it gave his
story interest to our minds, that time can never efface, and keeps it still fresh in
the memory, as when told to us thirty-two years ago.[43]

Despite the constant storm on the 29th, the company pushed
ahead for twenty-two miles. Dusk found them in what Dame called
Badger Valley (present-day Clover Valley) very near the site of
modern Acoma, Nevada. Here they found plenty of grass and fuel,
and the soil was very rich, but there was not enough water to consider irrigation. Only a few small springs were located where the
men dug holes for the water to collect in for the stock. The place was
named Cane Spring Wells.

April 30 proved to be a continuation of the bad weather the expedition had encountered almost from their departure. The wagons
remained in camp all day as a hard rain pelted the hapless company.
A small party made a reconnaissance of the country immediately
north of camp, hoping to locate a passable road; but the attempt was
futile.

The company pulled out of Cane Spring Wells on the 1st of May
and continued its southwest march down Badger (Clover) Valley. At
a place they named Cave Springs, near the future site of Barclay,
Nevada, the company rested and took in water. This place was
noted to have plenty of "water, good grass and wood."[44] But the
valley was very small and offered only the prospects of a very small
settlement. It was also not in harmony with President Young's instructions to find a place surrounded by a wide expanse of desert for
a defense.

The Southern Exploring Company now turned north, advancing
up a canyon and over a high divide twelve miles above Cave
Springs. This area was thickly covered with cedar and piñon. Colonel Dame described this trek as "a very rough pass, and through
the largest patches of Pinyon Pine and cedars I ever saw in the
Rocky Mountains."[45] From the summit of the divide, the company
descended a canyon running northwest for fifteen miles into Meadow Valley. Thirteen years later, this road was described by a
traveler in almost poetic terms in a letter to the *Deseret News*:

There is a very good road between here [Clover Valley] and Meadow Valley, and
for part of the way the scenery is grand beyond description. For some distance
the road follows down a large wash, on either side of which is a high and

precipitous bank of sand, or rather sandstone, warn smooth by the action of the water in some places, in others washed and warn until deep fissures and yawing chasms meet on every hand. Here the storms of the ages have carved the soft rock into almost every conceivable shape. Towering above may be seen huge castlelike piles with spires and turretts innumerable, while below are grotesque groupings of figures differently shaped from five to twelve feet high and appearing more like monuments in a churchyard than anything else. Close beside the road, like sentinels on duty, are tall and slender figures that look like a gust of wind would blow them over, while in the distance are groups of cone-shaped mounds appearing like the tents of a vast army. There is a wild, fantastic beauty about the scene that is rarely excelled in any country.[46]

The less artistic Colonel Dame simply reported: "Truly this is a country of hills and hollows."[47] The company traveled thirty-three miles since leaving Cane Spring Wells that morning and made camp in the wash just four miles east of Meadow Valley.[48]

An exploring party of seven horsemen had left the camp at Cane Spring Wells early that morning to follow an old Indian trail leading north. The party pursued the trail into the Cedar Range and climbed the slopes of one of the higher peaks, calling it Mount Lookout. Here Martineau took observations with a pocket compass and established their position as due west of Painter (Pinto) Creek. Cutting back to the west, the reconnoitering party intersected the canyon leading into Meadow Valley ahead of the main company and followed it into the valley, making camp for the evening. Martineau found four heavy, iron wagon tires when he entered the valley, which had been left behind by the Death Valley company. But in the morning, twelve Indians came into camp claiming that the iron belonged to them. According to their instructions from Brigham Young to "conciliate the Indians," Nephi Johnson purchased the tires from them. The Indians were also given some flour which they made into a mush and ate scalding hot from the kettle. From the natives, one of whom had never seen a white man before, they learned that the snow falls only three inches deep in the winter and that ash and cottonwood timber was available in the canyon which enters the valley from the south.

The main company arrived at the advance camp in Meadow Valley about 9 A.M. This valley was by far the most suitable for settlement than anything yet found. Dame, who was making an emigrant's guide entitled, "Guide for the Desert Camp," recorded in the manual that the valley was sixteen miles long and five to twenty miles wide with three hundred acres of meadow grass.[49]

A careful reconnaissance was made of the entire valley. Nephi Johnson, James H. Martineau, Ansel Twitchell, and Asahel Bennett explored the north end of the valley, while J. Ward Christian and James Cliff explored to the south. Martineau's report was even more optimistic than Dame's assessment. "There are several thousand acres of good grass," claimed Martineau, "the most of it fit for mowing, and a stream running through it."[50] The stream came from some large warm springs at the north end of the valley. As it ran south, the water "spreads over a marshy, wire and broadleaf grass bottom, forming a meadow half a mile wide," reported Colonel Dame. He also reported the stream to be larger than Center Creek at Parowan and sufficient to turn a small gristmill. Fish from three to eight inches in length were also found in the stream.[51] Although Dame did not consider the water from the warm springs fit to drink, other fresh springs were located around the valley. Near the springs, a small piece of land was found which appeared suitable for cultivation.[52]

But unlike George W. Bean, Colonel Dame seemed to be in no hurry to locate at the first possible location. He was not satisfied that he had found the place Brigham Young was looking for, and so, after more than a day surveying Meadow Valley, he prepared his company to move on farther into the desert. His temporary camp was situated about six miles south of the present site of Panaca, Nevada.

# VII

# THE MYTH
# AND THE SANCTUARY

While Bean and Dame were exploring the deserts of the Great Basin and adjacent country, the move south continued. By the middle of May, Salt Lake City and the northern settlements had been evacuated. But the objective point of the move seems to have been little understood, even by many of the Mormons. "Their destination is south, but where particularly even they themselves do not know," declared the *New York Daily Tribune* of June 12.

Many believed that Brigham Young was planning to settle the Saints in the Mexican state of Sonora. John R. Young has already been quoted in a previous chapter indicating his belief that Sonora was the object of the move south. On May 10, John Kay wrote to Thomas Williams that "we shall cut down our fruit trees, set fire to our houses, and move on slowly towards Sonora, although I believe the nearest way is to proceed via Jackson County, Mo. However, we can go anyway we please; we have the Territory on wheels."[1]

"The territory on wheels" was also the subject of much speculation outside of the Mormon kingdom. Many in the army and in the government were convinced that Brigham Young was leading a hegira to Sonora, often for the reason that they could not understand where else the prophet could be going. Captain Jesse Gove, of Johnston's command, wrote to his wife on June 4, with his usual display of contempt for the Mormons: "My opinion is that if they do not submit (which they will not) we shall pursue them and find ourselves in the vicinity of Sonora in hot pursuit."[2] After witnessing the evacuation of Salt Lake City, Governor Cumming wrote to the secretary of state on May 2 that "'Going South' seems sufficiently definite for most of them, but many believe that their ultimate destination is Sonora."[3]

Even before the evacuation of Salt Lake had been determined upon by Young, when desolation and scorched earth were simply alternative plans, the Eastern press had often predicted the Mormons' removal, frequently pointing to Sonora as the likely gathering place. "I find that the probability of Brigham Young leading his followers from Salt Lake to the Mexican province of Sonora has attracted the attention of the government," wrote a Washington correspondent in the *St. Louis Intelligencer* of November 23. Continuing, the *Intelligencer* urged the government to prevent a Mormon exodus to Sonora, if possible, because the country was in a mood to annex the province but would certainly forego the valuable acquisition should the Mormons take up quarters there.[4]

It appears that the public, both inside and outside of the territory, did not understand the implications of Brigham Young's "Sebastopol" speech of March 21, when he proclaimed their final destination was to be "in this territory." To further cloud the issue, the prophet occasionally joked about Sonora being his ultimate destination during the move south. In his Sunday afternoon Tabernacle speech on April 25, Young poked fun at the prognosticators: "I have a good mind to tell a secret right here; I believe I will tell it anyhow. They say there is a fine country down there; Sonora is it, is that the name for it? Do not speak of this out of doors, if you please."[5]

Other reports had the Mormons heading for Central or South America, Vancouver Island, Washington Territory, or Lower California. One report that the Mormons would flee to Alaska nearly caused an international incident with the Russians.[6] Such speculation was encouraged during the spring by Brigham Young's failure to publicly proclaim the exact destination of the new exodus. Only in his "Sebastopol" speech was even a general description of the location given, and the speech was never published except in the "confidential" circulars sent across the territory to church and military authorities. While the information quickly leaked out, it was often misunderstood and soon buried under the deluge of rumors spewing from the nation's Utah correspondents. Young's lack of detail on the destination of the move south was, of course, occasioned by the failure of Bean and Dame to send positive reports back to Salt Lake from the White Mountain country before new policies made the expedition obsolete. But Brigham Young ever maintained that the Saints would remain in Utah Territory.

From his many comments, both public and private, it is evident that Brigham Young considered Utah to be a special place given to the Saints by the Lord as a sanctuary or stronghold against aggressors. From the early days of the Mormon gathering in Utah, the church put a certain significance on the establishment of the kingdom in the Mountain West. Orson Pratt, the church's renowned propagandist, wrote several tracts explaining the Saints' unique position in the Rocky Mountains as the fulfillment of ancient prophecies.[7] Even during the Utah War, with pressure mounting to abandon the region, Brigham Young remained adamant that the Saints would not abandon Utah, and that the region contained a special significance for them. Writing to William Cox of San Bernardino on November 5, Young affirmed his belief that there "is no place for the saints to gather neither is there any other place except Utah."[8] And on September 13 Young asserted: "We are still on the backbone of the animal, where the bone and sinews are, and we intend to stay here, and all hell cannot help themselves."[9]

President Young's feelings about Utah surfaced again in May during a meeting with two businessmen, who had come to Salt Lake City to offer a proposal to the prophet. John B. Cooper and James M. Harbin, representatives of one Colonel Kinney of California, met with Young on May 24 to offer the sale of a huge tract of land in Central America to the church. Thirty million acres of the so-called "Mosquito Coast" were offered to the Mormons, whom Kinney obviously believed would be anxious to buy their way out of their present difficulties with the government. But despite the fact that the two agents did their best to promote the sale, describing the country in the most positive terms before President Young and other church authorities, Young finally told the pair that "if Mr. Kinney owned all of Central America, and would give it to me for nothing, I would not go there." When Cooper persisted, he was informed, "If you have any propositions to make, you will please to make them in writing . . ." but "you must make them in view that we will not move from this Territory as we are just where we want to be, and where we intend to stay, and all hell cannot move us from here."[10] John R. Young, who was present at the meeting, said he would never forget Brigham Young's reply to these two men. He remembered the president's response this way: "Gentlemen, God almighty made these everlasting hills to be bulwarks of liberty for the oppressed and down-trodden of the earth. We shall never leave here. . . . Gentlemen, you have my answer."[11]

The following day Cooper and Harbin delivered their written proposal to Young—thirty million acres of the Mosquito Coast for ten cents per acre. The proposition was promptly refused, as Young said it would be. Before returning to California, the persistent Cooper made one last attempt to sell the land, but the president turned him away cold: "I would not go to that country if it was covered 15 inches deep with gold and we owned it all. We are here and here we will stay in this territory."[12]

What neither Colonel Kinney nor his two agents knew was that by May Brigham Young was nearing a solution to the crisis which would not require removal of the Saints. But the colorful episode of the Mosquito Coast country serves to underscore Young's earlier remarks that Utah was a refuge for the Saints, a haven consecrated for the gathering of Zion. They might move, but they would not leave the territory. It must have seemed odd to the two agents, Cooper and Harbin, to listen to Brigham Young emphatically declare "We shall never leave here," while all the way through the settlements on their way to Salt Lake were scenes of refugees streaming south. It appears certain that somewhere in the fierce and unfriendly central valleys of the Great Basin Brigham Young envisioned a sanctuary for his besieged Saints. On March 21 he had announced his intentions to go there where he believed there was room enough for a half million settlers. Why did Brigham Young believe this? Where was this apocryphal oasis located? And did the prophet have a precise location in mind?

If Brigham Young did not have some exact location in mind for settlement, he at least talked like he did. In a packed meeting in the Tabernacle on October 18, Young claimed, "I know of places enough where I can hide this people and a thousand times more, and our enemies might hunt until doomsday and not be able to find us."[13] In his "Sebastopol" speech of March 21, he asserted that David Evans and company of 1855 "did not go to the mountain where they were sent, and made no settlement."[14] Colonel Dame had been told, "if you can't find the Place, I will go myself," in his meeting with President Young on April 7.[15] In each of these statements it appears that a particular place was envisioned. The reference to Evans's White Mountain Mission infers that a particular mountain may be central to the location.

It appears that Young did have a general location in mind. William H. Dame was instructed to take his company west from Pinto Creek and then north.[16] Bean alleges that he was told to explore the desert valleys west of Fillmore and Beaver.[17] If both of these men followed their instructions, they would wind up in approximately the same location. Later instructions to Bean contained orders to explore southwest from his location in Snake Valley, again pointing toward the same region. From these instructions it would seem that Brigham Young's legendary oasis would lie about two hundred miles west of Beaver City, which would also be consistent with Young's desire to establish the refuge beyond a desert barrier requiring eight days to cross. It appears likely that Brigham Young had at least a general idea of where his refuge was to be found.

Young's "Sebastopol" speech reveals more elaborate detail of the place he was considering. It was an area "larger than any of the Eastern States, that no white man knows anything about. . . . It is a desert country with long distances from water to water. . . . Probably there is room in that region for 500,000 persons to live scattered about where there is good grass and water."[18] The White Mountain district was, of course, one of the few places left in the Great Basin that had little contact with the white man. It is also clear that Brigham Young did not see the refuge as one large fertile area, but rather a series of oases scattered across a very large area, probably similar to the scattered settlements of the Wasatch Front. Unfortunately, Young grossly misjudged the capabilities of this land and its suitability for settlement.

Brigham Young's misconception of the Great Basin's interior desert lands probably derives from the same factors that caused the Death Valley company to plunge into the same region in 1849. When the forty-niners were persuaded to leave their guide and strike west across the desert, they were influenced by two "authorities": Elijah Barney Ward, the mountain man, and John C. Frémont, the Pathfinder.

Ward came to the Rockies in 1834 as a trapper and trader. He was one of the builders of Fort Hall on the Snake River, and from 1837 to 1848 he and John W. Patrick operated a trading post at Utah Lake. Ward became very knowledgeable of the surrounding country and its Indian inhabitants. When the Mormons arrived in the Great Basin in 1847, Barney Ward and his Indian wife and family joined them in Salt Lake. Three years later the mountain man was baptized into the faith and became an intimate friend of Brigham Young. His knowledge of the region was of great value to the Mormons, and he frequently performed valuable service for the church as an interpreter and guide.[19]

Ward firmly believed in a shortcut route to California between southern Utah and Walker's Pass in the Sierra Nevada. He even claimed to have traveled the route three times himself. During the summer and fall of 1849, he was very active in promoting the new route, called "Walker's Cutoff." Besides his contact with the Smith-Flake party that led to the Death Valley disaster, Ward encountered Thomas Forsyth, another well-known mountain man, near Bent's Fort on the Arkansas River the same fall. By the time Forsyth reached St. Louis, it was apparent that Ward had discussed the new route with him. Forsyth reported to the *Missouri Republican* of December 4 that "the Mormons have discovered a route occupying only some twenty or thirty days to cross the desert and Sierra Nevada, on which there is [an] abundance of wood and water at every stage, and of easy crossing."[20] Ward, who seems to have been everywhere that year, returned from the Arkansas in time to meet the Parley P. Pratt exploring party in December. Pratt had been ordered to explore southern Utah with the aim of locating settlement sites. Ward, with the Ute chief Wakara, encountered the Pratt expedition on the Sevier River, and here again Barney Ward freely discussed the geography of the region with the Mormons.[21]

The mountain man's opinions apparently influenced Brigham Young's conception of Great Basin geography. As stated above, Barney Ward became an intimate associate of the prophet, who placed great confidence in Ward. Brigham Young frequently employed him as an interpreter and guide with church exploring parties. In April 1851, Brigham Young personally led an expedition to Sevier Valley in which Barney Ward, Miles Weaver, and George W. Bean were the interpreters.[22] In June of the same year, Ward interpreted during an interview between Brigham Young and a delegation of Ute chiefs.[23] The following April, Ward again accompanied President Young on an expedition to Sevier Valley.[24] Throughout his life Barney Ward was devoted to the Mormon leader, who frequently employed his services. The mountain man likely shared all he knew about the unknown regions of Utah Territory with Young.

John C. Frémont also had an unmistakable influence on Brigham Young's misconception of the Great Basin's interior. Frémont's *Report* of 1845, detailing his second expedition, was damaging enough when he created a mythical range traversing the Basin at the 38th parallel; but his 1848 *Map of Oregon and Upper California* was even more harmful. While correct in detail for the areas he had actually explored, it, too, included the apocryphal mountain range, which he claimed to have seen on his exploring tours.[25] The range is shown to be about four hundred miles long, connecting the southern tip of the mountains below Cedar City to the Sierra Nevada Range of California. Along this hypothetical range are printed the words, "DIVIDING RANGE BETWEEN THE WATERS OF THE PACIFIC AND THE WATERS OF THE GREAT BASIN." A large area to the north of this range and west of the present locations of Fillmore and Beaver is designated "UNEXPLORED." This was the same unexplored region that Brigham Young ordered the White Mountain Expedition to investigate.

In Frémont's mind, the existence of this great east-west range was an established fact. He believed that the Great Basin had to be encircled by a chain of high mountains that isolated it from the Pacific slope and he saw what he believed. Frémont observed that "their summits white with snow, were often visible," and concluded that they "must have turned water to the north as well as to the south."[26]

Even though Frémont had not explored the Great Basin's interior valleys, he speculated about them in his *Report* of 1845:

> Of its [the Great Basin's] interior, but little is known. It is called a desert, and from what I saw, sterility may be its prominent characteristic; but where there is so much water, there must be some oasis. . . . where there is so much snow, there must be streams; and where there is no outlet, there must be lakes to hold the accumulated waters, . . . In this eastern part of the Basin, containing Sevier, Utah, and the Great Salt Lakes, and the rivers and creeks falling into them, we know there is good soil and good grass adapted to civilized settlement.[27]

In other words, if there were fertile, watered valleys in the Great Basin along the base of the Wasatch, there should be similar fertile oases at the foot of the great east-west range stretching across the Great Basin at the 38th parallel. It was the same conclusion reached by the Death Valley company. Was this the conclusion now reached by Brigham Young? Was this the place he informed his followers about in October when he told them he knew of places where "I can hide this people and a thousand times more"? And was Frémont's apocryphal mountain range the place he had instructed Evans's company to go, of which he later complained, "they did not go to the mountain where they were sent"?

Frémont's reports were given wide credibility. Frémont was the Pathfinder; he was the authority to which others turned. While he was correct in assuming that there would necessarily be river and lake systems in the interior of the basin, he greatly overestimated the amount of available water. All the major rivers and streams, with

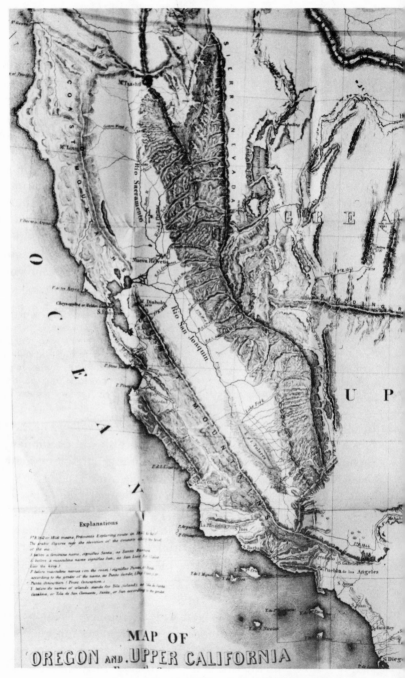

Fig. 9. Frémont's 1848 "Map of Oregon and Upper California," showing apocryphal east-west mountain range in southwestern Utah Territory.

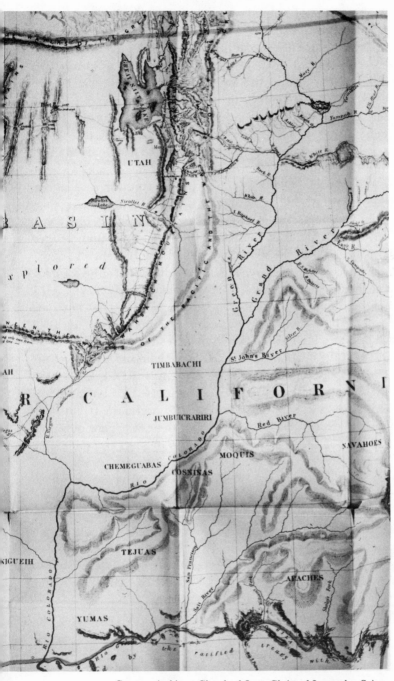

*Courtesy Archives, Church of Jesus Christ of Latter-day Saints.*

the exception of the Humboldt, emanate from the high mountains on the perimeter of the Basin. Frémont knew this, but contrary to Frémont's reasoning, these great peripheral ranges did not include a high east-west range at the 38th parallel. There was little snow and few streams of any size in that area. The lakes were usually dry, perhaps wet only a few months of the year.

It seems that Brigham Young and John C. Frémont had similar misunderstandings about the central valleys of the Great Basin. They both felt that there must be considerable fertile areas in the region west of Fillmore and Beaver. Young saw his refuge as a series of oases where perhaps half a million people could live "scattered about where there is good grass and water." Frémont was convinced there were streams and lakes, as well as fertile soil, in this region similar to what is found at the base of the Wasatch. Both of these men also believed that the region contained few Indians.

While no document has been discovered linking Young's conviction about the Great Basin with Frémont's maps and reports, we do know that the prophet had them and had read them. The church acquired a copy of the recently published Frémont *Report* in 1845, while still at Nauvoo. This document was read orally before the entire Quorum of the Twelve by Franklin D. Richards, and it was primarily the descriptions of Salt Lake and Bear River valleys that influenced the prophet's course in coming to the Salt Lake Basin.[28]

Frémont and other explorers continued to probe the Great Basin after the noted expedition of 1843–44, but there were few published descriptions to refute the errors in the *Report* of 1845 and the map of 1848. There were, in fact, some people who were promoting Frémont's writings for their own interests, not knowing that the Pathfinder was mistaken.

After his third expedition in 1845–46, Frémont published his *Geographical Memoir upon Upper California* which contained a more correct understanding of the contents of the Great Basin's interior. "The interior of the Great Basin, so far as has been explored, is found to be a succession of sharp mountain ranges and naked plains. . . . Sterility . . . is the absolute characteristic of the valleys between the mountains," admitted Frémont. But then he went on to say that although the basin is largely a desert, there were some "great exceptions . . . deserving the full examination of a thorough exploration"[29] And speaking of the mountains which constitute the rim of the Great Basin, which included his great east-west range, Frémont said:

> Snow abounds on them all; on some, in their loftier parts, the whole year, with wood and grass; with copius streams of water, sometimes amounting to considerable rivers, flowing inwards, and forming lakes or sinking in the sands. Belts or benches of good alluvion are usually found at their base.[30]

Again, the words of Frémont pointed toward the probability of finding fertile oases along the southern rim such as are found along the eastern rim. Besides these statements in his *Geographical Memoir*, Frémont retracted none of the earlier speculations contained in his *Report* of 1845. In fact, the error of the mythical mountain range was perpetuated in the later report, which was published "in Illustration of His Map of Oregon and California."

In 1854 Frémont's fifth expedition crossed the basin almost precisely where his fabled range was purported to be. In a letter to the *Daily National Intelligencer*, which was later printed as a Senate document, he described the country as "a high tableland, bristling with mountains. . . . The valleys are dry and naked, without water or wood. . . . Springs are very rare and occasionally streams are at remote distances."[31] But there was still no revision of his earlier assumptions of the character of the Great Basin's interior or the existence of the great east-west range. His report did not receive wide circulation. In 1854 there were other, louder voices being heard which advocated the oasis theory.

It might seem strange that in light of Frémont's later findings, and knowing the fate of the Death Valley company which had gone into the area, Brigham Young would still entertain notions of fertile valleys at the foot of a great mountain range spanning the breadth of the Great Basin. But myths die hard. So much credence had been given to Frémont's earlier theories of an east-west mountain range that Captain Simpson found it necessary to contradict them in his *Report of Explorations . . . in 1859*, a year after the White Mountain Expedition was sent into the region by Brigham Young.[32]

The voices clamoring for the central railroad route to the Pacific coast were loud in keeping the Frémont myth alive and well into the 1850s. Early in the decade, the various sections of the Eastern States began competing for the terminus of the proposed transcontinental railroad. Each section advocated a southern, central, or northern route that would bring the railhead to their area. The champion of the central route to the Pacific was the powerful Sen. Thomas H. Benton, of Missouri.

Edward F. Beale (the same who later commanded the Camel Corps) was the Superintendent of Indian Affairs for California in 1852. While in Washington that summer, he became infatuated with Benton's plans for the central route. Beale was ordered back to his post in California in 1853 "by the most expeditious route," but, for the purpose of promoting the central railroad route, he chose to go overland, even though the sea route was quicker. Beale was to send back reports to Benton who was to use them to further their cause. Along with his cousin, Gwinn Harris Heap, who served as a journalist, and a small party, they spent three months in the summer of 1853 traversing the country between Missouri and California. Heap's journal was first published serially in the *National Intelligencer*, but in 1854 it was published in book form with numerous appendices all suggesting that the central route, which included the central Great Basin, was the best route for the Pacific railroad. The book, entitled *Central Route to the Pacific*, was widely circulated and certainly overshadowed Frémont's meager article of the same year. It is probable that Brigham Young was familiar with the ideas advanced in Heap's book.

The journal mentions Walker's Cutoff, saying that Benton had wished them to try the route, as it was believed to be "a more direct way and over a better country."[33] But, as they could get no guide or information about the route, they proceeded to the coast on the Spanish Trail. Nevertheless, Heap asserted that "according to the accounts we had received, it conducts over a tolerably level, well watered, and grassy country."[34] Heap played a great role in the preservation of the Frémont myth by gathering up all of the information he could find about the region that supported the cause of the central route and putting it in his book.

In his appendices Heap made reference to the explorations of Frémont and wholeheartedly concurred with his early assessment of the Great Basin's interior. "This was the belief of Col. Fremont," wrote Heap,

who had examined Owen's River and Lake, and laid them down in his map of 1848, and also sketched a mountain running east and west, about latitude 38, along the southern base of which he judged (from the nature of the mountains anɩ valleys in the region) there must be a belt of fertile land, with wood, water, and grass, making a valley east and west; which was the course that the route for the road required. His views have been subsequently verified, and as early as 1849–50, by a party of emigrants, headed by the Rev. J. W. Brier. . . .[35]

Instead of dying a natural death, the Frémont myth was being magnified by a special interest group. The fate of the Death Valley company was downplayed by the inclusion of the testimony of the Reverend Brier, a survivor of the party.

It seems strange that in light of the disaster experienced by the Death Valley company and Brier's own near brush with death, he would give such a favorable report of the country. The Reverend spoke before a Pacific Railroad meeting in San Francisco on August 23, 1853. His comments were included in Heap's *Central Route*. Brier's appraisal of the route across the Great Basin was very misleading and, in fact, blatantly false in places. He cited the ease with which his party crossed the desert and he claimed to have found areas that were "very fertile" and a mountain range nearly one hundred miles long where they discovered creeks "large enough to run a mill."[36] Brier summed up the country by saying that "if the country east of the Wahsatch is equal to that part of the route west of the Wahsatch, I have no hesitancy in saying that, for distance and locality, it has greatly the preference over every other."[37]

Another letter included in Heap's book was from Richard S. "Uncle Dick" Wootton, a trapper from Taos, who claimed to have been over Walker's Cutoff within the past year. In his letter dated October 22, 1853, Wootton falsely asserted "there is a good wagon-road, and settlements all the way."[38]

There were others who contributed to the perpetuation of the Frémont myth. All of the most respected mapmakers of the day were turning out maps based on Frémont's 1848 map. Mitchell's maps of 1854 and 1856, Platt's of 1852, Bartlett's of 1854, Steptoe's of 1855, Lippincott's of 1857, and several others all incorporated Frémont's misconceptions.[39]

It is little wonder that Frémont's myth was becoming a fixed reality in the public mind. Brigham Young was no exception. As governor of the territory, he had undoubtedly seen many of these maps and was familiar with many of the false reports. Like the myth of the Buenaventura, the Frémont delusion died slowly. Some mapmakers continued to illustrate a shadow of Frémont's east-west range into the 1870s. There were many subscribers to the oasis theory, of which Brigham Young was but one. The mountain men Barney Ward, Dick Wootton, and even Kit Carson believed in it. The promoters of the central route to the Pacific publicized it. And now Brigham Young had set out to find it. In this respect, the White Mountain Expedition was the product of a popular geographical misconception.

# VIII

# A HUNGRY INDIAN

By May 3 Colonel Dame had completed his survey of Meadow Valley, so far the brightest spot of his own explorations. That morning he moved his company up to Bennett's Springs, eleven miles west, and camped. John Kay, one of the party, caused some worry in camp when he failed to arrive. While attempting another course, he became lost. Dame sent out some Indians with food and water for him, but Kay soon wandered into camp from another direction. Bennett's Springs, named for Asahel Bennett, were situated near the summit of Bennett Pass, a divide between Meadow Valley and the sterile Dry Lake Valley. Although these two large springs were slightly warm, they were considered sufficient to water up to ten acres of ground, and they were near plenty of good bunch grass and cedar for fuel.

Dame and Martineau proceeded to the summit of the pass where Martineau made observations with Dame's surveying compass. Looking west and a little north the colonel saw what he believed he had been looking for. At a distance estimated to be about 125 miles, they could see a majestic, snowcapped range which Colonel Dame pronounced to be the White Mountains. What the men were looking at were the 10,000-foot Grant and Quinn Canyon ranges, in reality only sixty miles away. To Dame it appeared that the desired refuge lay dead ahead. These high, snowy mountains must certainly contain the elements of life—water, grass, and fuel. Even the harsh desert which lay between them and the mountains seemed to be in perfect harmony with the prophet's defense plans—a desert that would require eight days to cross—for the Indians had informed him that there was only one small spring on their course, and it might be dry.

Dame thought it was now time to contact Brigham Young and relieve him of some of the anxiety which he had manifested before they departed on April 7. As the two Indian guides enlisted at Shoal Creek were anxious to return home, Dame took the opportunity to

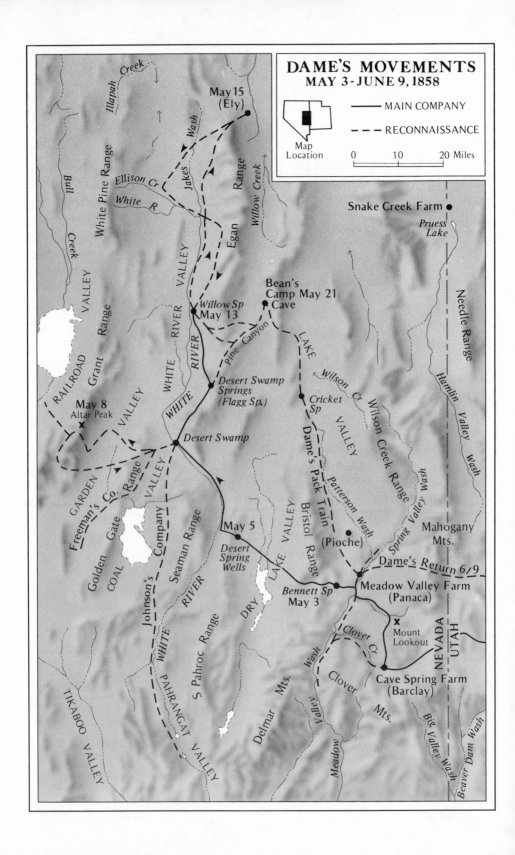

**DAME'S MOVEMENTS**
MAY 3 - JUNE 9, 1858

Map Location

MAIN COMPANY
RECONNAISSANCE

0          10          20 Miles

Illapah Creek

May 15 (Ely)

White Pine Range

Bull Creek

Ellison Cr.

White R.

Jakes Wash

Egan Range

Willow Creek

Snake Creek Farm

Pruess Lake

Needle Range

RAILROAD VALLEY

Grant Range

WHITE RIVER VALLEY

Willow Sp May 13

WHITE RIVER

Pine Canyon

Bean's Camp May 21 Cave

CAVE LAKE

Wilson Cr.

May 8 Altar Peak

Desert Swamp Springs (Flagg Sp.)

Desert Swamp

Cricket Sp

WILSON VALLEY

Wilson Creek Range

Hamlin Valley Wash

GARDEN VALLEY

Freeman's Co.

Coal Range

Johnson's Company

Golden Gate Range

Seaman Range

May 5

Desert Spring Wells

DRY LAKE VALLEY

Bristol Range

Dame's Pack Train

(Pioche)

Patterson Wash

Spring Valley Wash

Mahogany Mts.

Dame's Return 6/9

WHITE RIVER

S Pahroc Range

PAHRANGAT VALLEY

Bennett Sp May 3

Meadow Valley Farm (Panaca)

TIKABOO VALLEY

Delmar Mts.

Meadow Valley Wash

Clover Cr.

Mount Lookout

NEVADA
UTAH

Clover Mts.

Cave Spring Farm (Barclay)

Big Valley Wash

Beaver Dam Wash

send a lengthy letter to Young describing the organization of his
company and its movements up to the present. He also included a
description of the country they had traveled through. After discussing the possible merits of Meadow Valley, he announced the discovery of the high range saying they were "supposed to be the
White Mountains." "The prospects are bright before us," he exclaimed. "All feel anxious to reach the Big Snow Mountain; and
they desire to fill the mission assigned them. All feel to thank the
Lord for the strong hills and deserts. Tomorrow morning if all is well
we proceed on our journey. . . ."[1]

This letter took sixteen days to reach Brigham Young. Notwithstanding its positive tone, Young expressed dissatisfaction with
Dame's report.[2] Perhaps things were not progressing fast enough to
meet the urgency of the situation.

Several of the company took the opportunity to send messages
with the "Indian express," as it was called. Dame sent a letter to his
family which began: "Affectionate Wives, One hundred and fifty
miles from you on the side of a big mountain, by these springs, I find
myself, all well and hope you are well." Dame continued:

> I have just come down from the top of a big mountain looked hard to see you, but
> alas: the distance to great, though felt you were well and had not forgot to pray
> for me, I then looked west and saw the White Mountains about 125 miles off, one
> small spring from here to them, we shall start tomorrow. . . .[3]

It must have been assumed that a settlement would soon be made
and an express established between there and Parowan because
Dame then asked that his wives send him three pounds of sugar and
a copy of the *Deseret News*.

On the following morning, the camp moved out at 8:15 and
marched over the divide four and one-half miles west. From there
the company proceeded down a dry wash for nine miles into Dry
Lake Valley, a bleak desert with a huge, dry lake bed immediately to
the south. According to the Indians, the valley ran south to Las
Vegas. Although their guides reported a small spring lay between
them and their destination, each wagon took a full barrel of water on
board. Until this point, the company had been following Bennett's
trail of 1849 with only slight variations. "It helps & aids us very
much," wrote Dame of the trail of 1849. But from this point forward
the company was completely on their own in an unexplored country.
Colonel Dame had informed President Young that "if it [Bennett's
trail] still lies in our course we shall follow it across the desert if not

we shall turn to our course."[4] In Dry Lake Valley Bennett's trail veered to the southwest while Dame took a new course a little north of west.

Their guide was an Indian they had recently picked up in Meadow Valley. The guides were becoming increasingly valuable as the expedition penetrated deeper into the country known only to the Indians. In later years, Martineau recalled the process by which these guides were obtained:

> Whenever a guide was needed, we always found one; often the only Indian, as it seemed, in the whole country round about, and when he would leave us afraid to go any farther from his home, another was always found just in the nick of time to take his place, though sometimes we had to run them down by horsemen and capture them like we would wild animals.[5]

The company pressed on across Dry Lake Valley toward a gap in the North Pahroc Range on the other side. They skirted to the north of the great dry lake bed over sand and gravel. Vegetation was sparse, and water was nowhere to be found.[6] About 6 P.M. a dry camp was made at a place they called Rocky Point Hill, twenty-eight miles west-northwest of Bennett's Springs according to their own estimates.[7]

As the company traveled, an extremely well-disciplined system of exploration was developed. The company historian described it:

> The order of camp while travelling was as follows: The first ten had the train one day, and the 2nd ten the next. A company of mounted men went ahead of the train exploring, and two followed behind the train as rear guard and to pick up articles that might be dropped. At every camp a stake was driven by the Historian with the time of arrival of the company and distance to the next water.[8]

Martineau also mentioned that the animals were always guarded at night and while grazing.

The encampment at Rocky Point Hill was near the base of the North Pahroc Range, a relatively low divide. Here there was no water or wood and very little grass. No one knew how long it would be before water would be found, and the situation was the cause of some concern. Nephi Johnson and a few others went on ahead toward the mountains to scout for water. Six miles west of camp, at the foot of the North Pahroc mountains, the exploring party came across a lone Indian. Although there was no sign of water, the presence of the Indian and his little wickiup of brush convinced Johnson that water must be nearby. No one could live in the desert far from water. At first the Indian was terrified of the shovels carried by the party, thinking they were weapons of war. As he tried to make his escape, however, the party "headed him off at every turn and finally captured him."[9] After calming him down by making signs of friendship and giving him food, the desert native showed the explorers that water could be obtained by digging holes in a dry wash nearby. The thirsty party quickly dug a test hole two feet deep, and, true to the Indian's word, a little water seeped into it. The men hurried back to the main camp with the good news, arriving after dark.

On the morning of the 5th, the Southern Exploring Company moved up to the "dry" wash and commenced digging holes. The place was appropriately named Desert Spring Wells.[10] Twenty holes were dug in the sand—one for each wagon mess of three men. The men worked in shifts dipping the precious water out of the wells. All day long they laid by their wells with a spoon and tin cup in hand and a bucket by their side. "When enough water was collected to fill the spoon, it was emptied into the cup, and when at last the cup was filled, it was poured into the pail; but it took a long time to fill a pail," wrote Martineau.[11] Nine hours were spent filling the water casks.[12] Even then, "the horses had not half enough" to drink.[13]

It appears that Brigham Young's reasoning may have been correct. It would be very difficult to get a large army with animals through this country. While contemplating Young's strategy, Martineau was quick to point this out. "Was Brigham Young's reasoning correct?" he asked.

> Yes, surely. Here were but sixty men and sixty [one hundred] animals spending two days and a night [since leaving Bennett's Springs] in getting a drink around. How would it have been with six hundred or six thousand? They must all perish but a miserable few; and the greater the number of men the more certain their death.[14]

While the men were moving up to the wells, Dame, Martineau, Johnson, and George W. Sirrine were piloted to another small spring two miles north of the main camp. It was a "beautiful little spring holding about a tub ful of water, and so concealed by grass and bushes that a person might go within a rod of it without seeing it. This we named Secret Spring," wrote Martineau.[15] This feature of Secret Spring was typical in the Great Basin. Water was often nearby but was unknown except to those familiar with the area. According to Martineau, water was often passed by unnoticed "because of the entire absence of willows or growth usually seen about a spring or brook."[16] And even when water was found it was "almost always brackish, sulphurous and unpalatable."[17] In addition to locating the spring, the four men also ascended a nearby mountain peak in the North Pahroc Range to obtain a view of the surrounding country. From Desert Spring Mountain, as they called it, they could plainly see the Grant Range or "White Mountains" at an estimated distance of seventy-five miles.

After returning to camp, the guide brought in an Indian who lived nearby. All around his wickiup lay the long black hair and bones of his wife. He admitted to the explorers that she had died and he ate her during a time of famine. The previous winter had been very severe, and hundreds of these people had died during the cold months when the usual diet of insects, reptiles, and rodents was difficult to obtain. Those that survived, it was learned, had subsisted on grass and the inner bark of cedar and juniper trees. Although he first claimed that her death was natural, and later that other Indians had killed her, he eventually confessed to killing her himself for food.[18]

Despite the Indian's shocking admission, he was treated kindly by the company. Enough bread to last four or five days was given to him—or so it was believed. But the poor native, who was little more than a skeleton, began to down the food, with an appetite that amazed the explorers, until the entire provision was consumed. He then went into his wickiup and brought out his own stock of provisions which he ate before the whole company. Martineau, who had an eye for detail, recorded the menu of this unusual feast. His meal consisted of two large mountain rats, one mouse, five large lizards, one horned toad, and four large rattlesnakes. With the exception of the mouse, which was eaten raw, the entire dinner was buried in the hot embers of the campfire and roasted. All of these items were consumed whole—bones, scales, and entrails—with the exception of the rattlesnake fangs which he broke off on a rock. Martineau recalled that the "four snakes were puffed to double their natural size."

> He . . . commenced eating at the head, continuing in the same way to the tail, the oil streaming down his jaws. It was a most disgusting sight, and made some of our company sick who saw him. His horrified feast continued until he had finished everything, and yet he must have known that when we left him he would be perfectly destitute of food.[19]

During the night, the hapless Indian disappeared into the desert and was not seen again.

Almost without exception, the explorers of the interior Great Basin were appalled at the situation of the Indians. Jedediah Smith wrote in 1827, after his epic journey across the basin, that these Indians "appeared the most miserable of the human race having nothing to subsist on, (nor any clothing) except grass seed, Grasshoppers &c."[20] Frémont said in his *Report* of 1845 that "from all that I heard and saw, I should say that humanity here appeared in its lowest form, and in its most elementry state."[21] And in 1859 Captain James H. Simpson remarked that "these Indians appear worse in condition than the meanest of the animal creation."[22]

These desert Indians were often called Diggers, collectively, because of their habits of digging roots and foraging for insects and other small edibles. The natives are actually divided into two language groups, the Western Shoshoni and the Southern Paiute. The latter occupied the southern portions of the area explored by the White Mountain explorers, while the Shoshonis ranged across the northern region. These Indians were poor, even by Indian standards. They had no horses, no tribal organization, and few weapons. They wandered in family units across the deserts in search of the bare necessities of life, and, even in this, they were sometimes unsuccessful. A bad year or harsh winter killed them off by the hundreds. Their numbers were also decimated by the Mexican slave trade which had flourished for years between the Utes, Navahos, and the Mexican settlements. For years the stronger, horse-mounted neighbors of these Diggers had captured their children and sold them to slave dealers in California and New Mexico. Many of these poor natives eventually accepted this fate for their children and bartered them with the Utes and Navahos for jaded horses which they usually ate.[23]

George W. Bean, who was exploring the area north of Dame's operation at the time, made similar observations. In a report to Brigham Young, Bean stated:

> The Indians who inhabit this region are scattered. We found a few on every range of mountains in a most abject state of poverty, being almost naked and living on such roots, reptiles and insects as they can gather. They looked as poor and as weak, as a man who had suffered a month's sickness. The most of them call themselves Shoshones. They talk the Digger Tongue. A few in the south are Piedes, who exist in constant dread of the Tosanwick or White Knifes, Pahvantes and Utes, who rob them of their squaws and children, from time to time. They seemed much pleased on becoming acquainted with us, although at first, they were so shy that we were compelled to follow them, with horses till they could run no further, in order to get to talk to them.[24]

Bean's White Mountain company had encountered about forty of these Indians between Cedar Springs and Snake Creek before Bean returned to Provo to confer with President Young. It was not long before the force on Snake Creek began having trouble with the more treacherous Gosiutes and White Knives, both of the Western Shoshoni group. Snake Valley was a part of the traditional range of these Indians.

Despite the perfidious nature of some of the more aggressive bands, the natives proved to be of great service to the White Mountain Expedition. Martineau told of numerous incidents in which the local Indians aided the company in finding water. In one instance the explorers happened upon an Indian with an antelope upon his shoulders which he had caught in a snare. "Having been without water for thirty-six hours, and none being in sight anywhere, we were naturally anxious to interview him," wrote the historian, "but he fled as soon as he saw us, still carrying his antelope." It took three horsemen two miles in pursuit to bring him down, and for over a mile he had run with his prize still on his shoulders.

> Much terrified and doubtless expecting death, he was pacified by a gift of food, and made to understand that water was wanted. He turned, beckoning our men to follow him down into a plain apparently perfectly devoid of water; but after going about a mile they suddenly came to a little brook about two feet wide and six inches deep, flowing in a channel five or six feet deep, and so narrow that its presence would be unsuspected a little distance away.[25]

Martineau recalled another incident in which the Indians came to the rescue of the desert explorers:

> Our party was suffering for water, when we had the good fortune to find an Indian, who promised for a supply of food, to show us some, pointing, as he spoke, to the top of a mountain a few miles distant. A party of horsemen, supplied with canteens, as many as they could carry, went with him to find the spring. Upward we toiled for miles finding no rivulet or spring and we began to think he was deceiving us as he still pointed to the very top of the mountain, and we felt sure there could be no spring there. Arrived at the summit, the Indian lifted a large flat stone and disclosed a natural tank or hole in the rock containing about two barrels of pure, cold water. Lifting other flat stones we found several other tanks partly filled with water, cool and inexpressibly delicious to the thirsty, tongue-swollen soul. These holes are filled during the season of rains and are then carefully covered for preservation. And to get a drink one must spend nearly a day in a toilsome trip up and down a rugged mountain.[26]

On May 6 the Southern Exploring Company completed the filling of its water casks at Desert Spring Wells and continued its journey west toward the White Mountains.

# IX

# THE NEW POLICY

While Colonel Dame was organizing his men at Iron Springs for their trek across the desert, George W. Bean had arrived at temporary church headquarters in Provo. As Brigham Young had instructed him in his urgent letter of March 21, Bean was here to report the founding of his new settlement at Snake Valley. But it was now April 22, and things in the Mormon capital had changed considerably. Bean was updated on several important developments. For one thing, he had been unaware that Dame was exploring the country south of his own explorations. But the shocking news was that Brigham Young had stepped down as governor of Utah Territory—something of a jolt considering the political atmosphere when he departed Provo on March 20.

An express had reached Salt Lake City on April 8 announcing that Colonel Kane and Governor Cumming would soon be coming into the city unescorted by troops. On the following day a council meeting was convened in Salt Lake to discuss what action, if any, the church would take. It was certainly welcome news if Kane had at last made a diplomatic breakthrough, but the idea of a gentile governor replacing Brigham Young was naturally met with hostility, and some of the brethren would have liked to eject him. Brigham Young, however, seemed assured that "the Lord would overrule it for good which ever way it happened," but he did not want the governor warmly welcomed.[1] Three days later Cumming arrived in the city. George A. Smith scornfully recorded his arrival in the church records: "City corporation, Mayor, Alderman & some councilors went out to meet the animal, styled Gov. Cumming."[2] Such was the bitterness and utter contempt many of the Mormons held for the man they believed was a Missouri mobber. But the gesture of coming into the settlements without his bayonets could not escape the notice of the people of the territory, and slowly he began to gain their respect.

Alfred Cumming was generally treated with courtesy, but at the same time with great apprehension. Outsiders and gentiles were mistrusted and feared in Utah, and Cumming's influence with the army could not be ignored. Indeed, it was the army that was the real concern to the Mormons. No matter who sat in the governor's chair in Salt Lake City, Brigham Young was the real governor of the people, and Salt Lake was on the verge of becoming a ghost town anyway. Cumming was even to admit his impotence to Young on April 28, when he told the prophet, "I can do nothing without your influence."[3] But backed by the invasion forces of General Johnston, Cumming could be dangerous, and until the army was dealt with, the exodus would continue. In full operation when the governor arrived, the exodus continued until mid-May when Salt Lake County and all the settlements to the north had been virtually abandoned.

When Kane had arrived at Camp Scott on March 12, the situation appeared bleak. His first meetings with Cumming seemed unproductive, and when he approached Johnston two days later, he was met with hostility. After a week of talks, Kane considered his mission a practical failure.[4] But somewhere in his conversations with Cumming, Kane must have touched the governor. On March 24 Cumming wrote to Secretary Cass of his intention to go to Salt Lake City shortly, "where I can have communication with the people before the army advances."[5] Kane had not converted the governor to believe the Mormons were blameless in their difficulties with the government, but he did convince him that the Mormons were worth talking with. Neither was Cumming intending to negotiate with the Mormons. His intention was primarily to urge them to subordinate themselves to federal authority before the territory was thrown into bloody civil war.[6] Moreover, Cumming appeared in no real hurry to reach the Mormon capital; having delayed his departure from Camp Scott until April 5, he then made a leisurely hunting trip out of his journey through the canyons to Salt Lake.[7]

In the meantime the army was thirsting for blood. By modifying Cumming's position on the Mormon issue, Kane had succeeded in driving a wedge between the military and civil authorities. At Camp Scott Colonel Kane and Governor Cumming were detested by the soldiers as traitors who had been duped by, or sold out to, the Mormons. Kane was thought to be a Mormon spy by many in the military.[8] The letters of Captain Gove are filled with hate and contempt for Kane and Cumming: "If Gov. C. has been so far fooled by this nincompoop of a Mr. Col. Kane, he is a bigger fool than I thought him to be," wrote the captain on March 26. And on April 27 he wrote that Cumming "has made an ass of himself, to say the least of it." Cumming, it seems, was standing in the way of the military conquest so much desired by the Utah expedition.[9]

In Salt Lake City Cumming requested and received two interviews with Brigham Young and other church leaders on April 13 and 14. On the 15th the governor sent a dispatch to the seething General Johnston declaring, "I have been everywhere recognized as governor of Utah."[10] Having been among the Mormons only three days, this declaration would seem a bit premature. But Cumming's attitude toward the Mormons was rapidly changing. He found that he liked Brigham Young and his associates, and he sympathized with their grievances, or at least made a pretense of doing so. Cumming even went so far as to announce that the books and papers of the federal court were all accounted for and in perfect order. Since the Utah War originated in part over Stiles's and Drummond's charges to the contrary, such a declaration could seriously deflate the government's case against the Mormons. But Governor Cumming's appraisal of the court records was again premature. The Mormons had indeed destroyed some law books and at least temporarily removed the court records. Although the Mormons may have deceived the governor on this matter, Cumming was clearly anxious to establish peace at any cost, perhaps more than either side was willing to pay.[11]

Notwithstanding the *appearance* of amicable relations with the Saints and his success in gaining recognition as the governor of Utah, Cumming was deeply disturbed over the rapid depopulation of the northern counties. From the day of his arrival in the settlements, the roads were lined with refugees who seemed to have no destination in mind other than "south." In his numerous interviews with the leading churchmen in the city, he expressed his concern over the matter. "There would be nobody left here but renegades who followed the army for juries," he exclaimed in a private interview with Brigham Young.[12] Daniel H. Wells explained to the governor that "the people had resolved not to be governed by officers sustained by the bayonet."[13] And President Young informed the concerned governor that "if the troops were withdrawn from the territory, the people would stop moving; but that ninety-nine out of every hundred of this people, would rather live out their lives in the mountains than endure the oppression the federal government was now heaping on them."[14] On occasion Governor Cumming personally rode along the highway between Salt Lake and Utah County pleading with the people to return to their homes. But all was in vain. Brigham Young governed the people, and when he told them to move south, they moved. During the first two weeks of May, six hundred wagons per day passed through Salt Lake City heading south, and in one of his journeys on May 6, Cumming counted eight hundred teams between Springville and Salt Lake City.[15]

To add to the governor's frustration were the obvious plans of the Mormons to destroy Salt Lake. George A. Smith had little hesitation in parting with his new $12,000 home: "I think my buildings will make a good fire, should Johnston advance on a sudden," declared the apostle.[16] And when Cumming asked W. H. Hooper, secretary *pro tem* of the territory, why the government safe was located in his barn, Hooper replied, "We were going to burn the city shortly and did not want to burn any U.S. property."[17]

On April 25, three days after Bean's arrival in Provo, Cumming made a public address to the people of Utah. Boldly and single-handedly he confronted the issues before a radical assembly of three to four thousand Mormons in the Tabernacle. He told them it was his "duty to secure the supremacy of the constitution and laws." Cumming held back nothing, even though he fully understood the Saints' embitterment toward the government. The audience listened "respectfully" as he candidly explained the character of his administration. He also denied that the army was sent to destroy them, claiming it was sent to protect them. While his listeners did not particularly trust him, or even believe him, they admired his courage.[18]

Then the Mormons voiced their grievances, and the meeting became quite spirited, as the atrocities committed against them were recited again and again. Apostle John Taylor asserted that "these troops must be withdrawn before we can have any officers palmed upon us."[19] "We never said that we would not receive their officers," cried Gilbert Clements from the pulpit, "but, that we would not receive them at the point of the bayonet."[20]

It seems that Brigham Young lost much of the fire he possessed the previous fall. No longer did he speak of independence or violence; although he was still of the opinion that the United States was on the verge of collapse. His main goal was to keep the people and the army apart, but he shrank from taking any irretractable measures. He introduced Alfred Cumming as the governor of Utah, and, surprisingly, he reproved Apostle Taylor for inflaming the passions of the people with his recounting of their trials in Missouri and Illinois. Young spoke only of peace and the amicable settlement of the present difficulties. But the move south continued.

Later in the day President Young received a note from George W. Bean in Provo. The president was pleased with Bean's report of Snake Valley, mentioning to Wilford Woodruff: "They have found a desert as we have been looking for."[21]

Bean was getting anxious; he had laid in Provo for three days without receiving any word from Brigham Young. Something had changed. Where was the urgency of a month ago? Finally, on the 26th Bean sent a letter to the prophet, who was still in Salt Lake directing the evacuation, asking for instructions. The letter, which is reproduced in its entirety, is indicative of the dutiful nature of the man Brigham Young chose to find a refuge for the gathering:

> Provo   April 26th 1858
>
> Prest. Young
> Dear Brother. As I am anxious to return to the Deserts immediately I would like to be instructed upon the following points. Shall we extend our explorations North west of our present location towards Ruby Valley. Do you wish to know the distance North to Reddings Springs on the Beckwith route. Do you intend to send families across the Desert this spring. if so we must send a guide to meet them at the proper time and place. If we find a suitable place southwest for farming &c. shall we report to you immediately describing the extent of the same. and if not successful shall we continue on to the rim of the Basin. Shall the brethren go to building and making other improvements than farming at the present location. Do you wish to ratify or amend the election of Bro Edson Barney as President of that Mission. If you do not intend to return immediately to Provo I would be glad to receive an answer on those points with any additional instructions that you may give in relation to our future movements. I shall be ready to start as soon as an answer is received.
>
> Your Brother in the Gospel
> Geo. W. Bean[22]

Brigham Young's reply was sent two days later. It is apparent that Cumming had made great progress in allaying the fears and suspicions of the Mormon leader. All sense of urgency was gone in this communication with Bean. "We do not contemplate sending families across the Desert this Spring," wrote Young, "hence you need not hurry to send us word but send in every opportunity by those who may be coming back."[23] Here was a definite change in policy. Five weeks ago, on the day of his "Sebastopol" speech, Young's word to Bean was: "Send word immediately. . . . We are about starting five hundred families . . . bound for the Deserts." The prophet apparently no longer considered the White Mountain

Expedition the salvation of the kingdom, but this did not imply that the expedition or the move south were to be discontinued.

President Young did not consider his problems solved by any means—not so long as a hostile army sat on Utah's border. But his assessment of his situation had changed drastically since Governor Cumming had arrived. When Brigham Young informed Bean that families would not likely be sent across the desert that spring, he was admitting that the burning of the settlements was no longer considered probable, at least for the time being. The expedition could be useful, however. Since this massive undertaking was already in the field, it would be to their advantage to continue searching for the oasis in case it was ever decided to move there or even plant a settlement there. The move south was also useful. Although it was no longer considered a prelude to permanent resettlement, the exodus was still the kingpin of Young's public relations campaign being waged in the national press. It was also a demonstration of Brigham Young's power and influence. Perhaps most important, it reflected the prophet's resolve that his people not come in contact with the army. The bloody scenes of Missouri and Illinois must not be repeated, and the soldiers' influence in the territory must be abated whether the army proved to be hostile or not. If the army had to have Salt Lake, they could have it, but it was obvious from Young's recent instructions to Bean that he did not think this would actually happen.

In several respects, things had not changed materially. Brigham Young still governed the people, and he was still playing his options, emphasizing and de-emphasizing the facets of his plans that seemed likely to reap the most gain. But the prophet's options were becoming limited. When he gave up the governorship, he forfeited his command of the Nauvoo Legion. In the unlikely event of an armed conflict, Mormon resistance would have to be conducted underground. On May 21 Cumming reported that he was in total control of the militia.[24]

In his instructions to George W. Bean, Young ordered him to continue his explorations to the southwest and south in search of settlement sites. But he "need not look North or North West with a view of making settlements." In this way, Bean's company would be marching closer to the imagined oasis and also in the vicinity of Dame's explorations. Young closed his letter by saying that if it didn't storm, he would visit the explorer in Provo on Friday, which was two days away. The prophet was obviously no longer in any hurry; yet it was just three days since he had made allusions to going to Sonora in his Tabernacle address, an obvious deception. Friday rolled around, it stormed, and Bean departed for the desert without seeing Young.

Bean arrived at the White Mountain camp on Snake Creek about May 5. The men had not been idle in his absence. According to Orson B. Adams's map, a complete reconnaissance of Snake Valley had been made.[25] Parties had reached Salt Marsh Lake in the north end of the valley and as far south as Hamblin Valley Wash, a distance of seventy miles between the extremes.

Upon his arrival, Bean began to reorganize his company for the further exploration of the desert beyond them. The Iron County brethren, under the command of Orson B. Adams, were chosen to extend their explorations to the northwest. This was not done with the idea of planting new settlements, as Brigham Young had instructed Bean to look to the south and southwest for that object. Bean's motive was probably to connect their explorations with the known points on the Humboldt or Beckwith routes. His letter to Young of April 26 shows an interest in that direction when he asked if the prophet wished him to extend his explorations toward Ruby Valley or to find the distance to Reddings Springs on the Beckwith route. George W. Bean had been a member of the exploring party sent out by Steptoe in 1855 to find a shorter route to California south of the Great Salt Lake. It appears that Bean may have still been searching for the route in 1858.

The honor of searching for the oasis, with the intention of locating another settlement, fell upon the Beaver company. Bean personally lead this contingent to the southwest. About forty-five men from the Fillmore, Utah County, and Salt Lake companies were assigned to farm the ground at Snake Creek under the direction of Edson Barney, although he did not remain there. Barney later wrote that he chose Bean and a Brother Free to be his counsellors on the mission.[26] Bean, however, never did reside at Snake Creek for more than a few days.

The Iron County company, twenty-eight men in all, marched north toward a pass in the Snake Range. Crossing the site of present-day Baker, Nevada, they turned to the west and ascended the remarkably gentle grade of Sacramento Pass, the present location of U.S. Highway 50 and 6. This broad gap in the mountains

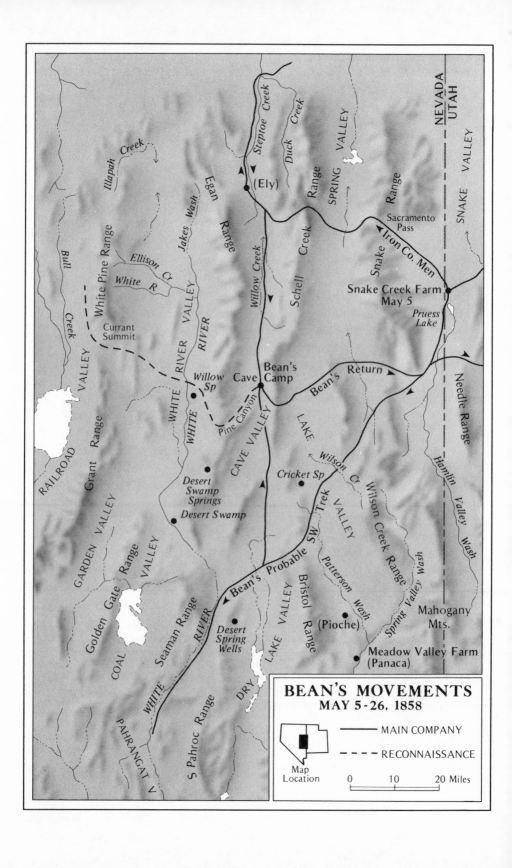

Illapah Creek

Steptoe Creek

Duck Creek

SPRING VALLEY

NEVADA
UTAH

SNAKE VALLEY

Egan Range

Range

SPRING VALLEY

Snake Creek

Sacramento Pass

Iron Co. Men

(Ely)

Willow Creek

Schell Creek Range

Snake Creek Farm
May 5

Pruess Lake

White Pine Range

Jakes Wash

Ellison Cr.

White R

Currant Summit

WHITE RIVER VALLEY

RIVER

Willow Sp

Cave

Bean's Camp

Bean's Return

Bull Creek

RAILROAD

Grant Range

GARDEN VALLEY

Pine Canyon

WHITE

CAVE VALLEY

LAKE

Needle Range

Hamlin Valley Wash

Desert Swamp Springs

Desert Swamp

Cricket Sp

Wilson Cr.

SW Trek

VALLEY

Wilson Creek Range

Spring Valley Wash

Golden Gate Range

COAL VALLEY

Seaman Range

RIVER

Bean's Probable

Desert Spring Wells

LAKE VALLEY

Bristol Range

Patterson Wash

(Pioche)

Mahogany Mts.

WHITE

DRY

Meadow Valley Farm
(Panaca)

S Pahroc Range

PAHRANGAT V

**BEAN'S MOVEMENTS**
**MAY 5-26, 1858**

Map Location

——— MAIN COMPANY
– – – RECONNAISSANCE

0      10      20 Miles

abounds in pine and juniper. Down the western slope of the Snake Range on an equally easy inclination, they found themselves in Spring Valley, a ten-mile-wide, flat, desert plain, bounded on the west by the Schell Creek Range. Most of the valley was a sea of low sagebrush, so typical of the valleys of the Great Basin. But near the center of the valley, and slightly north of their course, they discovered a large, grassy bottom interspersed with cedar trees. Nearby was a small spring which Adams called Desert (Layton) Spring.

Crossing the valley a few miles north of the present line of U.S. 50 and 6, the Iron County men proceeded westward up the slopes of the Schell Creek Mountains. Looking back, they could see the western slope of the towering Wheeler Peak looming over the valley. Driving up Cooper Canyon, as it is called today, was considerably more difficult than the gentle slopes of Sacramento Pass. A steep ascent was encountered just below the summit on the east slope. At the top the company dug four holes for the purpose of caching supplies,[27] before descending into what they thought was Ruby Valley. The explorers had actually reached Steptoe Valley, a high, relatively narrow plain, hemmed in by the high Egan Range on the west and the equally high Schell Creek Range on the east, which they had just crossed. Ruby Valley was a good seventy miles to the northwest. Somewhat of an anomaly, Steptoe Valley is one of the few valleys in the Great Basin's interior that is adequately watered. This is mainly because of its high elevation and close proximity to the surrounding mountains with their attendant runoff.

As the Mormons made their descent into the valley, they picked up Steptoe Creek (which they called Soap Creek) and followed it north. The stream widened to about five feet and a depth of one and a half feet with a rapid current and rocky bottom. They soon struck another stream flowing northeast issuing out of the Egan Range which measured a foot deep and six to ten feet wide. Adams, who was compiling a map of his explorations, named this stream South Creek, but on today's maps it is known as Murry Creek. As the explorers refreshed themselves by its banks, they stood precisely on the future site of Ely, Nevada. Both of the streams found by the Iron County men sank in the middle of the valley a few miles away, forming a bottomland of "luxuriant grass, intermingled with clover."[28] But Adams found the land too cold for farming purposes, there being frost every night. Had it not been for this and being outside of the arbitrary limits imposed by Brigham Young, it would have made an ideal place for a settlement (as the city of Ely testifies).

The expedition continued its northward trek up the valley past the present-day site of McGill. About seven miles farther, they turned east into the Gallagher Gap, a canyon in the Schell Creek Range. Undoubtedly the explorers were following up Duck Creek, a sizable stream, toward its source.[29] Adams called this stream North Creek, probably because this was the northernmost extent of his explorations. Going as far north as it seemed expedient, the Iron County contingent retraced its steps back down the valley and continued exploring south in hopes of linking up with Bean and his company of Beaver City men. It was now nearing the middle of May.

George W. Bean's southwest journey is not well documented. Unlike the party from Iron County who surveyed to the northwest of Snake Valley, Bean's contingent left no map which has been found today; although later in the month he wrote to Brigham Young that he hoped to "be able to make a full and complete map of this hitherto unknown country."[30] Many years later, in his autobiography, Bean claimed that after leaving Snake Creek he made his way southwest into the Pahranagat Valley of present-day Lincoln County, Nevada.[31] In his reports to President Young, Bean represented that he "crossed two valleys into the rim of the Great Basin, exploring right and left, for springs which we found at convenient distances, Plenty of grass and wood on the mountains, but the vallies were barren."[32] "Southwest of the White Mountains," wrote the explorer, "we find but little water and grass a few springs generally in the mountains some in the vallies but not very good, alkali being present."[33] Edson Barney recalled in later years that "Bro. George W. Bean and company returned from the southwest direction about 100 miles over the rim of the Basin."[34]

It would appear from Barney's statement that Bean did indeed penetrate the desert far enough to reach the Pahranagat Valley. Assuming this, Bean would have rounded the south end of the Snake Range and probably headed southwest across Spring Valley toward the gap between the Fortification Range and the Wilson Creek Range, the only good crossing to the southwest. Once through the gap, the company would have been in Lake Valley, a vast, sage-covered plain surrounded by cedar and piñon. From here Bean would have had a variety of options open to him to the southwest. He undoubtedly would have chosen to skirt the massive Schell Creek

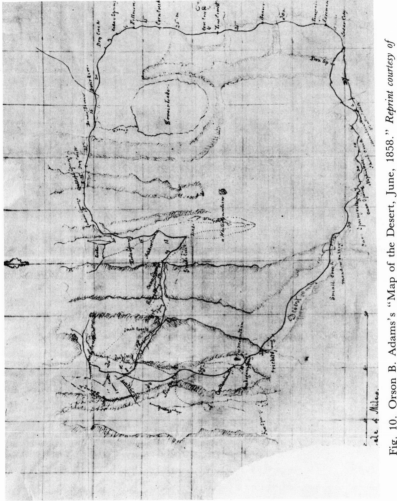

Fig. 10. Orson B. Adams's "Map of the Desert, June, 1858." *Reprint courtesy of Grabborn-Hoyem.*

Range to the south, and he probably struck the White River Wash—a usually dry streambed—and followed it south into the Pahranagat Valley. Unable to locate a suitable place for settlement of the Beaver City men, Bean turned the little company around and headed back for a rendezvous with the Iron County party.

# X
# MIRACLE ON ALTAR PEAK

Before parting company in Snake Valley, the two contingents of Bean's exploring company must have made plans to rendezvous two valleys west of Barney's settlement on Snake Creek. Adams's Iron County men continued their southbound trek down Steptoe Valley over a low divide and into Cave Valley, which they entered on the afternoon of May 13.[1] This elevated mountain valley had a natural, rugged beauty. Far greener than the other valleys in the area, lush grasses rippled across its 6,500-foot-high meadows. To the east stood the craggy, snow-covered peaks of the Schell Creek Range, and several springs were found in the valley. In short, it looked like a refreshing location for a camp. Within a day, Bean's division found its way into the valley, apparently from the south. United again, plans were laid to further their explorations to the west.

While Bean was pushing his way toward Pahranagat Valley, Colonel Dame's Southern Exploring Company was working its way toward the Grant Range (which Dame believed to be the White Mountains). Unlike Bean, Dame was unaware of the change in policy in Salt Lake City; consequently, his pace was relentless. At seven o'clock on the morning of May 6, the company retreated from their camp at Desert Spring Wells and crossed over the North Pahroc divide two miles from camp. Descending a canyon, they entered the narrow White River Wash and turned almost due north to follow its watercourse. After a hard march of twenty-seven miles, the company made a dry camp for the night. Had the party been but a few days later, they might have intersected George W. Bean's southwest reconnaissance.

On the morning of the 7th, the Southern Exploring Company continued its march up the White River Wash at 6:45. At this point the wash was little more than a canyon, but as the explorers advanced it began to widen considerably. Five miles up the trail, they came upon the first evidence of water in this valley. In an otherwise dry creek bed, they found "a little water standing in pools . . . with new grass along its edges."[2] The water was strongly tainted with alkali; nevertheless, it was a welcome find.

In this arid region, the explorers quickly learned how to survive on what was available. Martineau recalled that in the desert nothing can take the place of water. Although the company had an abundance of coffee and tea and a little brandy, "they cannot," wrote Martineau, "take the place of water to the thirsty—nothing can." He found that "men who use neither tea, coffee nor spirits, can endure the extremes of either heat or cold much better than can men who do use them."[3]

It was also discovered that the mules were far superior to horses for desert travel. The camp historian recalled:

> After a day's march beneath a burning sun without water, the horses, when unharnessed, would look about with the most forlorn appearance, give up entirely and seem as if ready to die; but the mules would have a good roll, shake themselves, nibble a dry greasewood, then look about them with an intelligent air—in short they never gave up.[4]

Martineau also found that the mules possessed a far greater ability to scent water than horses, and they were superior to dogs as sentries.

After watering their stock, the company proceeded up the wash finding more standing pools of water the farther north they got. As they rounded the north end of the Seaman Range to their left, the valley widened into a broad, flat plain. Looking to the west across the wide valley, they now had an unobstructed view of the so-called White Mountains, the object of their march.

At one o'clock the company camped on the edge of a "large wire grass meadow or slough full of strong alkali water."[5] This place was appropriately named Desert Swamp by the explorers. The meadow was watered by a considerable stream flowing from the north. Martineau recorded that it was "about 20 feet wide and a foot deep, with a good current,"[6] but Dame's report of the stream had it only half as wide.[7] The stream was strongly contaminated with alkali, however, and alkali beds were everywhere in the valley, which precluded any possibility of farming here. Typical of the Great Basin, this stream dissipated to nothing a few miles below the swamp, forming the standing pools found earlier by the explorers. This stream was the White River. It flows and sinks intermittently over a distance of 125 miles through eastern Nevada. Rising out of the White Pine Range, it is fed by numerous springs in the White River Valley and Pahranagat Valley in which vicinity it may flow during certain seasons of the year for several miles. Barring a heavy storm, it is almost always dry in the wash connecting these two valleys. The White River has been known to run dry for ten years at a time and then flow for a year or two.[8] Martineau found that above their camp the stream formed "large shallow ponds, which were much frequented by ducks."[9]

Dame wasted no time in organizing a reconnaissance of the White Mountains which were now only twenty miles to the west. Only one small divide, the Golden Gate Range, lay between them and their objective. After dinner the colonel and thirteen hand-picked men, including his trusted lieutenants, James H. Martineau and Nephi Johnson, struck out across the valley for these snowy peaks. The reconnoitering party headed toward a gap in the Golden Gate Range. Near the summit they discovered a rock arch "large enough for a covered wagon to pass under, presenting a very natural resemblance to a sleeping lion or dog with two faces, . . . guarding the way."[10] Now in Garden Valley, Dame continued his implacable march toward the Grant Range. Dame called the valley Wibe Valley on account of the abundance of wibe grass they found in the southwestern part, "which grows high and has seeds about half as large as a grain of wheat."[11] Reaching the slopes of the Grant Range, which Dame now calls Gray Head Mountain, the party camped for the night. Here they found plenty of grass and firewood but, disappointingly, no water. They had traveled, according to Martineau's estimates, twenty-two miles from their base camp at the Desert Swamp and thirty-three miles since breaking camp that morning at Desert Spring Wells.

In the morning the party again rose early and began searching south along the base of the mountain for a pass to the western slope of Gray Head Mountain. For nine miles they picked their way among the foothills through dense piñon and cedar, finally entering the mouth of a canyon for their ascent. This may have been Rimrock Canyon near the foot of Troy Peak; but the explorers called it Onion Canyon because of the abundance of wild onions they discovered growing around a nearby spring they had located a mile from its mouth. Martineau noted that the canyon "is full of the very best of bunch grass and would sustain a great many animals." He

Fig. 11. Arch discovered by Dame in the Golden Gate Range can be seen twenty-one miles southwest of Sunnyside, Nevada, at a place known locally as "the pinnacles." *By Todd I. Berens, April 1984.*

estimated that, with reservoirs, Onion Spring would be capable of watering several thousand head of stock.[12]

After reaching the head of the canyon, the company rested while the untiring Colonel Dame and a few others ascended another summit higher up in the range yet. But it was Dame's intention to reach the very top of this towering mountain range to make observations of all the surrounding country. Now only Dame, Martineau, and Johnson continued the assault on the summit, leaving behind the others, who declined to go on. Leaving their animals behind also, the trio struggled and clawed their way to the pinnacle. In places, snowdrifts six feet deep and fully exposed to the sun lay across their path. This mountain is a presently unnamed peak in the Grant Range immediately south of 11,298-foot Troy Peak near Cherry Creek Summit.[13]

From the top the view was breathtaking. To the north they saw a "high pyramidal peak perfectly white . . . , which Pres. Dame pronounced to be the White Mts." These mountains were estimated to be one hundred miles distant, and Martineau wrote, "we have since learned [it] must be a high peak on the Humboldt River." No doubt, Dame's latest candidate for the White Mountains was the Ruby Range.[14]

To the extreme west the majestic snow-capped peaks of the Sierra Nevada were clearly visible and correctly estimated to be 150 to 200 miles distant. Between them and the Sierras was "a perfect desert extending as far as the eye can extend." Immediately west of Gray Head was Railroad Valley with its huge, white alkali flat, by far the largest they had yet seen. Dame estimated its size to be "20 to 40 miles in extent." Looking to the east, the awestruck explorers saw the mighty Wasatch Range forming the eastern flank of the Great Basin. Its southern terminus below Harmony was easily discernable.[15] Here a geographic fact was established. They were now midway between the two great mountain ranges of western America. At this point, nearly one-third of the distance across present-day Nevada, Colonel Dame had indeed reached the center of the Great Basin, an area never before trod by the white man.

From their unique position on the top of a high mountain in the center of the Great Basin, these three men stood in reverence as they surveyed the great unexplored wilderness which surrounded them. They considered their mission: to find the refuge for God's people. "On this mountain peak," recalled Martineau, "the spirit of liberty

seemed to dwell; we seemed lifted above the sinful world and to be
nearer to heaven."[16] There was an abundance of flat stones lying
around on the summit, and President Dame began to gather them
up and build an altar. Apparently overcome by the grandeur of the
moment, the men commenced singing the Mormon hymn "For the
Strength of the Hills We Bless Thee," as they stood around the altar
of stones. The words of this hymn seem to have been written for this
exact moment. Indeed, they had only recently been published in the
*Deseret News* in January and were meant to reflect the Mormon feeling that Utah was a sanctuary from the enemies of Zion. Perhaps
one of the three men had cut it out of the newspaper and brought it
with him to the desert. The hymn is quoted in full as originally
published:

> For the strength of the hills we bless Thee!
> Our God, our fathers' God
> Thou hast made Thy children mighty
> By the touch of the mountain's sod.
> Thou hast fixed our ark of refuge,
> Where the spoilers foot ne'er trod.
> For the strength of the hills we bless Thee,
> Our God, our fathers' God.
>
> We are watchers of a beacon
> Whose light must never die.
> We are guardians of an altar
> Midst the silence of the sky.
> The rocks yield founts of courage
> Struck forth as by a rod.
> For the strength of the hills we bless Thee,
> Our God, our fathers' God.
>
> For the dark resounding caverns
> Where thy still small voice is heard;
> For the strong pines of the forests
> That by thy breath have stirred;
> For the storms on whose free pinions
> Thy spirit walks abroad.
> For the strength of the hills we bless Thee,
> Our God, our fathers' God.
>
> The royal eagle darteth,
> O'er his quarry from the heights:
> And the stag that knows no master,
> Seeks there his wild delights;
> But we, for thy communion,
> Have sought the mountain sod.

For the strength of the hills we bless Thee,
Our God, our fathers' God.

The banner of the chieftain,
Far, far below us waves:
The war-horse of the spearman
Cannot reach our lofty caves.
Thy dark clouds wrap the threshold
Of freedom's last abode.
For the strength of the hills we bless Thee,
Our God, our fathers' God.

For the shadow of thy presence
Round our camp of rock outspread;
For the stern defiles of battle
Bearing record of our dead:
For the snows and for the torrents,
For the free heart's burial sod.
For the strength of the hills we bless Thee,
Our God, our fathers' God.[17]

There is little doubt that these men understood the full significance of the words of this anthem. Dame, Johnson, and Martineau
then knelt in a circle around the altar while President Dame offered
up a prayer. The mountains and deserts were dedicated to God,
and he asked that they "be led to the place appointed by his holy
spirit that we might know the place when we see it."[18] Martineau recalled in later years that Dame specifically prayed that the
company might get a view of Pilot Peak, a prominent landmark on
the Hastings Cutoff far to the northeast. Apparently trying to get a
better fix on their position, the explorers strained to see the mountain. Although the sky was clear, the elusive peak remained invisible
to them. But after "having prayed God to open our way and our
understanding," they again scanned the northern horizon, "and
there, in plain view, we saw the mountain peak so much desired!"
asserted Martineau. "Perfectly and plainly it was outlined against
the sky." The account continues that the brethren "looked at each
other in astonishment and with gratitude to the Father who had
heard and answered our prayers, and had given us the knowledge
we desired." Martineau admitted that "some may smile in
derision," but, he avowed, "it is true, nevertheless. We ascended the
mountain with a certain purpose, and God in His mercy blessed us
according to our desires."[19]

A stranger sight has probably seldom been seen or heard in this region than the one presented here—three men, profiled against the desert sky on the pinnacle of a massive mountain peak, singing praises and praying to their God as they knelt around an altar of stones, while completely surrounded by a vast wilderness of mountains and deserts, many days from civilization. After this experience, the exploring company referred to this summit as Altar Peak.

Despite their sublime experience on the mountain, the explorers were agreeably disappointed with the prospects of making a settlement near this range. They discovered that Gray Head (Grant Range) was "only a single narrow mountain, and does not afford any streams of water except a small one running into Wibe Valley."[20] The water from the melting snows too often sank before reaching far enough into the valley to make irrigation projects possible.

Joining the remainder of his reconnoitering party, Dame emerged on the west slope of the range and pressed southward a few miles. Here Martineau's map shows something that is not indicated in any of the extant chronicles of the expedition. Apparently a trail was broken from the west side of the Grant Range down into Railroad Valley to a spring near the center of the valley close to the southern edge of the valley's huge alkali bed. In the absence of any further explanation it is surmised that this trail may have been a reconnaissance made by their Indian guide, or perhaps only representative of information supplied by him.

Soon the party turned east to recross the range. It appears likely that the explorers chose Ox Spring Wash to begin their ascent. Crossing over the summit, they descended a canyon which was almost certainly today's Cherry Creek Canyon. Martineau's journal states: "We descended into a kanyon (the head of Wibe [Cherry] Creek) and descended it to its mouth, about 12 miles."[21] In the canyon the men found abundant signs of copper and gold. The mouth of the canyon was described as being narrow—only about twenty feet apart, it was said—which consisted of "high ledges of gold bearing quartz."[22] Several men in the company who were deemed to be "experienced," were of the opinion that the ledges "promised a very rich yield of gold. But," wrote the historian, "we did not stop to prospect any."[23] The men of the White Mountain Expedition had a more important assignment; they still knew nothing of the new policies adopted by Brigham Young. The canyon's mouth was appropriately named the Golden Gate. It might be interesting to know if the nearby Golden Gate Range is a legacy of this expedition.

After traveling thirty rugged miles, most of it in the mountains, Dame's pack train bedded down for the night about a half mile below the mouth of the canyon on Wibe (Cherry) Creek. Early on Sunday morning, May 9, the party started east toward the main camp on the Desert Swamp.

By the second week of May, it was becoming increasingly apparent to both Bean and Dame that the White Mountain region was not what it was believed to be. The country just did not possess the resources necessary to sustain anything but the smallest of settlements, and those very few. As Bean reported on his return to Provo in April: "The difficulty was to find soil, timber & water *together*."[24] (Italics mine.)

# RENDEZVOUS
# IN WHITE RIVER VALLEY

Worried and perplexed, Dame made his way back to the Desert Swamp with his pack train. The reconnaissance of Gray Head had been disappointing. Mid-May was approaching, and the company had yet to plant a seed in the ground. The journey back to camp was a difficult one as well. The explorers chose to return by a different route a little farther to the south than the one they had taken west. After crossing the Golden Gate Range, they entered desolate Coal Valley. Here they endured considerable suffering from the intense heat. Martineau's estimate of a thirty-five-mile trek back to camp was obviously exaggerated by the suffering he endured. As the explorers looked across this flat, unforgiving wasteland, they saw a mirage resembling a beautiful lake five or six miles distant. What they probably saw was the sunlight reflecting off the large Coal Valley alkali flat to the south.

After a difficult march, they arrived in camp where they found all was well. The animals had been stampeded sometime earlier by the hordes of gnats that infested the "swamp," but all was now under control. Without wasting any time, Colonel Dame dispatched more reconnaissance parties in new directions to ascertain the value of the country. Ross R. Rogers, of Beaver, was sent with seven men to explore up the creek (White River) which fed the "swamp" from the north. Another seven men were sent to the southwest under the command of John W. Freeman, of Washington, to locate a large spring their Indian guide had reported about forty miles distant.

The sanctuary Brigham Young had spoken of must surely lie somewhere in this area; they had followed his instructions implicitly. For 225 miles, by their own estimates, they had penetrated the desert west and north of Pinto Creek, but, so far, all had been in vain. The area was cold, too. While suffering from the heat in the daytime, water would often freeze a half-inch thick in tin pans and cups during the night. It was frankly doubted that garden crops could mature under such conditions. There was also the problem of alkali impregnating much of the flat and irrigable lands.

The camp laid over all day on Monday the 10th waiting for word from the Rogers and Freeman reconnoitering parties. One of Freeman's men had returned during the night, but there was no news. His horse had only become lame. The wait continued on the 11th. The gnats at Desert Swamp were again becoming a problem. Finally, about 11 A.M. Freeman and company rode into camp from the southwest. The large spring could not be found. They had only discovered one small watering hole with hardly enough water to satisfy their own needs. The little company had either been to the south end of Garden Valley or into the barren wastes of Coal Valley.

About sunset the northern exploring party under Rogers returned to camp. They had been seventeen miles up the valley to the source of the water flow—several large springs at the foot of the Egan Range on the valley's east bench. The water from these springs flowed to the bottom of the valley where they formed a large wire grass meadow several miles long, before running south to the Desert Swamp. The little oasis was appropriately named Desert Swamp Springs. The water was estimated to be capable of watering fifty to seventy-five acres, but, as in so many other places, the alkali beds were so heavy that the land was useless to them.[1] They did find good grass and wood, however.

Dame had to make a decision. Where was the company to go from Desert Swamp? He had dispatched exploring parties, including himself, in almost every direction, towards every promise of water, no matter how slight. To the west of Gray Head he found only more desert worse than where they had already been. Freeman had found nothing in the south, and now Rogers offered little encouragement for putting in a settlement to the north. But the decision was not difficult. To the north there was at least flowing water—the lifeblood of the desert. There was also wood and grass available. The verdict was reached: At sunrise the Southern Exploring Company would march north.

The morning of May 12 saw the wagons of the frustrated company rolling up the White River Valley toward Desert Swamp Springs. These are the springs presently known as Flagg Springs located on the property of the Nevada Fish and Game Department's Sunnyside Wildlife Management Area, a fish and game refuge. These springs and others farther north provided the water for Sunnyside Creek, a major tributary of the White River. The river is now dammed five miles downstream to form the Adams-McGill reservoir. Several other dikes below the dam flood the valley bottom during the winter months. The area between the Mormons' Desert Swamp and Desert Swamp Springs is one of the wettest parts of the entire valley.

As the main camp was moving up to the springs, President Dame and eight others, including the faithful Martineau and Johnson, rode ahead of the company with five days' provisions. Their purpose according to Dame, was "exploring in the neighborhood of the White Mountain"[2]—in this case, the Egan Range which forms the eastern flank of the valley.

The pack train arrived at Desert Swamp (Flagg) Springs well ahead of the heavy wagons plodding up from the south. While the explorers found some rather large meadows in the valley bottom, the place was primarily an ocean of sage and greasewood ten to fifteen miles wide between the Egan and Grant ranges. Dame's exploring party stopped for about two hours at the springs to rest and feed the animals and then pressed on toward a large canyon in the Egan Range. Eight miles north of the springs the party turned east up Pine Canyon, so-called from its abundance of cedar and piñon pine, and camped a mile above its mouth. Like many of the mountain canyons they had discovered in this region, it was "full of bunch grass, capable of sustaining thousands of cattle."[3] But according to Dame, it "has no regular stream in it."[4]

On Thursday, May 13, the main camp, finding Desert Swamp Springs an undesirable location to settle, continued north another seventeen miles to Willow Springs. Like Desert Swamp Springs, Willow Springs spread out over the valley bottom creating a large wire grass meadow a mile across. But the climate was reported to be "very frosty,"[5] and, even though it was estimated that the water was sufficient to water several hundred acres, Martineau conceded that "the land is highly impregnated with alkali which is the prevailing characteristic of this country."[6] Dame believed that there was less alkali here than at Desert Swamp Springs, however.[7] What the desert camp had found was the springs known today as Immigrant Springs, which can be seen just west of Nevada Highway 318 on the property owned by the Utah-Nevada Livestock Company (UNELCO) sixteen miles south of Lund.

As the main camp was rolling up the valley toward Willow (Immigrant) Springs, Dame and party continued to wind their way up Pine Canyon—the present Shingle Pass—to get a look at the valley east of them. Suddenly they came upon a family of Indians who had not been aware of their presence in the canyon. The natives were terrified. Two small children ran up into the cedars one hundred yards away "screaming with all their might, and calling their parents to escape also."[8] But the parents remained at their camp desperately trying to conceal an infant. To be sure, they thought Dame's men would try to take the child, as these people had been the frequent victims of slavers. The explorers pacified them, however, by giving them some biscuits as quickly as possible. Once tranquility had been restored, the Paiutes informed Dame where a small spring could be found just over the divide, and the company departed. Near present Shingle Pass on the summit of the Egan Range, the water hole was located and named Indian Spring. Here they unsaddled their horses, rested, and ate their lunch. While there, the Indian family dropped in for another visit.

As in the past, the inseparable threesome of Dame, Martineau, and Johnson climbed a nearby mountain peak to view the country and get their bearings. Considering the talents of Johnson and Martineau, it is little wonder that Dame relied on them so heavily. Martineau, Dame's adjutant and closest advisor in the legion, was an excellent surveyor and the company's journalist. Johnson was an intrepid explorer and a superb interpreter. As essential as the Indians proved to be in guiding the company, they would have been worthless without the services of a good interpreter.

From this "high granite peak," perhaps Shingle Peak, the three explorers gazed down upon a high mountain valley which they called Three Butte Valley because of three small buttes in it. These buttes, which are plainly visible from the western slope of Shingle Pass, can be readily identified by a small sketch Martineau inserted in Dame's journal of the expedition. Across the valley lay the snow-capped peaks of the Schell Creek Range. This was Cave Valley, the same that was mentioned as the rendezvous point for the two elements of George W. Bean's expedition. Although they did not know it at the time, if it had not been such a hazy day, Dame's party might have been able to see Adams's company of Iron County men entering this unexplored valley from the north.[9] Looking to the north and five degrees west they "obtained a glimpse of a high snow peak . . . supposed to be a peak of the White mountain."[10] Here they were again viewing the Ruby Range far to the north. These were the

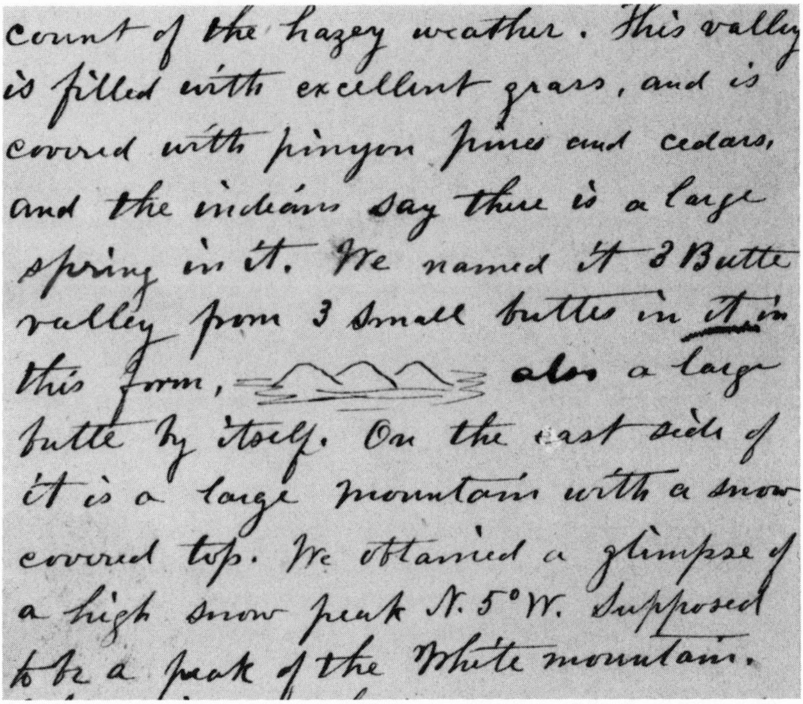

count of the hazey weather. This valley
is filled with excellent grass, and is
covered with pinyon pines and cedars,
and the indians say there is a large
spring in it. We named it 3 Butte
valley from 3 small buttes in it, in
this form, ⌒⌒⌒ also a large
butte by itself. On the east side of
it is a large mountain with a snow
covered top. We obtained a glimpse of
a high snow peak N. 5° W. Supposed
to be a peak of the White mountain.

Fig. 12. Martineau describes the discovery and naming of "Three Butte Valley" (Cave Valley) in Colonel Dame's "Journal of the Southern Exploring Company for the Desert." *Courtesy Archives, Church of Jesus Christ of Latter-day Saints.*

Fig. 13. The three buttes in Cave Valley. *By author, April 1984.*

same mountains that Dame pronounced to be the White Mountains from Altar Peak.

Unimpressed with the possibilities of making a settlement in Three Butte (Cave) Valley, and unable to get proper bearings because of the cloudy weather, they retraced their steps down Pine Canyon and advanced up White River Valley. Not far from the mouth of the canyon, they surprised five antelope at a spring on the east bench. As one might guess, they named this Antelope Spring. It is seen on today's maps as Silver Springs. The water was said to be sufficient to irrigate about twenty-five acres.

As they continued their northward trek, they intersected the trail of the main camp and followed it on to Willow Springs a few miles away. Here a tally was made of their mileage. The wagons had traveled 260 miles since leaving Parowan, and the pack trains had covered another 260 miles; but still they had not found anyplace to settle such as President Young had described. Now Dame decided to continue his pack train expeditions on a larger scale while the main camp was to lay by at Willow Springs for a few days.

On the morning of the 14th, Dame, Martineau, J. Ward Christian, Ansel Twitchell, George W. Sirrine, Francis Brown, Don Carlos Shirts, William Smith, Jesse B. Lewis, and John Topham set out again for the White Mountains. The inclusion of Shirts was to replace Johnson as the interpreter. Johnson left the same morning with a small company to locate a stream reported by the Indians one hundred miles to the south.[11] Each exploring company had a pack mule, a spade for digging for water, and "about a week's rations each."[12]

As Dame's party started north, undoubtedly for the Ruby Range, they discovered horse tracks heading west across the valley only five miles from camp. Colonel Dame was aware that Bean had left before him, and he must have known it was he who made them. George W. Bean and company were now ranging west out of Cave Valley. He had apparently crossed over Shingle Pass into the White River Valley shortly after Dame's exploring party had descended the canyon the day before. Apparently skirting Willow Springs to the north, he was unaware of Colonel Dame's presence in the valley, and he proceeded west toward a gap between the Grant and White Pine ranges.

Twelve miles north of Willow Springs the Dame party began to find water. First there was Deep Spring where they stopped at noon.

Then, thirteen miles further up the valley, they found a beautiful large stream. According to Martineau, it was "the first mountain stream we have seen since leaving Coal Creek [at Cedar City], (except Wibe Creek) and the brethren were so much rejoiced that with one voice it was named 'Eureka.' "[13] What the party had found was the upper part of the White River a few miles below the present-day site of Preston. The men believed the stream was capable of watering 2,000 acres of land, and the bottomlands here were "exceedingly rich, and would produce great crops," claimed Martineau.[14] The stream spread out over a meadow considerably larger than any previous meadow they had discovered, and, as a result, there was an abundance of native hay. And, unlike the valley further south, alkali did not seem to be a problem. Surely this was the best prospect for a settlement they had yet found, but the nights were very cold, with ice frequently forming in their drinking vessels. Also in this valley, the men found an Indian whom they wanted to question, but, like the others, he was very much frightened and scurried away. He was run down in the usual manner, but he was apparently Shoshoni, and Shirts found he could not interpret his speech.

Relentlessly, Dame pressed onward toward the north end of the valley. By 9 P.M. they finally reached the foothills of the Egan Range, which pinch off the north end of White River Valley and separate it from Steptoe Valley to the northeast. Tired and weary, the explorers made a dry camp among the cedars on the hillside. They had traveled forty miles that day—a record.

Camp was broken early on the morning of the 15th. The company advanced slowly toward the pass in the Egan Range. Their water supply was now getting low, and they hugged the base of the range hoping to find a spring or stream issuing out of it. High up on the mountainside, they finally located a "beautiful clear spring" (probably Lion Spring) which they called Crystal Spring because of the icicles formed along the stream running from it. They also found that these foothills contained an inexhaustible supply of bunch grass.

At noon they reached the top of the pass which is the present-day Murry Summit on U.S. Highway 6. Dame wasted little time in descending the canyon into the valley below. Martineau recalled, the descent was through "a long, narrow and crooked canyon, which could be easily defended if necessary."[15] The company was obviously still mindful of the Mormon defense strategy emphasized at the time of their departure. They were yet to learn of the drastic changes that had occurred in the Mormon capital in recent weeks and their effect on the search for the White Mountains.

Winding down Murry Canyon, the explorers named this defile Lone Rock Canyon because of a single, large boulder standing alone in the canyon bottom. It was estimated to be seventy-five to eighty feet long, fifteen to twenty feet thick, and forty feet tall. This "lone rock" is still seen today only a few yards from U.S. Highway 6 near Ely, Nevada, although it has become greatly diminished in size through the years.[16]

Below the rock was the head of a large creek which they naturally named Lone Rock Creek. Dame found the stream "capable of watering 1000 acres of land,"[17] if good land was available. Following the creek down to its entrance into Steptoe Valley, the party found the tracks of Bean's northwest contingent of Iron County men led by Orson B. Adams. This company had left the valley just a few days ahead of them. It was the same party that Dame had failed to see as he peered through the haze into Cave Valley on May 13. Dame's Lone Rock Creek was the same as South Creek on Adams's map, which is called Murry Creek today. Dame, like Adams, had arrived on the future town-site of Ely, Nevada. Dame correctly assumed that the valley had already been explored by Bean's men, and within the last ten days at that. He therefore withdrew his men back up the canyon four miles and camped.

The following morning was Sunday, but there was no time to rest. They crossed back over Murry Summit into White River Valley, but this time they crowded the west side of the valley on the high bench lands of the White Pine Range. They crossed a hill in this region that was covered with green stones which the company believed to contain 25 percent copper. Today the huge Kennecott open-pit copper mine is located just four miles away on the other side of the mountain near Ruth, Nevada.

About noon the men arrived back at Eureka Creek, the large stream they had discovered the day before. But this time they were on the west side of the valley where the creek issues out of the White Pine Mountains. In reality, the explorers had found Ellison Creek, a major tributary to the White River, and were not on the same stream they had previously discovered. A large wire grass meadow was found where the water spread out over the ground and sank. The grass was reported to be about two feet high. Two miles below, the stream rose to the surface again. Working their way down

Fig. 14. Murry Rock near Ely, Nevada—William H. Dame's "Lone Rock" in 1858. *Courtesy of Effie O. Read.*

stream, the company struck camp about 8 P.M. where the creek sank a second time. Again, the night was cold, freezing water in their cups.

Monday the 17th saw the men continue their return march to the base camp on Willow Springs. Following the approximate route of Nevada Highway 318 through the future town-sites of Preston and Lund, they discovered several large springs but no land considered suitable for cultivation. When they arrived at their base camp, they found that George W. Bean and a company of men had passed through on their way east. The tracks that Dame had discovered a few miles north of camp were made by Bean's westward advance. After making a reconnaissance of Railroad Valley, probably via Currant Summit on the present U.S. Highway 6 right-of-way, he recrossed the valley, intersected Dame's tracks, and traced them down to Willow Springs where he found the main camp. "We obtained considerable news regarding the church," wrote Dame of Bean's visit to his camp.[18] No doubt, Bean had informed Dame's men of Brigham Young's surrender of the governorship to Alfred Cumming and the prophet's relaxed stand on locating a refuge in the desert. Young's instructions to Bean of April 28 were also discussed, and it now appeared they were farther north than they should be, as President Young wanted any new settlements made south or southwest of Snake Creek. This would preclude any attempt to settle in the Eureka Creek country, which had the best water and land. Bean also described the position of his own base camp. Surprisingly, the two forces had established their camps within twenty miles of each other. Bean was encamped in Cave Valley to the east, which Dame had called Three Butte Valley; to Bean it was Pockage Valley.

Nephi Johnson and company had not yet returned from the southern country, and Dame decided to lay by on the 18th and await his return. He hoped that Johnson had located the valley they had been looking for. On the 19th it was decided to relocate the Desert Camp at Desert Swamp Springs, seventeen miles south. Willow Springs was too far north according to the latest instructions.

As yet, Bean and Dame had not met. Bean had returned to his base camp in Cave Valley before Colonel Dame had returned from Steptoe Valley. Nevertheless, there was considerable communication between the two camps. Beaver, Parowan, and Cedar City had each sent a company on both expeditions and many of the men from one camp had friends in the other. Colonel Dame himself had a cousin, Wesley William Dame, in Bean's expedition. Consequently, there was some traffic between the two camps. Several of Bean's men visited Willow Springs, and a number of Dame's men, including Martineau, crossed over into Cave Valley to see a large cave near Bean's White Mountain Camp.[19]

As the wagons retraced their ruts to Desert Swamp (Flagg) Springs, Martineau and others veered off to the east toward Cave Valley. But Martineau wanted to attempt a new route across the Egan Range by ascending a small wash just north of their old crossing of Pine Canyon. Near the summit of the range, he discovered a "fine spring issuing from a bed of granite."[20] In the tradition of the expedition, it was named Granite Spring. Today it is known as Big Spring. Late in the afternoon, Martineau and his associates arrived safely at Bean's camp.

There was also some communication between Bean's camp in Cave Valley and Barney's settlement on Snake Creek. Barney wrote that he left Snake Creek and "took ten men and proceeded to Cave Mountain about 100 [sixty-five] miles from Snake Creek."[21] Edwin Stott, of Fillmore, was probably one of these men, as he was reported to have been in Cave Valley for a time.[22] Barney was in the camp when Martineau arrived, and passed on considerable news of the Snake Creek mission. Fifty or sixty acres had been successfully cleared, and the grain was mostly in. But he reported the nights were very cold, and water was scarce. And while the brethren were generally faring well, some were suffering from colds and rheumatism. The Indians were also growing bolder day by day, especially the Gosiutes and the White Knives or Tosanwicks. The latter was a particularly aggressive Shoshonian band that ranged south out of the Humboldt River country. They had acquired their name from the beautiful white flint they obtained from the nearby mountains and fashioned into knives.[23] These Indians had stolen some of the horses from Snake Creek. All but one, which the Indians had slaughtered, were recovered, however.[24]

On May 20 Nephi Johnson's exploring party rode into Desert Camp from their excursion far to the south. In later years, Johnson recalled that "we went without food on the way back. . . . When we arrived in camp we were a hungry crowd."[25] His report of the country was for the most part favorable. He had been deep into the Pahranagat Valley, one hundred miles to the south. By his own esti-

Fig. 15. Upper Pahranagat Lake (called Johnson Lake by Nephi Johnson, its discoverer, in 1858), near Alamo, Nevada. *By author, June 1979.*

mates, "this place [was] within 2 days ride of the crossing of the Muddy, California road." Here he discovered a large stream and good land believed "sufficient to support 2000 people."[26] In places the stream was waist deep and several yards wide. There were also fish in the stream measuring up to a foot in length, which meant that the stream did not dry up later in the summer like so many of the basin streams do. But Johnson found the valley thickly settled by Indians. The natives had planted wheat which was just heading out—an indication of the valley's mild climate. They had also successfully cultivated squash, corn, and watermelons. The Indians were not unfriendly, and they had, in fact, invited the Mormons to come and settle in the valley on free land.

Johnson continued to follow the stream south, actually the lower end of the White River, to a lake about two miles long, which Johnson named after himself. He also discovered a smaller lake of about one hundred acres and named it Rush Lake because of the tall bulrushes surrounding its shores. These lakes, the Upper and Lower Pahranagat Lakes, can be viewed today from U.S. Highway 93 a few miles south of Alamo, Nevada. The bulrushes still grow thick around their banks.

The Johnson pack train had reached the Pahranagat Valley by retracing the expedition's tracks back to Desert Swamp. But instead of following the White River Wash south, Johnson rounded the west side of the Seaman Range and proceeded south through Coal Valley. Near the valley's southern end, the exploring party made for a gap in the Seaman Range (probably Seaman Wash) and emerged on the east side of the ridge back in the White River drainage. Wending their way down this dry wash on the location of present-day Nevada Highway 318, they descended 2,000 feet in elevation into the north end of Pahranagat Valley to the present location of Hiko, Nevada. Here the climate was markedly warmer. The Indian wheat was already heading out, while in the high valleys to the north, Dame was yet circumspect of planting due to the cold climate. As they entered the Pahranagat Valley from the north, the party was also struck by the drastic changes in the types of vegetation seen. The sage and greasewood of the north quickly gave way to creosote, cacti, and yucca varieties—joshua trees and Spanish bayonets.

Johnson, no doubt, discovered Crystal Springs in the north end of the valley and Ash Springs five miles below. These were named Stewart's Springs and Grapevine Springs respectively. Obviously, William C. Stewart, of Cedar City, was a member of the exploring party. The grapevines apparently found at Ash Springs were another indication of the radical change in climate here. These springs revive the practically dry watercourse of the White River, creating a luxuriant meadow in the valley bottoms. The explorers reached the Pahranagat Lakes by taking a course similar to the present route of U.S. Highway 93.

Johnson began his return to Desert Camp on May 18. Martineau's map indicates that the party returned by the same route they went out on.[27] Besides the positive report he brought back to camp, there was also a piece of disturbing news to tell. The Desert Swamp, so full of water just ten days ago, was now all but dry! The water from Desert Swamp Springs was sinking before it could reach the "swamp." In a country where the limited water resources fluctuated so rapidly, it would be difficult to assess the land for settlement potential. Water in these ever-changing interior valleys might be abundant when a crop is sown, but vanish in a week with a sinking stream.

On the afternoon of Johnson's arrival at Desert Camp (the 20th), visitors from Bean's White Mountain Camp also began coming in. Martineau returned bringing with him, among others, the tireless George W. Bean. After weeks of exploring around each other and intersecting each other's trails in the desert, Colonel Dame and Captain Bean finally came face to face.

# XII

# THE GREAT CAVE

The rendezvous of Dame and Bean in White River Valley had significant consequences for the future of the White Mountain Expedition, as they now combined their information and their resources. In the evening a parley was held to discuss the available options. George W. Bean, Edson Barney, and John Riggs of the White Mountain Camp all spoke, as did William H. Dame of the Southern Exploring Company. President Barney wanted to know if the colonel "had found any places for farming, more than we wished to occupy this season."[1] In response, Dame recounted the history of their travels, telling Barney, "the last mountain stream of water I had crossed was Coal Creek at Cedar City."[2] He explained that most of the streams he had found were "small spring branches, running through heavy saleratus bottoms a short distance, and sinking," but, added Dame, "he could have his choice of any of them."[3] Bean also informed Dame that the tracks the colonel had discovered at the northern terminus of his explorations were indeed made by his company, as he had assumed, and that this was "Ruby Valley or White Knife Country."[4] In this, as has already been discussed, Bean was mistaken. It was Steptoe Valley, not Ruby Valley, that the explorers had penetrated.

Willow Springs, Eureka Creek, and Steptoe Valley all had sufficient water and land to justify making settlements, but they lay too far north of the area intended by President Young. These areas were also considered very cold, and to plant in such areas would be risky. The country to the west was deemed to be a great sterile desert by Dame, who had surveyed the country from Altar Peak, and by Bean, who had recently taken his own observations in Railroad Valley and from Currant Summit in the White Pine Range. In Railroad Valley Bean had met with Indians who informed him that he was "on the borders of a great desert, between us and the Sierra Nevadas."[5] No doubt, the Indians had described Ralston Valley, Death Valley, and the Great Amargosa Desert to Captain Bean. His own findings confirmed this report: "We took observations from the highest peaks on this tract of desert, which served to strengthen our faith in these statements," he later reported to Brigham Young.[6]

The so-called Johnson's Lake Country looked promising for a settlement. The weather was warm and conducive to raising a variety of crops, and the soil and water were also good. But the Indians there were so thick and their grain and vegetables so scattered up and down the stream that Dame thought it "best not to move our camp there this present season."[7] Dame had been ordered by Brigham Young "to conciliate the Indians . . . & exercise a salutary influence over them." He knew he could not establish a settlement in Pahranagat Valley without offending or possibly fighting the Indians, even though they had offered free land to the Mormons. Dame admitted, however, that this valley "seemed the only prospect west of our present location," in a letter written to Young from Meadow Valley on May 26.

After reviewing their explorations, President Dame suggested that they each choose a place to settle and go there. President Barney proposed that the colonel have the first pick, and accordingly, Dame chose Meadow Valley for his own men. Barney then chose Cave Springs for the twenty-eight Parowan and Cedar City men of Bean's exploring company to be organized under Charles Hopkins of Cedar. This left only Bean's company from Beaver unsettled. Captain Bean announced his intention to explore a range of mountains southeast of the Snake Creek farm in the hope of locating the seventeen Beaver City men at some place suitable for cultivation in that vicinity. Bean was looking at the Wah Wah Range of western Millard County, Utah. If all went as planned, the White Mountain Expedition would found four settlements on the desert, although none of them offered the defense situation that Brigham Young had hoped for.

The explorers determined that the only country between them and the southern Utah settlements they had not explored was an area to the southeast. Bean had come in from the north and Dame from the south, and while their routes eventually crossed in some places, neither had made an assessment of a substantial part of the area known today as Lake Valley. Colonel Dame, therefore, asked for nine men to forge a new trail to Meadow Valley while the wagons retraced the old trail back to the valley. The new trail would traverse

Cave Valley, cross the Schell Creek Range, and then proceed south to Meadow Valley. Samuel Hamilton, James Cliff, Ansel Twitchell, Joseph Nelson, John Couch, Ross R. Rogers, J. Lewis,[8] and, of course, James H. Martineau and Nephi Johnson volunteered to break this new trail.

Another important event occurred at Desert Swamp Springs on May 20. At 6 P.M. Martineau took a series of observations with President Dame's surveying compass and copied the diagram into the company journal.[9] The headings from the springs to all the prominent landmarks in the region were carefully recorded. Martineau's intention was obviously to aid the future traveler of this area in finding his way. It is doubtful that these observations were ever used for that purpose, but they were of supreme importance to this study. Since the appellations given to physical features of this country by the White Mountain explorers have rarely survived, the problem of identifying the mountains, valleys, and springs would have been a fruitless task, in many cases, had it not been for these headings and the many other records, journals, and maps which Martineau meticulously prepared. One of the landmarks recorded by Martineau was Gunsight Mountain at south 12° west. This peak, known today as Gap Mountain, is not large, but it stands apart from the Egan Range about eight miles south of the springs making it quite noticeable. This mountain is distinguished by its clefted summit resembling a gunsight, and so it was named by the White Mountain explorers. It was for the same reason that it is today called Gap Mountain. While this characteristic is plainly visible from Desert Swamp (Flagg) Springs, it is not noticeable from other large springs in the area. This was a major key in determining the identity of Dame's Desert Swamp Springs. Once Desert Swamp Springs, the radius point for the readings, was tentatively identified as Flagg Springs, the remaining landmarks fell into place along the headings drawn by Martineau on May 20. Other landmarks he diagrammed were Gray Head (Grant Range) at S 73° W, Willow (Immigrant) Springs at N 5° W, Eureka Mountain (White Pine Range) at N 35° W, and Mt. Whitney (Whipple Peak) in the Egan Range at E 25° S, obviously named after Francis T. Whitney, a member of Dame's expedition from Parowan.

On Friday, May 21, the explorers began their drive toward their final destinations in this wilderness. The main company withdrew to

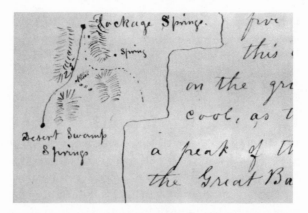

Fig. 16. Martineau's sketch of the route from Desert Swamp Springs to Pockage Springs in Dame's "Journal." *Courtesy Archives, Church of Jesus Christ of Latter-day Saints.*

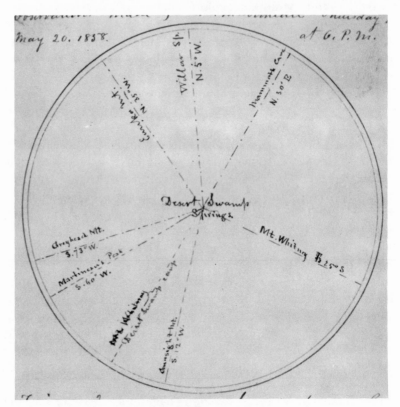

Fig. 17. Compass headings drawn by Martineau in Dame's "Journal." *Courtesy Archives, Church of Jesus Christ of Latter-day Saints.*

Meadow Valley by way of the Desert Swamp, variously reported at seventeen or eighteen miles to the south. They found the place as Johnson had reported on his return from the south—nearly dry.

Fig. 18. White River Valley near Sunnyside, Nevada, looking south toward Gap Mountain (called Gunsight Peak by Martineau). *By author, June 1979.*

Dame's pack train was enlarged by the addition of two more volunteers, George W. Sirrine, of Washington, and Charles Carter, of Parowan. Also accompanying Dame's party, for the time being, were Bean, Barney, Riggs, and others of Bean's company who were heading back to the White Mountain Camp in Cave Valley. Crossing Pine Canyon (Shingle Pass) they proceeded to Bean's base camp. Dame found the place situated on the east side of the valley at some springs. Less than a mile away was the large cave that Martineau and others of his men had gone over to see on the 19th. Now President Dame and his exploring party decided to tour the great cavern.

The letters and journals of the explorers are replete with descriptions of this cave. To many of them it was the highlight of the expedition. The cave's length was variously reported by different individuals, but all the descriptions were similar. George W. Bean reported the discovery of

a large cave having numerous smaller branches. The main cave is half a mile in length and varying in breadth from five to sixty feet. The smaller caves or branches are from ten feet to one hundred yards in length and from ten to twenty-five feet wide; they are from seven to twenty-five feet high. The first half is perfectly dry, the remainder have a damp clayey bottom. And we found three pools of water, cold but having a mineral taste. . . . There was also the track of a wild animal, supposed to be that of a wolverine. The air in most parts of the cave was good, but rather warm in some places. The entrance was about four feet high and six feet in breadth.[10]

Bean called this place Pockage Cave from the Indian word "pocket" meaning hole or cave.[11]

Martineau described the cave as having been explored "more than a mile without finding any sign of its end."

It has hundreds of passages branching off in every direction. About ½ a mile from the entrance is a clear, cool spring of excellent water. It stands in a little pool. The roof of some of the appartments is so high that it could scarcely be perceived with 6 candles, and is ornamented most beautifully by thousands of stalactites and stalagmites. . . . The floor in many places is a peculiar reddish clay, with veins and spots of a bright red in it. There are tracks of some large animal plainly visible in the damp clay, which resemble bear tracks.[12]

Martineau surmised that the clay on the cave floor contained mercury. Bean packaged up some of the sticky stuff and eventually carried it to Provo where he offered it to a local potter named Roberts. The clay was tested and found to be of a "most excellent quality for potter's ware."[13]

As Colonel Dame's party groped their way through these subterranean passages they were awed by the natural beauty they beheld in the flickering lights of their candles. Again, the words of the hymn, "For the Strength of the Hills We Bless Thee," were impressed upon their minds. As on Altar Peak the verse seemed to have an uncanny pertinence to their present circumstances. In one of the largest rooms the brethren assembled and sang this hymn, their voices echoing down the halls of the eery cathedral.

> For the dark resounding caverns
> Where thy still small voice is heard;
> For the strong pines of the forest
> That by thy breath are stirred;
> For the storms on whose free pinions
> Thy spirit walks abroad.
> For the strength of the hills we bless Thee,
> Our God, our fathers' God.
>
> The banner of the chieftain,
> Far, far below us waves:
> The war-horse of the spearman
> Cannot reach our lofty caves

Thy dark clouds wrap the threshold
Of freedom's last abode.
For the strength of the hills we bless Thee,
Our God, our fathers' God.

Notwithstanding an Indian taboo against entering the cave, the explorers found thousands of human footprints in the fine, moist clay bottom, as well as evidence of fires in many places in the cave. Yet when Bean prevailed upon the Indians to guide him through they steadfastly refused, telling him they had not dared enter the cave for generations. Both Bean and Martineau recorded the ancient Indian legend surrounding this mysterious cave in their writings. Bean wrote:

> They have a legend, that two squaws went into the cave, a long time ago, and remained six months. They went in perfect nudity and returned dressed in fine buckskin, and reported they had found a large and beautiful valley inside clothed with vegetation, timber, and water, and filled with game of the choisest specie. Also, a band of Indians in an advanced state of civilization; being dressed like white men. They asserted the tracks we found were made by these subterranean inhabitants.[14]

"All the Indians firmly believe this story and will not enter it," wrote Martineau in the company history.[15] But Bean noted that one brave, after watching the explorers return safely from the cave after an hour, did accompany them on their second expedition into the cave. This was apparently before Martineau's arrival in the area.

The superstition of Bean's Pockage Cave lasted for many years. Miners traveling through Cave Valley in the 1860s reported the legend was still very strong among the natives. One group of miners was able to hire the services of an Indian guide for "an enormous quantity of cold grub," who claimed to have "been in the cave a day's travel." Their account of 1866 continues:

> He told us all manner of stories about the cave. He said that after traveling three days we would come to a new world, where there was another sun and moon, and another race of human beings, who had horses, cattle, sheep, etc. and plenty of women. Before entering the cave we supplied ourselves with thirty candles and the Indian carried a bundle of dry grass to scatter along our path, so we should have no difficulty in retracing our steps—a wise precaution, as we afterward found. . . . We explored the cave a distance of 2,785 feet, by measurement with a tape line. We were unable to go farther for lack of light, as there were a great many angles and side chambers where we deemed it prudent to place lighted candles in order to find our way back. This was all the more necessary as we observed our guide was confused, and might easily be lost. In making a sharp curve he stopped, and throwing up his hands called out, "Lights ahead! See!

Fig. 20. The author inspecting formation in Cave Valley Cave in May 1977.

Fig. 19. Formations in Cave Valley Cave. Called "Pockage Cave" by George W. Bean in 1858. *By author, May 1977.*

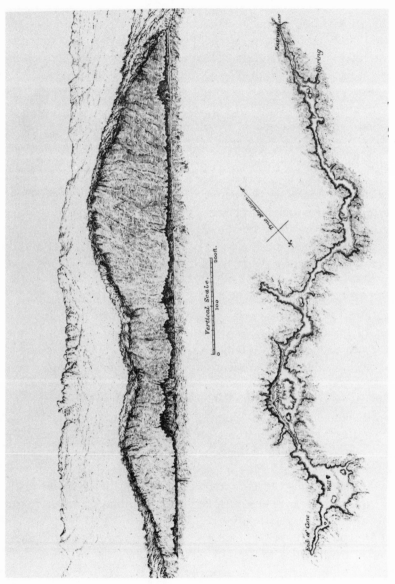

Fig. 21.  Diagram of "White Mountain Cave" from Wheeler's Report.

See!" We found we had been following him in a large chamber, perhaps 250 feet wide, and he had got himself turned around and was doubling on himself, and the lights we saw ahead (ours of course) he supposed belonged to the people of the other world he told us about.[16]

This superstition probably remained strong as long as the Indians roamed freely across these valleys. James H. Martineau claimed as late as 1890, "To this day, no Indian will venture to enter its gloomy recesses, fearing he may be spirited away as were the squaws."[17]

George W. Bean was an astute observer when it came to matters of this nature. He noticed that "great quantities" of clay had been removed from the cave, and he surmised that the large amount of ashes he found were from fires built to fire the clay or light the passage for its excavation. Broken clay pottery was frequently seen by the explorers as they traveled across the deserts; yet, the local Indians did not make or use pottery. These Paiutes informed Bean "that all such, as making pottery, mounds, inscriptions on rocks, and the like, were done by the Tribe of Moquis [Hopis], in ages past. Indeed, all advanced evidences of industry are credited to that people, who were the old settlers of this mountain region."[18] And so the mystery was correctly solved. "I am satisfied," concluded Bean, "they [the human footprints] were made by Indians in former times, going into the cave to get clay to make earthenware, as numerous pieces of broken ware are scattered over different portions of the country. It was probably a tribe called Moquis (or white Indians of the Colorado Valley); as we learned they once inhabited this country."[19]

The cave discovered by the White Mountain Expedition is the one presently known as Cave Valley Cave, one of the longest single shafts in the West.[20] Its entrance on the property of the Cave Valley Ranch is in the foothills of the Schell Creek Range on a low hill jutting into the valley. Despite its size, Cave Valley Cave is not well known today because of its remoteness, being far from paved roads and cities. But the cave is accessible to the determined and has many beautiful formations and curiosities.[21]

After exploring the cave, Dame's pack train camped for the night at the nearby White Mountain Camp. Bean's encampment was situated by four or five good springs, and the ground was free of alkali. A meeting was called, and Bean's men were informed of the decisions and plans made the previous night at Dame's camp on Desert Swamp Springs. Dame and his party would cross the moun-

tains into the next valley east, breaking a new trail to Meadow
Valley. The twenty-eight Iron County men in Bean's expedition
would follow Dame's trail south to Meadow Valley, and from that
point they would be piloted to Cave Springs in Badger (Clover)
Valley southeast of Dame's settlement. There they would establish a
farm under the command of Charles Hopkins of Cedar City. Captain Bean would take the Beaver company with him to the Wah Wah
Mountains to attempt a settlement somewhere in that region. And
Barney was to return to his post at Snake Creek.

In the morning, before the brethren departed for their final
destinations, Bean and Barney penned a letter to Brigham Young
and gave it to Colonel Dame who was expected to run an express
into the settlements after reaching Meadow Valley. They described
the ramblings of their company since their last communication with
the prophet when Bean was in Provo almost a month ago. They also
told of their inability to locate the desired refuge:

> Southwest of White Mountains [Snake Range] we find but little water and grass
> a few springs generally in the mountains some in the vallies but not very good,
> alkali being present. Our N.W. and western most points of exploration are about
> 200 to 225 miles distant on a straight line from Cedar Springs [Holden] and
> Fillmore and this distance brings us into a dry country. Mountains low, no
> water, grass, nor wood for many days travel except we should keep N.W. along
> the rim of the Basin which here runs up to the south side of Ruby [Steptoe]
> Valley.[22]

Speaking for themselves and for Colonel Dame they declared, "we
have thus far been agreeably disappointed in our expectations of
finding hiding places as regards to the most necessary items. water,
grass and wood but land suitable for cultivation is very scarce indeed
and the climate is very cold. there being frost every night as yet."

Dame's pack train, Barney and his men, and the Beaver City contingent commanded by George W. Bean began their trek together
by marching toward Patterson Pass in the Schell Creek Range
southeast of their camp. Bean called the gap Pockage Pass.
Hopkins's Iron County detachment was to follow later which would
leave the White Mountain Camp in Cave Valley abandoned. The
company reached the summit of Pockage (Patterson) Pass at noon, a
distance of ten miles. The men dined at a spring on the mountainside a mile north of the pass. Afterward, President Dame, Martineau, Johnson, and Rogers ascended a "high and very steep
mountain" in company with George W. Bean who showed them the

country to the north that his men had explored. He then showed them the White Mountain (Wheeler Peak) where his own settlement was nestled at its eastern base. This mountain was magnificently clothed with timber and draped with a heavy mantle of snow. To the south they could see their destination—Meadow Valley—about seventy miles distant. Here Martineau continued his observations, taking bearings with the surveyor's compass to the major land forms and making notes for his map. In this way he insured the accuracy of the map which would aid a later generation to prove the trails of the White Mountain Expedition. The explorers named this 10,063-foot mountain Pinnacle Peak; it is now known as Patterson Peak in the Schell Creek Range. Descending the mountain's eastern slope into Lake Valley, the exploring parties divided. Bean and Barney proceeded east across the valley, while Dame turned to the south and traveled along the valley's western bench. Hoping to find water, Dame's company plodded south down the present course of U.S. Highway 93 until 10 P.M., when they finally camped at the foot of the small Fairview Range. They had logged thirty-two hard miles since leaving Bean's camp in Cave Valley.

The light of dawn found the twelve men again pressing southward. Within a mile of camp they discovered a "considerable spring" on the mountainside. The explorers had found Pony Springs, but the Mormons called this welcome find Cricket Spring "from the great number of those insect about."[23] It had been a long dry march from the spring on Patterson Pass to these springs, and Dame feared the Hopkins company might pass by this oasis and find itself in serious difficulty. Accordingly, he assigned John Couch and Samuel Hamilton to stay behind at the springs and guide the Iron County detachment to the water, then bring them into Meadow Valley.

Five miles south of Cricket Spring they suddenly came upon another spring—a very small one almost hidden by the sagebrush. The little pool was surrounded by wire grass and a few wild rosebushes. Predictably, the waterhole was named Rose Spring, and the company pressed on.

Mile after mile, Dame pushed relentlessly down Lake Valley. A rich covering of sage and greasewood spread across the wide valley. But as the company advanced toward the south end of the valley the cedars and junipers on the bench became more abundant, sometimes flowing down the hillsides and spreading into the valley itself.

They continued to follow the present-day course of U.S. Highway 93 past the Bristol Range on their right and on to the Pioche Hills. Here the company of twelve made for a gap between the hills and the Highland Range near Arizona Peak, being led by an Indian they had found earlier in the day. The explorers were guided to a beautiful spring in a high "mountain cove." This spring, known to-day as Highland Spring, was called Cove Spring by Dame and is found six miles west of modern Pioche, Nevada. On this divide be-tween Lake Valley and Meadow Valley, they found plenty of wood, water, and grass, all of which were essentials to the desert traveler. It was again ten o'clock in the evening before the expedition camped for the night. Since sunrise they had logged an incredible forty-five miles through an unknown country. They were now very close to their destination.[24]

On Monday morning, May 24, Colonel Dame and company slipped over the divide into Meadow Valley and located a site for a farm. The wagons had not yet arrived from Desert Swamp Springs, but they were believed to be somewhere near.

# XIII

# THE MEADOW
# VALLEY FARM

While the Dame pack train was wending its way toward Meadow
Valley, Barney reached the farm on Snake Creek. He did not stay,
however. Instead, he appointed David E. Bunnell of Provo to take
charge of the mission while he commenced his return home.

Bunnell was forty-nine years old at the time of his call to the
White Mountain Expedition. The Springfield, New Jersey, native
had been a staunch and faithful Latter-day Saint since 1831. Much
of his early life was spent in Michigan and later in Nauvoo where he
witnessed the persecutions of the Saints. He came to Utah in 1852,
settling in Provo where he practiced his trade of carpentry prior to
enlisting for the expedition.

Barney's return home is somewhat unclear. In his "Biographical
Sketch," written many years later, Barney contended, "I took four
wagons and ten men and went southeast to the sink of the Beaver
dam [Beaver River] and from thence home."[1] Since Bean explored
to the southeast, eventually striking the Beaver River, it is considered possible that Barney simply attached himself to Bean's company for his homeward trek. Other factors, however, indicate he
may have explored a new trail across the desert. One is his assertion
that he took four wagons and ten men with him. Bean had seventeen
men with him. Another is the report Barney and Bean wrote to
Brigham Young from Cave Valley on May 22, in which they discussed their plans: ". . . we intend to run two wagon trails across
from this neighborhood to the vicinity of the settlements. Col. Dame
will make another which will be five trails across the unexplored
region."[2] The five trails spoken of would be the two westbound
routes of Dame and Bean, the eastbound routes of the same, and one
other—apparently Barney's. Barney and Bean inferred to Young
that they would run two trails themselves. The exact route Barney
used is unknown.

Of Bean's movements, we can synthesize a little more. Bean had
hoped to settle the Beaver company somewhere near the Wah Wah
Range. Logic indicates he exited the south end of Snake Valley strik-

ing southeast for the Wah Wah Range. This would put them in Pine Valley, a broad desert plain fifteen miles wide and covered with scrubby sagebrush. Although we have no actual account of Bean's activities in this region, he must have spent some time exploring the Wah Wah Mountains. Ten days were spent covering the distance between Cave Valley and Beaver City about 170 miles away. This pace would have allowed for several days to examine the prospects of settlement in the Wah Wah Mountain region or other desert ranges. Bean found the Wah Wah Range an uninviting place, however, and the area was passed up. Bean reported "finding grass and water at convenient distances on the mountains, also plenty of wood; but no land suitable for farming."[3]

Giving up all hope of finding a place to settle the Beaver company, Bean proceeded "in the nearest possible direction for Beaver Canyon."[4] Lt. George M. Wheeler of the U.S. Army Topographical Engineers, who explored this region eleven years after Bean, apparently uncovered evidence of Bean's trail or was informed of his route. In his *Preliminary Report upon a Reconnaissance through Southern and Southeastern Nevada*, published in 1875, Wheeler stated:

> The Mormons, looking forward to active operations with the troops ordered to their section under General Johnston in 1857, and for secure shelter in case of being driven from their mountain homes, sent out two expeditions to seek for fertile mountain retreats to the westward.
>
> One party, consisting of twenty-six wagons, leaving Beaver City passed west to Hawawah [Wah Wah] Springs, then across Desert and Lake Valleys, until the pass where the Patterson mines are now found [Patterson Pass]. . . .
>
> Our return trip from Hawawah Springs to Cave Valley, followed their route very nearly.[5]

Although Wheeler had the company traveling east to west rather than west to east over this route, this document sheds considerable light on Bean's movements in southwestern Utah. It appears that Bean took the logical route toward Beaver City, finding Wah Wah Springs along the way. His trail was basically the same as Utah Highway 21 from the southern end of Snake Valley to Beaver City.

Crossing the Wah Wah Range, the company found themselves in Wah Wah Valley, another bleak expanse of open desert. To the north lay the Wah Wah Valley Hard Pan, an old lake bed, clearly visible from the elevated points along their trail. Twelve miles across this valley, they rounded the southern terminus of the San Francisco Mountains by traversing a low, cedar-covered divide. Here, on the eastern foothills of the San Francisco Range, they were very near the future site of the rich Frisco mining camp (now a ghost town). Descending from these hills, they marched out onto the Escalante Desert and struck the lower Beaver River sixteen miles below the canyon where the river makes its northern bend. This would place the company very near the present-day city of Milford, on the eventual route of Utah Highway 21. They found the lower Beaver Valley to contain "a great amount of good farming land" with "grass and wood in abundance."[6] The Beaver City men followed the river downstream past the site of present-day Minersville to Beaver City, where they arrived on the last day of May. While Bean did not report this last desert crossing as unusually difficult, he did mention that the company traveled for distances of fifty miles without finding water.[7]

Five days after arriving at Beaver, George W. Bean was at church headquarters in Provo to make his report to Brigham Young. Bean received his interview with the prophet on June 7. Recounting the history of his travels, he described the country in general terms with few exceptions. The great cave had made an obvious impression on him. Bean portrayed his cave in great detail. He claimed since leaving Provo two and one-half months ago, he had "travelled about eight hundred miles in a country never before trod by white men, so far as we have any knowledge. In the course of our travels," continued Bean, "we crossed seven ranges of mountains and the same number of valleys."[8] Wilford Woodruff, who was apparently present when the report was made, alleged that Bean "explored the whole desert to near Carson Valley."[9] It is doubtful that Bean really believed his westward penetration was near Carson Valley. Woodruff's remark was apparently his own interpretation.

Back in Meadow Valley, Dame's men divided up the work necessary to establish the new settlement. Since the main company had not arrived with the bulk of the manpower, much of the heavy work had to wait. Some of the men began to engineer a ditch to bring water to the tillable land a mile and a half away. Others, like Martineau, Rogers, and Lewis, commenced making a complete reconnaissance of the surrounding country to determine the full extent of its resources.

Dame ordered these three to the far south end of the valley and to the narrow canyon which continued below. Passing down the valley for sixteen miles, they found large portions of it covered with grass, but the soil was white with alkali. The party entered Meadow Valley

Wash, a narrow, rocky canyon, about ten miles south of the site of modern Panaca, Nevada. They wound their way through the wash another fourteen miles, passing by the future site of Caliente, to a spot a few miles north of present-day Elgin. Here they camped, having covered thirty difficult miles.

On the morning of May 26, the little exploring party continued to wind down the wash. They soon discovered a small Indian farm among the ash and cottonwood trees. Near the present-day site of Elgin, they halted their southern advance while Martineau and Rogers climbed a nearby mountain to take observations. No end to the canyon could be seen—just a continuation of the long meandering wash and a "succession of rough and broken mountains." It was decided, therefore, to return to Meadow Valley immediately.

This excursion did produce some useful results. Grand Echo Canyon, as they called the wash, was found to contain 2,500 acres of excellent mowing grass which Martineau estimated would yield four tons per acre. The wash consumed the runoff from the springs in Meadow Valley, but the stream here would spread out and sink only to rise again and sink a few miles farther down the canyon. At each sink a lush meadow was created. Martineau's party also found considerable stands of ash and cottonwood timber which would be in demand for construction of buildings as well as for tool handles. Furthermore, Martineau believed the canyon could be made impregnable if fortified in the tradition of Mormon defense tactics.

The reconnoitering party arrived in camp at sundown and found the teams and wagons had finally arrived from Desert Swamp Springs. The main camp had spent one night at the Desert Swamp, now dry. Pressing on, they recrossed the North Pahroc Range and made their way to Desert Spring Wells, where three weeks before they had so patiently laid by for hours dipping water from the holes they dug in the sand. But the wells had also gone dry. The Great Basin was entering its dry season and water was critical. Some of the company's animals received little or none. The night of the 24th was spent at Bennett's Springs, and they arrived in Meadow Valley the following day.

The Southern Exploring Company was united again. Unlike Bean, who liked to drop off his companies one at a time as soon as settlement sites were located, Dame kept his force together while scouts ranged over the surrounding country. While Bean attempted

Fig. 22. Caliente, Nevada, about 1900. Built on ground first charted by the White Mountain Expedition in 1858. *Courtesy Utah State Historical Society.*

to put his men into three different settlements, Dame concentrated his entire expedition in Meadow Valley.

President Dame spent the morning of the 26th making a reconnaissance. The colonel went to the north end of the valley and probed the Pioche Hills about four miles north of camp. Here he found a beautiful canyon with a good stream of cool water and an abundance of cottonwood and box elder. The stream, called Box Elder Creek on Martineau's "Chart," was estimated to be capable of watering twenty acres. Dame had found what is called today Condor Canyon.

Word was soon received in camp from one of Hopkins's company. The Iron County men had depleted their water and needed help. Dame himself went north to pilot the unfortunate company into the valley. Somehow, Hopkins had failed to find Cricket Springs and had traveled sixty-nine miles without finding water. The twenty-eight-man party had slipped past Hamilton and Couch unnoticed. The beleaguered company arrived late in the afternoon. They planned to rest and recuperate until the 28th before continuing their journey to Cave Spring.

While Dame was guiding Hopkins into camp, the rest of the company spent the day leveling for the ditch. It seemed, however, that problems might force them to abandon this project if not the entire Meadow Valley venture. The farm land was a mile and a half from the water, and it was now doubtful whether the land could be sufficiently leveled to allow the water to flow onto the necessary ground.

President Dame was depressed over the prospects of the settlement. He decided to send an express through to Parowan with a letter to be forwarded to Brigham Young. That evening he penned the letter dated from "Desert Camp, Meadow Valley, 147 miles from Parowan. He began by reciting a history of his wanderings since his last communication from Bennett's Springs, more than three weeks before. Then he explained the present situation:

> This day we have been leveling for [a] water ditch, but I find ourselves defeated in reaching the desired spot with our water, one mile and a half distant. Tomorrow we will try on the other side of the valley. Either of these ditches, if they could be made to reach the small pieces of tillable land would have to pass through saleratus beds nearly shoe mouth deep. If this last fails, I hardly know whither to turn or where to go to put in our crops.

There was also a touch of sarcasm in this letter, understandably induced by Dame's failure to locate the sanctuary:

We have found in our explorations some high mountain springs with the best of range for stock around them, a good place for saints to live, provided they would bring their bread and dinner with them. All of the low country are like the head-waters of the Salmon River—saleratus, saleratus. . . . Our farming prospects for this season look very gloomy and dull.[10]

Notwithstanding these disappointments, Dame remained resolute to do the will of God as spoken through his holy prophet. Dame was absolutely loyal to Brigham Young. Despite his long ordeal, Dame declared, "I am ready with my company to go any course or any distance which you may suggest. I expect to remain here until I have received word from you." Colonel Dame continued:

This is a country, I think, Uncle Sam, can't come here without a great deal of trouble. We have ascended the highest peaks—descended the lowest vales, found every little spring or watering that we could hear from our Indian guides. . . . I think a trail can be made from here due east or a trifle north to Parowan. If you wish this done, or any other trail made, or any other course we are prepared to make it. We have a chart and sketch of our journey and country in progress; as soon as we can complete it, we will forward it to you. We have travelled with our wagon train 380 miles; with our exploring parties aside from this 790 miles, total 1170 miles in one month. The bearer of this letter will remain in Parowan until this can go and reach you, and an answer return to him for us. Good health prevails in our midst. The Lord hath blessed us all the day long, for which we acknowledge his hand.

Before sending this report into Parowan, Dame and others wrote personal letters to their families and friends. President Dame wrote one letter to Calvin C. Pendleton, his personal friend and first counselor in the Parowan Stake presidency. Another letter was sent to his wives. James H. Martineau also took the opportunity to send a letter to his family. For his young children, he sent some beautiful crystals he had found in his travels.[11] The letters, including Bean's to Brigham Young of May 22, were sent into Parowan with Ansel Twitchell who arrived at his destination on Sunday morning, May 30.

For the first time in weeks, news of the desert company was received in the settlements. Twitchell's express arrived in Parowan just a day before Bean rode into Beaver. While Bean traveled to Provo to make his personal report to Young, the written correspondence from Parowan also began working its way north. Soon the whole southern country was aware that their men were establishing three new settlements somewhere in the White Mountain country to the west of them.

Dame's letter to Pendleton was received just in time to be read before the congregation at afternoon services in Parowan, Dame's home. Other letters were anxiously received by the wives and families of the explorers, and letters were quickly posted for return to Meadow Valley. A look at some of these letters reveals not only the thoughts and concerns of the families, but in some cases, the feelings of the husbands as well. Susan E. Martineau, the twenty-one-year-old wife of James H. Martineau and younger sister of Nephi Johnson, wrote a tender letter to her husband on May 30 which is quoted here in part:

> We received your letter this morning and was happy to hear of your being in such good health and spirits and we think of you when we sit at the table and wish you were here. We think of you almost every hour of the day almost and wonder what you are doing whether you have anything to drink &c. . . .
>
> Kanosh [the Ute chief] paid us a short visit and said you had gone to find a place for the women and children and he would stay here and fight with the men. Susan told him about the cave and he said it was good. he enquired very particularly about you and asked when you were coming home. . . .
>
> Oh james, if you get a chance send some more of those pretty stones the children were very tickled with the crystals you sent them and Moroni lost his and wants me to write to father to send him another.[12]

Lounna, one of William H. Dame's wives, also wrote as soon as she received a note from her husband. "You dont say much about you[r] country," wrote the nearly illiterate Mrs. Dame.

> but I think I know pirty well wat you think abou[t] it if you dont say m[u]ch about it. . . . dont you worry any thi[n]g about hom[e]  you have noed me long enuf to now I will do as near as you would as I can  you hav[e] anuf to think of afairs whair you are. . . . take care of you self tell it rit for me to go thar.[13]

Mrs. Dame apparently thought she would soon be joining her husband in Meadow Valley. While Brigham Young had already determined a hegira to the deserts was unlikely, the people had not been informed of the new policy. On May 30 Salt Lake City was nearly abandoned. As far as the people knew they would be resettling in the deserts. Why else would they be leaving their homes and heading south? There had been no *official* policy changes since the "Sebastopol" speech of March 21.

Information on the events transpiring at the Snake Creek farm while Dame was establishing the mission in Meadow Valley is sketchy. It is known the men successfully planted and cultivated (for the time being) fifty or sixty acres of ground in the vicinity of present-day Garrison, Utah. To do this required the installation of ditches and other improvements. We also know the settlers were somewhat plagued by cold weather and bands of marauding Indians. Little else has been discovered for the period while Bunnell presided at the camp.

The Meadow Valley settlement, meanwhile, was working hard to bring the water from the creek to the farming ground. As the leveling and digging continued on May 27, President Dame with seven others started south to further explore Grand Echo Canyon. Four miles into the canyon, Dame camped for the night.

On the 28th the exploring party pushed down the canyon again to the location of present-day Caliente. But instead of continuing south as Martineau had done, Dame struck east going up a side canyon. This narrow canyon was Clover Valley Wash, an extension of Clover [Badger] Valley, where Hopkins was just now arriving by the established trail to begin his settlement. They followed up Clover Creek which Dame reported to be "a good stream" in places. More stands of ash and cottonwood were also found in this canyon. Their march took them along the present line of the Union Pacific railroad until they decided their trek through the rocky streambed was too rough, and they cut across a steep mountain and descended into Clover Valley. After a difficult twenty-five-mile march, they arrived at Hopkins's camp on Cave Springs near the present site of Barclay, Nevada.

After spending the night in the camp of the Iron County explorers, Dame and party followed the old, direct trail back to Meadow Valley. Traveling ten miles north, they again ascended the slopes of Mount Lookout taking more observations. The party rode into Desert Camp in Meadow Valley on the evening of the 29th after a strenuous thirty-two-mile march.

The men at camp had kept themselves quite busy. On the 28th work commenced on a dam to raise the water level and force it through the ditch. Some hauled rock for the dam while others cut brush. Everyone had plenty of work to do. A forge was built, and others installed the bellows, anvil, and vice. Many thought these efforts were all in vain. Ross R. Rogers thought "the prospect rather doubtful" for getting the water down to the field.[14] Nevertheless, he and other men still continued to level the ground. While Dame was on Mount Lookout on the 29th, his faithful company was erecting the blacksmith shop itself. It was merely an open pavilion or "shade" made from poles stuck upright in the ground, with cross-poles lashed across the top and piled with brush. Some of the men hauled wood for a charcoal pit.

When President Dame arrived that evening, he announced that "in consequence of the lateness of the season & the urgent necessity of getting in our crops . . . we will begin the water ditch tomorrow and also build the dam."[15] Although the next day was Sunday, a day when virtually all work in the settlements ceased in observance of the Sabbath, the men of Desert Camp commenced their diggings in earnest. There was time for nothing else. The first day a ditch four feet wide and one and a half feet deep was completed for nearly half a mile. The dam across the creek was also built to a height of seven feet. Water was now running in the ditch, but there was still over a mile to dig. Monday morning brought more of the same. While most of the men were working on the ditch, a few men with three teams began hauling in pickets for a public corral one hundred feet in diameter and capable of holding one hundred horses. During the evening of the 31st all the men drew lots to determine which plots of ground they would farm.

Tuesday was the first of June, and still it would be a week before the ground would be prepared for sowing. James H. Martineau, with Colonel Dame's help, began the work of surveying the field and staking out twenty lots—one for each wagon mess of three men. These lots were originally five acres each—twenty rods by forty rods. But clearing a five-acre lot proved to be too big of a task if crops were ever going to be planted this season. The number one lot had been drawn by Samuel White, Nephi Johnson, and Joseph Hunter. After much hard work they were able to strip only one-third of an acre of its native brush, and the men voted to have the lots reduced to only three acres. On the 2d Martineau resurveyed the field, laying it off in three-acre parcels measuring twelve rods by forty rods.

The field was heavily covered with sage and greasewood, and clearing it was a difficult task. Each man had one acre to clear by himself before plowing could begin for a total of sixty acres—about the same size as the Snake Creek farm. But because of the position of the ditch it was possible to irrigate almost twice as much land as had been laid off in the survey. Despite the considerable labor involved in clearing the land, several of the men asked for and received permission to extend their lots into this unsurveyed area.

On Thursday, June 3, the men began clearing their lots, while a few continued to work on the corral, and some repaired the ditch where the bank was too low. Such was the scene for the next several days. A bowery for public meetings was also erected. In a crude fashion, Meadow Valley began to take on the appearance of civilization.

Sunday was an eventful day for the weary Meadow Valley pioneers. The men were awakened at 3 A.M. by an express rider from the settlements. Twitchell had returned carrying the mail, although he did not wait to receive Brigham Young's reply as he had been earlier instructed. During the afternoon the ditch was completed in an all-out effort, and Sunday services were held for the first time since beginning their desert odyssey. There was much to be thankful for. Not a man had been lost. The Lord had provided for their needs, and it now appeared the ditch was a success after all. Perhaps the settlement would survive.

Monday, June 7, saw the explorers-turned-farmers commence the sowing of their crops. The first seeds planted by the Southern Exploring Company were sown on the precise location of present-day

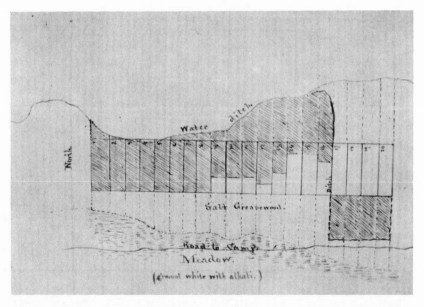

Fig. 23. The Meadow Valley plat surveyed by James H. Martineau, from Martineau's "History of the Mission Exploring the Southwest Deserts of Utah Territory &c in 1858." Shaded areas probably represent areas planted. *Courtesy Archives, Church of Jesus Christ of Latter-day Saints.*

Panaca. Within two days the men had sown forty acres. There was also a small Indian farm about two miles from camp. Two acres had been planted in a little cove where Dame found "corn stalks that the Indians had raised last year, that would measure about ten feet."[16]

The hard work completed, and their goal of getting the seeds into the ground realized, Dame decided it was time for a reorganization. In the evening he announced his intention of leaving the valley on Wednesday the 9th, and he called on eight of the men to accompany him to establish a new, direct route to Parowan. Ross R. Rogers, Nephi Johnson, Samuel Hamilton, Martin Taylor, Don Carlos Shirts, John Osburn, John Lewis, and John Couch received the assignment. Martineau was conspicuously absent from this party; his services were undoubtedly required in Meadow Valley, but it was J. Ward Christian, the captain of the first ten from Beaver, to whom the responsibility of the mission had temporarily fallen. Old Father Sheppard, the company chaplain, was also given permission to return home and rest himself. The following day, James Cliff, of Cedar City, also received permission to return home upon his own request. Dame saw a need for cows to be brought into the new settlement, and he called upon his men to donate any they thought their families could spare. Eighteen cows were pledged to be forwarded to Meadow Valley as soon as men could be sent to bring them.[17] Before leaving he advised his men not to plant any more after June 17.[18]

June 9 saw the Dame party get underway as scheduled. In doing this, Dame had, for some reason, actually disregarded his own declaration to Brigham Young that he would "remain here until I have received word from you."[19] The colonel took two wagons with him and ordered two barrels of water secured to each. They struck a course almost due east on the present line of Nevada Highway 25 heading for Panaca Summit. It was not long before they ran into difficulty. On this final leg of their journey the hand of fate seems to have turned against them. Perhaps it was the excitement of going home, or maybe it was a simple misunderstanding, but instead of two water barrels on each wagon, the men had only brought two barrels total. This went unnoticed until it was too late to rectify, and soon it was discovered that the water had leaked out of one of the casks leaving them with only one barrel for eleven men and fifteen animals in a desert that would take at least four days to cross. It was now imperative that they locate additional water sources along the trail, but none could be found. The party passed the site of modern

Fig. 25. Cover of Martineau's "History of the Mission Exploring the Southwest Deserts of Utah Territory &c in 1858." Shows actual sketch of the Dame company. Note Deseret Alphabet. *Courtesy Archives, Church of Jesus Christ of Latter-day Saints.*

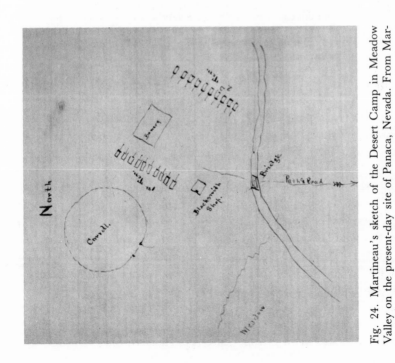

Fig. 24. Martineau's sketch of the Desert Camp in Meadow Valley on the present-day site of Panaca, Nevada. From Martineau's "History of the Mission Exploring the Southwest Deserts of Utah Territory &c in 1858." *Courtesy Archives, Church of Jesus Christ of Latter-day Saints.*

Modena, Utah, near the Utah–Nevada border, and entered the Escalante Desert on the approximate line of today's Utah Highway 56. They had hoped to make Little Salt Lake Pass west of Parowan, but they now faced the prospect of crossing fifty miles of bleak desert with no water. On the third day out of Meadow Valley, the party was forced to turn south and bear toward Iron Springs where the expedition had organized in April.[20]

Upon reaching Parowan, Dame made arrangements to have the cattle forwarded to Desert Camp. Jesse N. Smith, one of the Parowan men who failed to make the original expedition because his animals were in Salt Lake with the exodus, was ordered to proceed to Meadow Valley with the cattle and to take charge of the mission.

Shortly after his return, Dame received a letter from President Young in response to his communication of May 26. In this letter dated June 9, Young appeared to be well pleased with Dame's exertions. ". . . your report from Desert Camp, May 26, afforded much gratification," wrote Young, "and the energy and perseverance of yourself & company, in given operations, are highly commendable. In regard to your further movements," he continued,

> it will probably be best for you to at once arrange to leave enough of your company, selected from those who can most conveniently tarry, to farm as much as the soil and water will admit and explore around for secure places for caching, and yourself and the rest of the company return home; and you, so soon as you have prepared your map pay me a visit.[21]

Young's letter also contained another positive note. Peace commissioners from President Buchanan had arrived in Salt Lake on the 7th of June. "I propose going to G.S.L. City tomorrow, where we shall, probably soon be able to learn a few items which may have a bearing on our next movements," declared the prophet to Colonel Dame.

Things seemed to be looking brighter for the beleaguered churchman. The government, it appeared, may be suing for peace. Perhaps his tactics were bearing fruit. Hostilities appeared more remote than at any time since July of 1857. William H. Dame's report of May 26 was negative; so was Bean's report of May 22, as was his oral report of June 7. Dame was exasperated with his failure to find good places for settlement, and it was doubtful, when he last reported to President Young, that Meadow Valley could even be irrigated. Yet the prophet was satisfied. Young wrote to Bishop Tarleton Lewis of Parowan that "late reports from bros' Dame and

Bean are highly satisfactory, demonstrating that there are places undesirable to all who value earthly comforts and riches above the blessings flowing from obedience to the gospel."[22] But the reason for Brigham Young's change of heart was not at all the discoveries of Dame or Bean on the southwest deserts; his optimism no doubt sprang from the arrival of the presidential peace commissioners in Salt Lake City. Brigham Young was by now aware that the White Mountain Expedition had failed to find the oases of Barney Ward and John C. Frémont.

# XIV

# A PLAN FOR PEACE

With affairs in Parowan settled, Col. William H. Dame and Nephi Johnson left for church headquarters on June 18. Five days later they arrived in Provo carrying the map and other papers supplied by Martineau before leaving Meadow Valley.[1] Dame lightly penciled in his last movements between Meadow Valley and Parowan, writing "Low Mountain Pass" above the line of his new trail. On June 24 the two men personally reported their mission to Brigham Young and presented him with Martineau's "Chart" and a detailed description of the country containing an evaluation of its water, grass, soil, and wood resources, as well as the native inhabitants.[2] Young approved of their labors, and the two Iron County men returned home on July 2, their mission terminated.

At this point President Young was all but indifferent toward his White Mountain Expedition. What had been for a few brief weeks a key element of the kingdom's defense strategy, was now only a few pitiful farms so scattered and distant and on land so marginal as to make them almost worthless. Two thousand miles of desert had been searched—a tremendous price for such little gain. In the whole expanse, the expedition had found no more than 150 acres worth farming in a two-and-a-half-month search. But at this late date, the failure to find fertile valleys for settlement meant little.

The situation had altered drastically since the dark days of last winter when each succeeding California mail brought more dismal news for the Saints. In April the Mormons had swallowed their pride and allowed Alfred Cumming to enter the territory as their governor, but the people had sworn never to submit to or accept a federal occupation force in Zion. Even with a gentile governor in Utah, Brigham Young had by no means forfeited his leadership of the people. President Young still headed the church, and in so doing he controlled the hearts and minds of the people. In essence, Cumming governed Utah only to the extent that Brigham Young allowed him. There were other changes, too.

Many of the threats that had alarmed the Mormon hierarchy a few months ago had failed to materialize. One of their greatest fears, that of becoming surrounded by hostile forces, was now dispelled. The California mail arrived in the city on May 4 bringing news that the proposed movement against the Saints from California had been scrubbed—the victim of a political scandal involving the awarding of government contracts. It seems, too, that General Scott had never been fond of the idea, believing it was impractical.[3]

Amasa Lyman also returned from his reconnaissance of the Colorado River with a favorable report, allaying all worries that an invasion could be launched from that quarter. Lyman had reached the Colorado on April 13 with his force of eighteen men selected largely from the ranks of the dismantled San Bernardino colony.[4] Unlike Ives, who considered a wagon road from the Colorado River to the Salt Lake–California road quite feasible, Lyman found the country a difficult obstacle for any traveler, much more so for an army. His diary pronounced the region "very barren and desolate in the extreme, without a single spring, and scarcely any grass. . . . The whole country all around the Colorado, on both sides, presents the same barren, rocky mountainous, desert aspect. . . ."[5] Obviously an army would have a difficult time in the area. It was just such a buffer that Brigham Young had hoped to find to keep the troops and his people apart. He also wanted a defensive site located where the militia could make a stand against government steamers attempting to land soldiers on the river. Here again, Lyman was successful. Lyman found the site on April 17 in Pyramid Canyon after a difficult march down the river's west bank. "Noticed one place in particular, . . ."; wrote the apostle, "which affords excellent facilities for commanding the river, as the channel is, at this point, on this (west) side of the stream, and the adjacent rocks and ravines afford protection and shelter for a great number of men."[6] Like the White Mountain explorers, Lyman was unaware that his mission had been made obsolete by events in Salt Lake City. Nevertheless, it was good news for Brigham Young when Lyman made his report on May 22. The fear that Utah was vulnerable from the south, the same concern that had Brigham Young scrambling for alternatives in March, had melted away for good.

There was other favorable news reaching church headquarters at this time. The May 4 California mail also carried word that Congress had again defeated the president's request for four additional regiments to subdue the Mormons. Upon hearing the news, Hosea Stout wrote: "News from the W[est] favorable to us. Congress has refused to grant a dollar or another man to president B. in addition to the regular forces & expenditure of the army to aid him in his tyrannical crusade against us."[7] Had the mail carried more recent dispatches, the Mormons' optimism might have been dampened a bit. On April 9 Congress did pass an act allowing for the addition of two new regiments of volunteers for the purpose of "quieting the disturbances in the territory of Utah."[8]

Governor Cumming also proved to be a valuable asset to the Mormons. Not only did Cumming lend a sympathetic ear to their grievances, but he manifested a determination not to interfere with the church nor treat the Mormons as rebels. This unlikely friend was also converted to the Mormon view that peace was unattainable in Utah so long as the Saints were threatened by a federal army. On May 2 Cumming wrote to Secretary Cass:

> . . .there are among the Mormons many brave men, accustomed to arms and to horses; men who would fight desperately as guerillas, and, if the settlements are destroyed, will subject the country to an expensive and protracted war, without any compensatory results. They will, I am sure, submit to trial by their peers, but they will not brook the idea of trials by "juries composed of teamsters and followers of the camp," nor of an army encamped in their cities, or dense settlements.[9]

Cumming's letter could not have been written better by Brigham Young himself. After doing what he could to gain the confidence of Mormon leaders and urge their cooperation in defusing the potentially violent confrontation, Governor Cumming returned to Camp Scott in an attempt to dissuade General Johnston from advancing his army before a peaceful settlement could be arranged. Cumming left Salt Lake City with Colonel Kane on May 13. The governor realized he had no real authority to prevent Johnston from marching if he was determined to do so, as Johnston was under orders from the War Department to establish a military post at or near Salt Lake City. But perhaps he could persuade the general to adopt a more liberal interpretation of his orders. His poor relationship with Johnston made this a difficult task; nevertheless Cumming was determined to defuse the Utah powder keg.

Alfred Cumming occupied the unique position of being the only principal character on the scene who had a dialogue with all the parties involved. But the burden was great. On the one hand he had the difficult task of convincing the Mormons to act with prudence and to obey federal law; on the other he had to somehow deter the inflexible General Johnston from acting too hastily, lest the peace he had been nurturing be shattered in an instant. Johnston, in truth, did not want a civil war, but he felt that the Mormon "rebels" should be chastised or the Constitution would be compromised.[10]

At temporary church headquarters in Provo, Brigham Young had sufficient reason to be optimistic when he learned of the peace commissioners' arrival in Salt Lake City on June 7. The plan to fight the invading army had long ago died along with the flamboyant claims of independence and returning to Jackson County. The alternative strategy had also been seriously impaired with the failure of the White Mountain Expedition to locate a suitable refuge on the desert. Young now had good reason to believe the destruction of the city would not be necessary. All indications pointed toward a peaceful adjustment of the difficulties. It now appeared that the government was suing for peace at that very moment.

Brigham Young would not have been so optimistic had he known that the peace commissioners did not come to Utah to investigate the charges made against the Saints, as Dr. Bernhisel had been advocating untiringly in Washington; nor were they sent to negotiate with the Mormons. The peace commissioners were sent to offer a simple deal, the terms of which were not negotiable. In exchange for dutiful obedience to federal laws and authority, including the acceptance of the army in the territory, the president would pardon the Mormons for all previous crimes of treason and guarantee nonintervention in their religion.[11] There were no concessions.

Neither did Brigham Young understand the real motivation behind the president's appointment of a peace commission for Utah. In truth, the Mormon policies of resistance to the federal troops followed by a calculated evacuation of northern Utah did not evoke the sympathy in the East Brigham Young believed it had.[12] Church historians have gone to great lengths to attribute this apparent reversal in Buchanan's Mormon policy to widespread criticism of the president for his belligerent stand against an innocent, persecuted people. Indeed there were some who were critical of the president's policies. But there was no wholesale denunciation of the president, and, contrary to Roberts's assertions, Buchanan was not flinching from overwhelming criticism in the national press.[13] True, public opinion was now divided, and some articles had appeared critical of the president's policies, but the mood of the public was still decidedly anti-Mormon. Only occasionally were favorable comments based on genuine sympathy for the Mormons. Mishandling of the crisis and economic matters were generally the concerns of the president's detractors. Some newspaper editors and congressmen were beginning to ask why it was necessary to engage in an expensive military occupation of Utah at all. Nevertheless, there was no united outcry from the public, and it is doubtful that such a diversity of opinion would have influenced the president. Buchanan's actions demonstrated no real urgency to bring the war to a close.[14]

The appointment of a peace commission for Utah was based primarily on practical rather than humanitarian concerns. The Utah expedition had been an expensive undertaking from the start, especially since it followed on the heels of the financial panic of 1857. When the army failed to reach Salt Lake City in the fall of 1857, Buchanan found himself in the embarrassing situation of asking Congress for additional troops and funds to subdue the Mormons. Largely due to political and economic concerns rather than any sympathy for the Mormons, the president's appeal for additional assistance met with antagonism in Congress and was delayed for several months. By the time Congress approved the enlistment of two additional regiments of volunteers and appropriations for the nearly bankrupt expedition, Buchanan had already appointed the peace commissioners. His motive in encouraging a dialogue with the Mormons might have been to correct his oversight of sending an army to Utah before investigating the charges of sedition in the territory.[15]

Early in April President Buchanan selected Lazarus W. Powell, of Kentucky, and Maj. Ben McCulloch, of Texas, to carry the offer of peace to the Mormons. Powell was a U.S. senator-elect from his home state and had recently served as governor. McCulloch had gained some fame for his valiant service in the Texas Rebellion and the Mexican War. Luckily for the Mormons, neither of these men had any axes to grind with them nor any political advantages to be gained by this assignment. Both were considered men of "distinction and national reputation."[16] The commissioners carried the president's pardon dated April 6.

Powell and McCulloch arrived at Camp Scott on May 29, where for several days they listened carefully to the divergent views of Johnston and Cumming. Although the commissioners were decidedly in agreement with Johnston's point of view, they did extract a pledge from the general that he would not march until he had received word from them or Governor Cumming. On June 2 Powell and McCulloch departed for Salt Lake City, followed the next day by Governor Cumming and his wife.[17]

Brigham Young did not rush to Salt Lake to meet the commissioners. In fact June 7, the day of their arrival, Brigham Young was in Provo conferring with George W. Bean who had just returned from the desert with his report. It was not until June 10 that Young went to Salt Lake City. A meeting with the commissioners was scheduled for nine o'clock on the following morning in the Old Council House.

This first meeting was attended by a large number of the "leading brethren"—too many, perhaps, to carry on the delicate talks. The commissioners presented the pardon to the Mormons which, if accepted, implied that the Mormons were guilty of many serious charges. Powell declared that the commission was not empowered to treat with the Mormons; they must either accept or reject the offer, but to accept was to bind them to give proper allegiance to the government and to accept the federal army which would have to fulfill its orders and march to Salt Lake City sooner or later. The meeting got off to a poor start. Brigham Young learned by an express which arrived that morning that, despite the assurances of the commissioners, Johnston had given the order for the army to march on the 14th. The commissioners were positive the report was false, and they earnestly denied it; nevertheless, it was true—Johnston was preparing to advance.[18]

The pardon itself was a lengthy document, and one that the Mormons found as offensive as it was long. Most of the Mormon delegation considered the pardon a studied insult, which, according to their observations, contained forty to fifty false charges. The president used most of the proclamation to justify his belligerent course toward the Mormons, hashing through most of the old charges against them, including the accusations of treason and rebellion. The first paragraph begins:

> Whereas the territory of Utah was settled by certain emigrants from the states and foreign countries, who have for several years past, manifested a spirit of insubordination to the Constitution and laws of the United States. The great mass of these settlers, acting under the influence of leaders to whom they seem to have surrendered their judgement, refuse to be controlled by any other authority.

They have been often advised to obedience, and these friendly counsels have been answered by defiance. Officers of the federal government have been driven from the territory for no other offence but an effort to do their sworn duty. Others have been prevented from going there by threats of assassination. Judges have been violently interrupted in the performance of their functions, and the records of the courts have been seized and either destroyed or concealed. Many other acts of unlawful violence have been perpetrated, and the right to repeat them has been openly claimed by the leading inhabitants with at least the silent acquiescence of nearly all the others. Their hostility to the lawful government of the country has at length become so violent that no officer bearing a commission from the chief magistrate of the union can enter the territory and remain in safety; . . .[19]

After asserting his purposes and right to send troops to Utah Territory, Buchanan then accused the Mormons of attacking the government supply trains—the only charge to which the Mormons admitted. "Fellow citizens of Utah," the president declared, "this is rebellion against the government to which you owe allegiance. It is levying war against the United States and involves you in the guilt of treason." The Mormons, of course, could not accept this view. They saw themselves only as defenders of a peaceful territory assailed by an armed mob who would trample the Constitution, destroy their religion, and take their lives.[20] Perhaps the most insulting of the president's accusations was the contention that "You never made a complaint that was not listened to with patience." The Mormons had long been angered over the government's failure to listen to their grievances and to intervene when they were being driven by mobs. The Mormons perceived government inaction as a desire to injure them.

More than three-fourths of the way through the proclamation the president announced the intention of the document: "And being anxious to save the effusion of blood, and to avoid the indiscriminate punishment of a whole people, for crimes of which it is not probable that all are equally guilty, I offer now a full and free pardon to all who will submit themselves to the authority of the federal government."

The meeting did not go well. Not only was Brigham Young angered by intelligence of Johnston's intention to advance, accusing the commissioners of bad faith, but, to his bitter disappointment, he discovered that the commissioners were not interested in investigating the serious charges leveled against the Mormons, many of which Governor Cumming was prepared to refute. The church president emphatically denied the church's guilt as alleged in the proclamation and proceeded to rip the administration's intentions of sending an army to subdue his people. Young made it clear that he had no hatred of the government itself. The Constitution was sacred; only corrupt men in office defiled it. Eventually the meeting evolved into a harangue of the injustices perpetrated against the Saints in Missouri, Illinois, and Utah. In short, the Mormons refused to play the part of a defeated people.[21]

But all was not as hopeless as it might have appeared. During the evening serious talks were conducted between the commissioners and Brigham Young, Heber C. Kimball, Daniel H. Wells, and George A. Smith. In the absence of a large audience, there was no necessity for the ostentation which prevented constructive dialogue in the earlier meeting. Here the issues were confronted and resolved. The Mormons had no illusions about the necessity of accepting the troops into the territory. Their only alternatives were a resumption of active resistance, a move fraught with disastrous consequences, or a continuation of the policy of self-imposed exile, an increasingly unpopular policy at home. It was reluctantly agreed that the troops would be allowed to enter the valley unmolested. But many thorny issues had to be resolved. The problems of protecting the citizens, the route of the march, and the ultimate question of where the troops were to be quartered were serious concerns to the Mormons. Throughout the campaign the Mormons had received continual reinforcement of their perception of the army as a wicked, licentious rabble bent on malevolent deeds in Utah. According to Cumming, it was widely believed in Utah "that the approach of the army to their settlements would be the signal for the commission of every species of crime that an infuriated soldiery might perpetrate."[22] Working into the night the issues were decided. The soldiers would march through the city, but they would not be quartered there. The commissioners also guaranteed the strictest order and discipline of the troops for the protection of persons and property and expressed this concern to General Johnston in a dispatch the following morning.[23]

The meetings of the following day were largely for show. At 10:15 A.M. the Council House was again thronged with people, but discussion had ended and a tentative agreement reached. Speeches were made giving acceptance to the presidential pardon. In so doing the church had swallowed considerable pride. To partake of the pardon was tantamount to admitting guilt, since one is not pardoned for crimes not committed. But the Mormons denied guilt, even though they accepted the pardon as a matter of necessity. The army also had to be admitted—another bitter pill, as the people had vowed never to accept the troops under any circumstances. Now they would be marching through the streets of their capital city. But the Mormons, too, received some promises. The army was not to be quartered in the city, and the soldiers would not be allowed to plunder. And of course there was the matter of rebellion and treason to be forgotten by the government and a pledge to refrain from interfering with religion in the territory.

In speeches made during the day, church leaders would not admit defeat. In one eloquent address, George A. Smith assented to the pardon but claimed the document contained forty-two false charges. "I am a man of peace, not of war," proclaimed the apostle.

> I accept the pardon. I may have some serious objections to the form in which it is couched, and to the forty-two false accusations therein. But friends, should we throw ourselves in the attitude of defense against the advancing columns of the army, it brings on hostilities and bloodshed immediately. Let us drop upon this army and crush it to pieces, and it will not end there. One hundred thousand men would probably be sent here to exterminate us, and to wipe out the administration's disgrace, . . .

Smith's speech exhibited little of the radicalism displayed in the fall of 1857 until he reached the emotional issue of the conduct of the troops who were poised to march through the city:

> When I say, walk in gentlemen, fulfill your orders and don't interfere with our gardens, fields and pastures, and I want it perfectly understood that the first man that ravishes or seduces a wife or daughter of mine, I fully intend to blow out his brains. Hundreds with the army came for that purpose.[24]

If Smith's opinion of the army had not improved significantly, his attitude toward Governor Cumming was much improved. Just two months to the day had passed since an angry George A. Smith had bestowed the epithet "The Animal" on the governor in the church's historical journal. But on this day Smith expressed his satisfaction that Cumming was a "manly, free, generous spirit." He admitted that until he had seen his face he was convinced that the president had appointed one of the Jackson County mob to be their governor. Once past this misunderstanding, Smith learned to like him. He had been impressed with Cumming's entrance into the valley without a military escort.

Later in the day Brigham Young delivered an oration reminiscent of the fervent discourses of the previous fall. "He spoke in the power of God," remarked Apostle Woodruff, "those Commissioners heard the voice and roar of the Lion."[25] Young claimed the Mormon people had always submitted to the Constitution and laws—"We always have, and always expect to."

> I have no character, no pride to gratify, no vanity to please. If a man comes from the moon and says he will pardon me for kicking him in the moon yesterday, I don't care about it, I'll accept of his pardon, it don't affect me, one way or the other. . . . Twenty-eight years ago, it was revealed to me that I should live to see the world arrayed against this people. . . .
>
> Our necks shall not be given to the halter. Col. Johnston said that not a soldier of the army should be quartered in this city. I'm tired of this city. I had not finished my house until I wanted to leave it and build better. I'm a man of enterprise. My duty on this earth is to build up. I call forth the enterprise and energy of this people. Don't be concerned. We shall live. I could select one thousand of our boys from 15 to 18, who could whip all the armies that could be sent here. We'll live and prosper.
>
> The battalion was raised to prove my loyalty to the constitution, they want my neck to prove my loyalty. I'll see them in hell farther than they can get in a days journey first. They war with God, but can't dethrone him. We will not be governed by them [unrighteous officials]. . . . If the nation will not harken to our petitions as Joseph Smith prophesied, that government will be broken and not a potsherd left. . . .
>
> Don't be concerned, brethren, we have to do right and God will sustain us; trust in God and keep your powder dry.[26]

Thus was the confused and stormy end to the so-called Utah War; neither side admitting defeat, both sides claiming victory, and everyone frustrated and embarrassed. The Mormons had been unable to make good their extravagant claims of 1857, and the administration found itself guilty of shooting first and talking later. The ill-starred Utah expedition was angry over being deprived of a military victory.

On June 26, two days after Dame and Johnson made their report to Brigham Young, the troops of General Johnston marched through the otherwise vacant streets of Salt Lake City. It was a disappointment for the would-be conquerors. One soldier wrote, ". . . it was like entering a graveyard. Silence reigned supreme. If a plague had threatened it instead of us, it could not have depopulated it more."[27] The troops passed through the city, crossed the Jordan River, and camped on the west bank. A week later a military reservation was established in Cedar Valley west of Utah Lake near present-day Fairfield, about thirty-five miles from Salt Lake City. But the soldiers were fuming. An officer of Johnston's command wrote to his wife on July 2 that the Mormons "are impudent and rebellious still. They say they will accept the pardon, but the President is a fool; that they will not obey anyone but Brigham Young. They don't want the army and won't have it. Such is the result of the pardon, a miserable policy which the government ought to be damned for.[28]

The ordeal of the Saints did not immediately end with Johnston's swift passage through Salt Lake City. Thousands were still in exile in the south, and the men and boys of the White Mountain Expedition were still in the southwest desert. Brigham Young was well aware of the contempt the army held for him and the Mormon people; therefore he refrained from giving the order to return home until he could be certain of the army's intentions. Although the troops had acquitted themselves with strict discipline on their march through the city, Young remained unconvinced. On June 27, the day after Johnston's entrance, Young wrote to James Ferguson that it was not advisable to return to the north until it could be determined whether the troops would really behave as Johnston had pledged and whether reinforcements had actually been ordered back. ". . . then we can return with a feeling of assurance that the President is sincere and intends to carry out his pledges made through the commissioners," reasoned the prophet.[29] The Mormons had too often been the victims of treachery and broken promises in the East to accept these pledges at face value.

Notwithstanding his benevolent statements about Governor Cumming in recent days, President Young did not entirely trust him either. Young directed William C. Staines, at whose home Cumming was lodging, to gather information for him. On June 17 he communicated to Young the discovery of a letter in the governor's room while the latter was absent from the home. The letter was only Cumming's angry response to General Johnston for beginning his advance without receiving word from the authorities in Salt Lake. The June 15 correspondence should have provided Young with proof of Cumming's sincerity toward the Mormons, but Staines remained resolute to continue his surveilance. In closing his communication with Young, Staines dutifully informed the churchman, "I shall endeavor to keep the wax out of my ears and the dust out of my eyes the Lord being my helper."[30]

On June 30 Brigham Young approved the return of the exiles to their homes. There was really no other choice. The White Mountain had failed to provide a practical alternative for the people to settle, and there was mounting pressure from the people to end their self-imposed exile.[31] These refugees were just surviving in their makeshift accommodations in Utah County. The war had been a trying period for them, but the last two months were the most severe. Thousands lived in squalor along the Provo River bottoms and along the shores of Utah Lake west of Provo. The lucky ones had constructed board shanties, while the less fortunate had to be content living in dugouts, tents, and wagon boxes; some even lived in holes in the ground. Driven from their normal labors, many found it difficult to obtain proper clothing and other necessities. Adding to this misery, many of the exiled Saints failed to plant any crops, believing they would be driven away before they could harvest them.[32] In ensuing weeks, 30,000 men, women, and children trudged wearily back to their homes in the northern settlements. As they walked along the road, many were scorned and ridiculed by contingents of U.S. troops they met along the road because of their shabby appearance.[33] "They are the most destitute looking set I ever saw," wrote one soldier,

> pigs, poultry, white-headed children, mothers and wives all heaped promiscuously together in the wagon, with barely sufficient clothing to cover their nakedness. To judge the men by their appearance, one would think that their coats were made from the same pattern that Joseph wore, from the many colors they contain, or else bed quilts are a spontaneous production in this section of the country. It is said that some of the women were so naked they avoided the road. . . .[34]

But the Mormons held their heads high. To their way of thinking they had won a victory, or at least convinced themselves they had not been beaten. In the fall when Brigham Young said, "Stop!" the army stopped, and it was not until the prophet said, "Come in," that the troops could march into the valley. Their faith in Brigham Young remained unshaken.

Although a chapter in the history of Mormon–federal conflict was brought to a close, the conflict persisted. The underlying issues were not resolved, only postponed. As the historian Furniss noted, the peace of 1858 was in reality "an armed truce" rather than a solution to the problem.[35] Nearly half a century elapsed before the conflict was over.

# XV

# ABANDONMENT

Despite the proclamation of peace in Salt Lake, little had changed for the settlers on Snake Creek, Meadow Valley, and Cave Springs. Their mission was unimportant now—the remnant of an antiquated policy. Nevertheless, their struggle for survival was just as real now as the day they left their homes.

Little is known of the mission at Snake Creek other than that it was still functioning under David E. Bunnell's care. We also know that Hopkins's men put in some crops near Cave Spring in Badger (Clover) Valley. But because of James H. Martineau, one of those peculiar individuals who kept accurate records under the most adverse conditions, we have a near complete history of the Meadow Valley settlement.

There was no let-down in the work when President Dame left the valley on June 9. Indeed, the success of the mission, as well as their own well-being, depended on their work and constant vigilance. The day following Dame's departure, the remaining forty-nine men turned out to finish the corral. On Sunday the 13th, it was voted to sustain Lyman Curtis, James H. Martineau, and Jabez Nowland overseers of the ditch. William C. Stewart, Silas Harris, and John Topham were elected watermasters. The following Tuesday a tremendous rainstorm, called "a perfect deluge" by Martineau, left water standing "several inches deep on level ground" and washed out the ditch in several places.[1] On Wednesday all hands turned out to make the necessary repairs. In addition to their labors on the public works, the men had their field work to attend to. There was little time for idleness at Meadow Valley.

By June 17, the day President Dame had counseled his men to cease planting, there were fifty-four acres of crops in the ground and doing well. Martineau even termed them "luxuriant." The new settlers had planted wheat, corn, peas, beans, squashes, melons, cotton, sugarcane, hemp, flax, potatoes, "and a great variety of other vegetables," all of which were developing well at this point.[2]

Friday, the 18th of June, saw the men scrambling to recover their animals which had stampeded during the morning. All were retrieved before dark, however. The 19th brought three Indians into camp with information that some men from the settlements would be arriving shortly. About noon George W. Sirrine and Charles Carter returned to camp carrying the mail, newspapers, and a copy of President Buchanan's proclamation.[3]

The men were gathered together, and the proclamation was read to them. The explorers had mixed feelings. They now knew with certainty that the object of their original mission was obsolete—all their hard labors and months spent in the wilderness away from families and civilization for a few acres of grain and vegetables. But to their joy, it also meant they might be going home soon.

Jesse N. Smith, the man designated by Colonel Dame to take command at Meadow Valley, arrived in camp on the evening of June 25, bringing five men with him. Smith was a young man—only twenty-three years old—but already he was a high priest in the church and a counsellor to Dame in the stake presidency at Parowan. Smith had also been elected to a term in the territorial legislature from Iron County. Born in New York State, he was a cousin to both the Prophet Joseph Smith and Apostle George A. Smith, and as a boy he had experienced the sufferings and expulsion of the Mormon people in Missouri and Illinois.

Smith took leave of his home in Parowan on June 21, six days after receiving his assignment from Dame. He had no idea how long he would be required to serve. Accompanied by Marius Ensign, also of Parowan, he proceeded to Cedar City where he was joined by John Hunter. At Pinto Creek they overtook three other men destined for Meadow Valley, who were driving the stock donated by the company. These three were members of the original expedition who had returned to Parowan with Colonel Dame. Of them, only John Lewis, of Washington, can be identified. The company now consisted of six men, one boy, two wagons, seven horses, six mules, nine cows, and three calves.[4] They reached Shoal Creek at noon on the 23d where they fed three Indians who came into camp. They spent the evening at Nephi's Spring where more Indians came into camp who were also fed. Three of them remained overnight. By sunset of the following day, they arrived at the camp at Cave Spring. It is probable that Hopkins had released himself from the mission by now, leaving Orson B. Adams in charge. Smith calls the Cave Spring Farm, "Orson B. Adams' camp."[5]

The company reached Meadow Valley at dark on the night of June 25—a dry march of thirty-five miles, which nearly caused the cattle to drop. A meeting was called by John Ward Christian in which he announced that President Dame had appointed Jesse N. Smith to take charge of the mission. Smith then read a list of the names of thirty men who were to be discharged and sent home. Two days later the men set out for their homes with others going home for temporary visits.

Shortly before this, Brigham Young ordered similar reductions for the brethren at Snake Creek. In a letter dated June 21 to Bishop Brunson, of Fillmore, and Bishop Farnsworth, of Beaver, he outlined his plan for the future of the Snake Creek farm, stating that Colonel Dame would receive instructions to take charge of all the Iron County men.[6] This placed the men at Cave Springs in Dame's care despite the fact that they were originally organized under Bean. Officially, Snake Creek was to be abandoned as soon as the crops could be harvested. Young also wished the brethren to give the Indians "all the surplus vegetables and a portion of the grain." In the meantime, he ordered the Fillmore and Beaver settlements to supply replacements for the men who wanted to return to their homes. This was especially important, reasoned Young, for the men from the northern cities whose families were still in exile. Probably anticipating the return to Salt Lake in the near future, he knew that the men would be needed to help their families move north. Farnsworth and Brunson were also required to regulate the officers of the mission as they saw fit, because Edson Barney and George W. Bean would not be returning.

The two bishops responded with their usual alacrity, organizing and outfitting relief companies. The Beaver company consisted of twelve men, "well fitted out," who departed for Snake Valley on July 6. They were led by James Low, the veteran of the original Beaver company under Bean which returned after failing to find a suitable location for settlement.[7] The particulars of the Fillmore relief company are obscure, but Brunson reported to Brigham Young that the company started within four days of receiving the prophet's instructions; therefore, they were probably on their way before the end of June.[8]

President Young apparently gave Dame orders similar to those he gave Brunson and Farnsworth, because the colonel quickly sent a letter to Jesse N. Smith, upon his return to Parowan, instructing him to remain until after the harvest, then bring in the grain and abandon the settlement. Smith received the letter on July 10 while visiting the brethren at Cave Springs.[9]

Dame was also pressing Bishop Farnsworth to furnish an additional eight men for Meadow Valley. This irked the bishop, as he felt the resources of his tiny village had been stretched to the limit. He also felt that Colonel Dame had not dealt fairly with him. Beaver was one of the newest and smallest settlements in the south. Yet, as he complained to Brigham Young, "On the Colonel's first demand, he was furnished from Beaver with fifteen men, five wagons, five horses, and twenty mules, while his own settlement [Parowan] and Red Creek [Paragonah] together furnished only nine men, three wagons, and fifteen animals."[10] Farnsworth also asserted that Beaver had outfitted seventeen men for George W. Bean's expedition. "And in as much as we are called to sustain the Snake Creek mission," he cried to President Young, "and many of our brethren are without homes, and our fields which were made this season are unfenced, . . . I find great need of what substantial men I have left." In consequence of this, and from his interpretation of Young's instructions of June 21 (which he believed required only Dame and Iron County to support the Meadow Valley mission), he denied Colonel Dame's request and sent a letter to Meadow Valley, authorizing all those from Beaver to return home if they wished to do so, without being released by President Dame. The letter arrived late in June; but the men had a strong sense of duty, and, according to the company historian, "They all preferred remaining until they should be discharged by the same authority which had called them to the mission."[11]

At Desert Camp the men were occupied with the usual labors of establishing a settlement on virgin ground. They hauled wood to burn into charcoal for the blacksmith's forge, they cultivated and watered their fields, and they chased down their stray animals.

June 27 was a Sunday, and services were held in the evening. Orson B. Adams and two others from the Cave Spring farm were present. President Smith decided to transfer ten men from Cave Springs to the larger settlement in Meadow Valley, but when they had not arrived in Meadow Valley in two weeks, Smith and three others went down to Cave Springs to inspect the situation. All but ten of the original twenty-eight men had been released, and four of the ten were on furlough in the settlements at the time. The Cave Spring farm had been a failure; Smith closed down the settlement and transferred the six remaining men to Meadow Valley. Besides Adams, the group included Urban Van Stewart, Josiah Reeves, William Walker, Lafayette Guyman, and William Roberts (a stepson of Adams).[12] The group arrived at Desert Camp on July 12. Reeves and Walker eventually became discouraged and left the mission without being released. President Smith tried to dissuade them, but on July 19 the two homesick boys left for Iron County.[13]

Cave Springs was not the only settlement on the verge of collapse. It now looked as though there would be little or no harvest at Meadow Valley. The crops which were earlier described as "luxuriant" were withering as a result of the alkali in the soil. Most of the experienced men in camp felt it was unlikely they would ever mature, and President Smith called them "backward and worthless" on July 10, the day Dame's instructions arrived to abandon the settlement after the harvest.[14] Three days later Smith maintained there was "slight prospect of raising any grain."[15]

Martineau affirmed that the soil was impregnated with "black alkali," which began to rise as soon as the water was turned on it. The ditch itself, nearly two miles long, crossed a heavy alkali bed which also contaminated the water. The crops grew well at first but eventually became retarded in growth, and then began dying rapidly.[16] By mid-July an estimated four-fifths of the produce had been destroyed "and a fair prospects for the remainder to go."[17]

Not only did the alkali affect the grain and vegetables, it also affected the health of the men who consumed the alkali-tainted water. The men in camp "became seriously affected" by "sores which caused an intolerable itching."[18] It was eventually discovered that strong doses of sour buttermilk went a long way toward curing the ill effects of the alkali. The cows sent by Dame proved to be a great blessing to them.

An express was finally sent to Colonel Dame on July 19, explaining the pitiful situation at Desert Camp. Orson B. Adams and William Roberts were the letter carriers.[19] Despite these hardships, Martineau was able to write, "The hand of the Lord was over the camp for good, and his blessings attended us continually as nearly all the brethren testified frequently."[20]

In other events, the men continued to come and go between
Desert Camp and their homes in large numbers, as the crops
withered and died leaving little for the brethren to do. A few found
time to scratch their names in the soft rock of a white butte near
camp.[21] As Adams was being sent off with the express for Colonel
Dame, J. Ward Christian and five others arrived from the settlements with letters. About the same time Francis T. Whitney and
eleven others were sent home to visit their families. By July 20 only
thirteen men and boys remained in camp to tend the dying fields.[22]

While Smith waited for further instructions from Dame, he decided to explore the canyon to the south to procure some ash timber
for pitchfork handles, hay rakes, and other implements. No doubt,
Martineau had informed Smith of the stands of ash he had seen in
Grand Echo Canyon (Meadow Valley Wash). This excursion nearly
proved fatal, however. Smith, accompanied by J. Ward Christian
and Samuel D. White, started down the valley on the morning of
July 22. They soon entered Meadow Valley Wash which seemed to
impress Smith with its natural beauty. "The valley soon closed in
making a romantic canyon," Smith wrote in his diary. And the next
day, "the scenery of the canyon became more and more magnificent, the sides rising almost perpendicular, the walls rich in various
colors, rising to a great height, the narrow, flat and winding bottom
covered with a dense growth of willows and grass."[23]

On the afternoon of the first day, the party surprised a couple of
Indians who were very much frightened. They were quickly pacified
with a few crackers, however, and they were soon joined by other Indians, three of whom spent the night with them at their camp near a
small spring.

In the morning the Indians invited the explorers to accompany
them further down the wash to see their wickiups, corn, and ash
timber. While Christian stayed behind with the team and wagon,
Smith and White unknowingly followed their Indian "friends" into
an ambush. As they worked their way down the canyon, the two
men became alarmed at the number of Indians who were increasing
rapidly around them. Finally, two or three miles from camp, several
braves sprang onto the trail in front of them, while a dozen more
closed the circle behind them. The Indians first demanded the shirts
off their backs. One Indian who appeared to be in authority grabbed
White as if to rip the shirt from him. It was a tense moment, and the
two white men knew they would have to acquit themselves well to

emerge from this scrape in good health. Samuel White, who knew the Indian tongue, attempted to appeal to the honor of the ones who led them into the trap, claiming they were "there by their invitation, to see the country, drink water with them, etc."[24] But their captors only laughed in their faces saying "there was nothing to see neither corn, ash timber, water, wickiups, or anything else." The two explorers were clearly caught at a disadvantage. Smith was wearing his revolver and was also carrying a knife, while White had a small axe. Their foes, however, outnumbered them six or seven to one, all of whom were armed with bows and arrows except one who carried a gun. Notwithstanding the poor odds, the two decided to "fight it out with our shirts on," making preparations to do so. When the Indians perceived that their quarry was unwilling to lay down without a fight they had second thoughts and began making "professions of friendship." The invitation to go on with them was renewed. Not wishing to provoke the Indians, they proceeded on a little further, leaving their abashed hosts at a convenient moment with a brief exchange of courtesies.

Arriving back at camp, they cut the wood, loaded it on their wagon, and headed north, making camp about seventeen miles from the Meadow Valley farm. Because two of the mules bolted at daylight, the trek back to Desert Camp was a slow one. While Christian went in pursuit of the animals, Smith and White proceeded with only the two remaining mules to pull the heavily loaded wagons over the unbroken ground. It was late in the day of July 24 when they reached camp, but, to be sure, Smith and White were more than content just to be out of the canyon with its treacherous inhabitants.

Earlier in the day, an express arrived from Colonel Dame, John W. Osburn having carried the mail into Desert Camp about 2 P.M. The message, which arrived on the anniversary of Utah's struggle with the government, was as anticipated: Dame ordered the immediate abandonment of the mission. What few crops remained were to be given to the Indians. Considering the situation at Meadow Valley, Dame had no reasonable alternative; yet he still found it difficult to close down the mission ordered by Brigham Young. Before issuing the order, he had conferred with Apostles Amasa Lyman and George A. Smith, who were then in the south, and he issued the order only upon their sanction. Soon afterward he explained his actions in a letter to the prophet dated July 31. After commending his men to Young, asserting they "have done as they were told and still hold themselves in readyness for any call," he justified his decision: "I saw no other way to do. If I have done wrong, please inform me that I may make amends."[25] But Brigham Young remained silent, and the mission was closed.

The morning after Dame's instructions were received, the brethren gathered together what they could salvage and began the trek home. Early on the morning of their departure, President Smith sent for the Indians to come into camp. Pursuant to his instructions from Colonel Dame, he turned the fields over to the natives, telling them that if they continued to water the crops they might raise something to harvest. The men wasted no time in leaving camp. When assembled, the return company consisted of fifteen men, seven wagons, twenty-six horses and mules, fifteen cows, and four calves.[26] Some of the company arrived home on July 28, while others herding the cattle arrived home the next day.

For most of the company it had been a tour of three months; but for some, like Orson B. Adams, who had begun with George W. Bean and was subsequently transferred to Cave Spring and then Meadow Valley, it was considerably longer. Adams recalled that he had been absent from home four months and two days.[27] Martineau calculated the distance traveled by the Southern Exploring Company during this time to be 1245 miles.[28]

The Snake Creek farm fared no better than its sister mission. Near the end of June, Bishop Brunson, of Fillmore, received an express from David E. Bunnell stating that "the water had dryed up so that there could not much be raised."[29] According to the express carriers, the creek had entirely failed so that it was impossible to irrigate the wheat again. After conferring with Apostle Orson Pratt, who had been in Fillmore since the exodus, Brunson concluded to send Samuel P. Hoyt with three men to Snake Creek to assess the situation. Riding there as quickly as possible, they were empowered to call in the mission if conditions were as bad as had been reported. The reports proved accurate, and the mission was abandoned. According to one observer, the last remnants of the expedition arrived home in late July and early August.[30] Some of Bean's original expedition, such as David E. Bunnell, had been out since late March, making the duration of their tour about four months.

The men of both contingents endured considerable hardships on their desert journey. Willingly, they exposed themselves to a hostile environment, suffering from heat and cold, alkali sores, crop failures, and privations of every sort. But for the most part, the men of the White Mountain Expedition performed this difficult assignment without complaint.

# XVI

# SUMMARY
# AND CONCLUSIONS

The White Mountain Expedition was conceived as an alternative solution to a difficult problem: How to keep Israel intact while a hostile army invaded Zion. When Brigham Young determined that fighting the army was pointless, he turned toward the interior deserts of the Great Basin, hoping to find a refuge for the embattled Saints. For a few anxious weeks in the spring of 1858, this alternative plan became the hope of salvation for the Mormon kingdom. The White Mountain Expedition proceeded to the southwestern deserts of Utah Territory, penetrating deep into unexplored country. Even when the danger was past and a desert sanctuary had become unnecessary, the expedition moved ahead surveying and mapping this vast *terra incognita*.

The significance of the White Mountain Expedition, therefore, is threefold. First, the expedition was related to a concept in Mormon history of abandonment and resettlement, which, in 1858, could have resulted in the permanent removal of the Mormons from the Salt Lake Basin. Secondly, its achievements in Great Basin exploration, although not widely recognized, were considerable. Finally, the expedition demonstrates the Saints' unwavering allegiance to Brigham Young.

The resettlement concept was nearly as old as Mormonism itself. Establishing Zion on the fertile plains of Jackson County, Missouri, in 1831, the Saints soon found that hostility from the "Old Settlers" made their homesteads untenable. By 1833 the Mormons were re-established in the adjacent counties, but again, open hostilities and the threat of extermination brought them streaming into Illinois, where, on a bend in the Mississippi River, they built the city of Nauvoo in 1839. Seven years later western Illinois was on the brink of civil war; and once again the Mormons had to go, this time electing the quiet seclusion of the Great Basin. Before long the Mormon church was again embroiled in conflict, with the church and federal government each trying to wrest political control of Utah Territory from the other. The difficulties of the 1850s were rooted in the church's Zionistic concept with its unquenchable desire for isolation and political control at almost any cost, the American public's ignorance and hostility toward Mormon beliefs and practices, and the government's insensitivity to Mormon problems.

In the long history of Mormon-gentile conflict, the Utah War of 1857–58 was distinguished in several ways. For one thing, the scope of the confrontation had escalated. No longer were the Mormons contending with mobs or militias. This time they had incurred the wrath of the United States government and would now have to contend with the national army. Also, the Mormons had increased their capacity for defense. After each flight from their homes the Saints had emerged stronger than before. Seeming to thrive on persecution, the Mormons in 1857 were stronger and more numerous than they had ever been. No longer were they the newcomers in another's land. Now they were the "Old Settlers" in a land they saw as consecrated for their own use. The land was also far removed from their enemies and otherwise strategically advantageous.

In this situation, removal from their Wasatch homes seemed only a remote alternative, and the Saints bid defiance to the advancing army. With the woeful news of invasions from California, the Colorado River, and other localities, however, Brigham Young became preoccupied with the idea that his enemies had surrounded him. Perceiving his position as increasingly vulnerable, Young became apprehensive about engaging in hostilities with the U.S. troops, and the resettlement option again took on appeal. When Colonel Kane's mission appeared fruitless and Cumming had yet to prove himself an ally, there seemed to be no reasonable alternative. Inspired by the heroic defense of Sebastopol during the recent Crimean War and probably by a prophetic dream in March, President Young finally determined upon a course of defense. Once again the Saints were to abandon their homes. But this time they were prepared to lay waste to their settlements as they commenced a tactical retreat into the little-known interior of the Great Basin. In this way Young hoped to preserve the gathering and defeat the enemy in a single stroke.

Brigham Young had conceived the idea—with considerable help—that somewhere in the unexplored recesses of the southwestern deserts there lay substantial tracts of land suitable for settlement. He envisioned a series of oases capable of supporting the entire population of Utah, while surrounding them with the security of a harsh desert, impenetrable by a large force. And so, as in the past, the Mormons prepared to retreat to a new location. The plan was a long shot, desperate, perhaps even naive, but Brigham Young saw no remaining options that would both preserve the kingdom and protect the Saints from their enemies. The charge of the White Mountain Expedition was to search out and find the refuge for the besieged Saints—prelude to a fourth attempt at abandonment and resettlement in three decades of conflict.

Brigham Young's strategy might have been different had he been correctly informed of the region's true nature. Not only had Young been misled by exaggerated reports of troop movements, he had also been misinformed about the interior regions of the Great Basin. Thus, the White Mountain Expedition was founded on two false suppositions: There was no reasonable alternative to flight, and there was indeed a place to go. The profuse writings of John C. Frémont and information supplied by the mountain man, Elijah Barney Ward, were no doubt influences on Young's perception of Great Basin geography. Just as Frémont and an earlier generation of explorers had been fooled by the myth of the Buenaventura, Brigham Young was duped by the promoters of the "Oasis Theory." Many others had been deceived by the same sources, beginning with the Death Valley company in 1849. On the eve of the Utah War, in fact, the recently published map of the territory of Utah by Rogers and Johnston indicated a vast void west of Utah's southern settlements with only this description paraphrased from Frémont's map of 1845: "It is surrounded by lofty mountains and is believed to be filled with rivers and lakes which have no outlet to the sea, deserts and oases which have never been explored. . . ." It is not difficult to understand how Brigham Young became preoccupied with the concept of an interior oasis. As early as 1855 Young had sent a company to find the fertile region. Now, with a hostile army on the fringes of the territory, he again turned to the desert—perhaps the only real estate open to large-scale Mormon settlement in the United States.

With the failure of the expedition to discover the sanctuary, and receiving positive assurances from Alfred Cumming and the peace commissioners, Brigham Young accepted the unwanted and distrusted army into the territory. The Mormons returned to Salt Lake City in the summer of 1858, never again to abandon their homes, thus ending the resettlement process of nearly three decades. From time to time when confrontations arose, Brigham Young threatened to evacuate the territory, but the threats were never acted upon.[1]

The expedition itself occupies a unique place in the history of exploration in the Great Basin. In spectacular fashion, the White Mountain Expedition explored a large portion of the last virgin territory in the United States south of Alaska. Large areas of present-day western Utah and eastern Nevada were charted and mapped for the first time. Information on the White Mountain country was severely limited in 1858. Evans had explored the route from Antelope Springs (near the House Range) to Snake Valley in 1855. The Death Valley company and Frémont's fifth expedition paralleled Dame's route between Cedar City and Meadow Valley, as Martineau's discovery of the old iron wagon rims in Meadow Valley testified. And in 1827 Jedediah S. Smith, the first non-Indian to enter the inhospitable central regions of the Great Basin, traversed a portion of the White Mountain country on his return from California. It was not until the discovery of Smith's journals in 1967 that his exact route across the Great Basin was traced; he crossed the White River Valley from west to east in the vicinity of present-day Lund, Nevada, thence across Steptoe and Spring valleys to the Snake Range. As the Mormons did in 1858, Smith took Sacramento Pass into Snake Valley. While Smith's route did not often parallel the White Mountain trail, it did intersect it at points along the northern tier of the Mormons' explorations.[2]

The White Mountain Expedition, with a combined force of over 160 men,[3] combed virtually every inch of the country from the southern Utah settlements west to Nevada's Railroad Valley and from Duck Creek on the north to the Pahranagat lakes in the south. Their own calculations placed their explorations in this region in excess of two thousand miles in a period of four months—by far the most extensive examination of the Great Basin's interior to date. Exploring nearly every mountain, valley, stream, and spring in the region, they produced accurate journals and maps of their findings. Climate, soil, water, grass, fuel, Indians, and potential for settlement were all diligently recorded. These accomplishments qualify the Bean and Dame ventures for comparison with some of the more commonly known explorations of Frémont, Smith, and Bonneville.

Unlike these previous expeditions into the Great Basin, the Mormons were not looking for a convenient trail to California, nor were they searching for a means to extract the basin's native wealth; they were searching instead for a place to establish settlements. Eventually the explorers selected the best land they could find and cleared three farms—the first agricultural attempts in the region. With the exception of the White Mountain Mission of 1855, previous entrants into this region had only a transitory interest in the land over which they traveled.

Had circumstances been different, had the expedition not been cloaked in secrecy, its accomplishments would almost certainly have attracted wider notice. While the whole world was aware that the Mormons had fled their homes, few outside of Utah knew anything about the expedition scouring the deserts for a refuge to hide the people. Indeed, Capt. James H. Simpson, the army engineer who explored the Great Basin in 1859 in search of a wagon route to Carson Valley, could not, at first, account for a portion of the White Mountain trail he discovered in Steptoe Valley. Ironically, Simpson had hired George W. Bean to guide him, and although Bean was leading the engineers over a segment of his own trail from the previous year, Bean told the captain nothing about its origin until after their return to the settlements, allowing Simpson to believe a story concocted by a Mormon mail agent in Ruby Valley that the trail had been forged by a California-bound emigrant train which had not been heard from since leaving Fillmore. Until he was enlightened by an Indian in Steptoe Valley who had witnessed the White Mountain Expedition, and Bean later confirmed the story after their return, Simpson was as ignorant as was the rest of the world concerning the Mormons' efforts to explore the Great Basin's interior in 1858.[4] Bean's lack of candor with Simpson and the mail agent's outright falsehood is clear evidence of the covert nature of the expedition. Why Bean did not at first admit his part in the venture to Simpson is uncertain, but it clearly demonstrates the Mormons' mistrust of the government if not the public at large. When Simpson finally published his *Report of Explorations* in 1876, he gave little credit to the Mormon expedition which preceded him, preferring instead to berate the Mormons for their lack of honesty with him. The entire region explored by Bean and Dame south of his own explorations was labelled "UNEXPLORED" on the detailed map accompanying his report. And so, Simpson, one who might have shed some light on the White Mountain Expedition, said little, perhaps fearing the Mormon accomplishments might detract from the significance of his own expedition.

For several years mapmakers apparently learned nothing of the discoveries of the 1858 expedition. Except among the Mormons, Frémont's reports remained the authority on this region. Johnson's *Map of California and Territories of New Mexico and Utah*, published in 1862, continued to show a void in the central Great Basin region with this paraphrasement of Frémont: "This vast unexplored region of country is supposed to be inhabited by tribes of Indians. Altitude 5,000 feet." Other maps continued the use of Frémont's great apocryphal east-west mountain range well into the 1860s.

Information about Mormon activities in the White Mountain country was not easily obtained, and then it was grossly inaccurate. In the summer of 1858 a newspaper correspondent with Johnston's army reported: "At the White River Mountains, west of Fillmore, a settlement was attempted, but an Indian, through a trifling business transaction, got dissatisfied, which finally led to shooting, a fight, and the departure of the settlers."[5] Such was the limit of knowledge received by the outside world of the White Mountain Expedition. The story may have its foundation in the Indian depredations reported by returnees from Snake Creek. The history of the Snake Creek farm is still somewhat obscure.

When Capt. Richard F. Burton, of the British army, visited Salt Lake City in 1860 to take notes for a book, Orrin Porter Rockwell, whose understanding of the White Mountain country probably came from his associate, George W. Bean, advised him to "shun the direct route, which he represented to be, 'about as fit for traveling as is h--l for a powder magazine,' and to journey via Fillmore and the wonder-bearing White Mountains."[6] But as Burton noted, an emigrant company had lately tried this route and was obliged to abandon it on account of the death of the cattle. The White Mountain trail had apparently become known for its natural wonders and was perhaps used as an emigrant trail, although certainly not to any great extent, and not likely after the completion of the Pony Express trail and the railroad in the 1860s.[7]

Without doubt, it was the great cave that became the object of interest, as information about the White Mountain Expedition leaked out. During his expedition in 1859, Captain Simpson reported hearing from the mail company of a great cave three days' travel south of

Steptoe Valley, which was said to have been discovered by persons from Fillmore. Although he did not venture to the cave, Simpson reported that persons had traveled up to three miles in the cave without reaching its terminus.[8] Burton also heard about the cave: "At the western extremity of the White Mountains," wrote the captain, "there is a mammoth cave, of which one mile has been explored; it is said to end in a precipice, and the enterprising Major [Howard] Egan is eager to trace its course."[9] Egan was active in the mail contracting business at the time. The route he established ran about eighty-five miles north of the cave.

Eventually, as miners and stockmen fanned out across the Great Basin in the mid-1860s, a degree of awareness of the Mormon expedition and their discovery of the cave spread although their information was sketchy. On March 2, 1866, the *Reese River Reveille*, an Austin, Nevada, newspaper, published a letter from a miner dated "White Mountain Cave, 22d February 1866." The letter's author also used the term "White Mountain Range" in the body of the letter. Although he did not specifically mention the Mormon expedition, the use of the White Mountain terminology indicates the expedition was probably known to them. Another miner found the cave in 1866 while on his way to the Pahranagat mines. In a letter dated July 18, 1866, and published in the *Union Vedette* (Fort Douglas, Utah) of August 13, he indicated the cave was widely known at the time. In fact, the term "Cave Valley" was already in use, and, according to the article, was named because of "the celebrated cave in it." His description of the cave and the Indian legend surrounding it leave no doubt as to the cave's being the same one found by George W. Bean's men eight years before. The miner's statements show a crude connection between the cave and the White Mountain Expedition. "The story is," he wrote, "that here is where Brigham Young was going to secrete his treasure and best looking 'spirituals,' to keep them from stampeding to Johnston's army." Although the legend of the White Mountain Expedition had obviously become corrupted, its allusions to a refuge or hiding place were unmistakable.

It appears that the facts of the 1858 expedition were never really known to the outside world. Perhaps Lt. George M. Wheeler, of the U.S. Army Topographical Engineers, came the closest of any to identifying the areas explored by the White Mountain companies. In his *Preliminary Report* of his explorations made in 1869, Wheeler

correctly reported the Mormon discovery of Meadow Valley, Pahranagat Valley, and Sierra [White River] Valley, but in other areas
in his brief statement, he was far from correct.[10]

Contemporary Mormon accounts of the expedition seem no more
accurate. Joseph Fish, who lived in Parowan in 1858, was to write
late in life that "some seem to think that they went to a place called
the White Mountains, some considerable distance north of Pioche.
But there is evidence that at least they made a camp for some time
near the present town of Panaca."[11] While these assumptions were
basically correct, they point out how little was actually known. Even
members of the expedition could not state with accuracy where they
had been in relation to settlements which were later to crop up in the
Great Basin's interior. As was noted, Nephi Johnson alleged in his
memoirs that he had penetrated the desert to where Rhyolite,
Nevada, now stands, far to the west of his actual route.[12]

With information and documents lacking or unavailable, the
history of the White Mountain Expedition all but died. To date, the
expedition remains generally obscure. Even the identity of the White
Mountain cave was forgotten, now being called Cave Valley Cave
after the name of the valley, when the valley was actually named for
the cave by miners in the 1860s who had a vague knowledge of the
expedition. With one exception—at Meadow Valley—even those
who now reside where the White Mountain explorers camped can
trace the histories of their towns no further than the first miners and
stockmen to enter the area. The towns of Preston and Lund in White
River Valley are good examples. These towns were settled by Mormons in the 1890s (after earlier entries during the 1860s) near the
White Mountain camp at Willow (Emigrant) Springs and Dame's
Eureka Creek, but there is no reference to the 1858 expedition in
their local histories or traditions.

At Meadow Valley, on the other hand, where Dame planted his
Desert Camp in 1858, the present residents of Panaca, Nevada,
recognize the deeds of the White Mountain Expedition who first
settled on their townsite.[13] The first *permanent* settlers of Panaca were
Mormons who arrived in 1864. One report claims that it was Urban
Van Stewart, a member of Bean's company, who led these settlers to
the site of Dame's old Meadow Valley farm.[14] Another account
alleges that a former member of the White Mountain Expedition
returned to Meadow Valley after ten years and retrieved a small box
of flour he had cached.[15] In any event, when the company arrived on

the ground, they found remnants of ditches, corrals, and other improvements, and they apparently knew who made them. The first settlers of Panaca sowed their grain atop the corn stubble left by the original White Mountain Expedition and used the same ditches.[16] The name of Lafayette Guyman was found etched in the side of a white kaolin butte just out of town.[17] Guyman was a seventeen-year-old boy from Parowan when he began his march with George W. Bean in 1858. He was one of the Clover Valley settlers under Charles Hopkins who was subsequently recalled to Meadow Valley. Other names were also found, but the action of the water on the soft rock had rendered them illegible. During its early years, Panaca derived its livelihood from selling produce to the miners at Pioche and other mining towns which sprang up in eastern and southern Nevada. As the story of the White Mountain Expedition was handed down over the years, it was supposed that the expedition assumed its name "because of the white kaolin hills bordering Meadow Valley."[18]

Eventually, all three White Mountain farms became the locations of permanent settlements. The history of Panaca has already been discussed; however, the settlement process did not stop with Meadow Valley. Using Panaca as a base, the settlers leapfrogged into adjacent valleys. Eagle Valley, eighteen miles north of Panaca, and Spring Valley, five miles farther north,[19] were settled by the Mormons, although they were very small settlements. In 1872 only fifteen families resided in Spring Valley. Today it is the site of only a few ranches.

Fanning out across present Lincoln County, Nevada, the Mormons also settled in Clover Valley in 1865 where Dame's Cave Spring rises. In 1871 sixteen families made their homes in Clover Valley near the place where Charles Hopkins planted his settlement thirteen years before. Today the tiny railroad towns of Barclay and Acoma stand in the valley. Barclay is about one mile west of Hopkins's attempt at settlement.

The Snake Creek farm was resettled in later years as the town of Garrison, Utah. The valley was settled mostly by non-Mormons, especially in the early years; consequently, no tradition of the Snake Creek farm seems to have survived to the present day. Not only did these non-Mormons have little information about the White Mountain Expedition, but there was probably little physical evidence of the settlement on Snake Creek. The first permanent settlers arrived in 1869, eleven years after the mission was recalled. The fields and ditches of George W. Bean's exploring company had likely been reclaimed by the desert from which they were hewn. One report asserts that fifteen or twenty families resided in Snake Valley by 1873, with quite a number of bachelors.[20]

Despite the claim by Assistant Church Historian Andrew Jenson in 1941 that "the mission . . . brought about no results for practical purposes,"[21] the *Deseret Evening News* of November 9, 1917, claimed otherwise: "The White Mountain Mission," declared the *News*, ". . . resulted in the settlement of Spring Valley, Clover Valley, Panaca and Eagle Valley."[22] It is difficult to determine the effect the White Mountain Expedition had in settling Lincoln County in the 1860s. In all probability, the location of the mines would have prompted the settlement of these valleys sooner or later to supply the needs of Pioche, Ely, and the Pahranagat mines. Orson B. Adams admitted that the expedition "did not appear to be of any practical value," but he blamed fate rather than any other failure. In spite of his own vain attempt to establish a settlement in Clover Valley, Adams argued: "Some of the places we found have since been settled. Had the saints not returned to their homes the object of our explorations would have [been] realized."[23]

Probably because of the confidential nature of the White Mountain Expedition, most of the credit for exploring this region has gone to others. The Simpson expedition of 1859 and the Wheeler surveys of 1869–79 were both government projects. The names they gave to the physical features of this land in their published reports have remained to the present day in most cases. The 13,061-foot White Mountain of George W. Bean is today called Wheeler Peak. In some instances Wheeler used names already in local use, but rarely is the White Mountain nomenclature preserved. Only a few examples have survived to the present day. Most of them lie in a path between Cedar City and Meadow Valley. Because the Mormons who settled this region were somewhat familiar with the findings of the White Mountain Expedition or were former members, Meadow Valley, Nephi Springs, Cave Spring, and Bennett Pass and Springs are still found on today's maps. And despite Colonel Dame's naming of Badger Valley, Jesse N. Smith, Dame's successor to the mission, used the term "Clover Valley" in his journal, the term that is still used today.[24]

The origins of the place names "Snake Creek" and "Snake

Range" have long been misunderstood. They are often attributed to the range's supposed snakelike course. But Helen S. Carlson disputes this theory in her book *Nevada Place Names*: "Although the Snake Range is said to have been named for its sinuous course, early historian Myron Angel refers to the range as the *Snake Creek Range* . . . an indication that the mountains may have been named for the creek."[25] Carlson was absolutely correct in this assumption, as George W. Bean applied the name to Snake Creek in 1858, and the term "Snake" may go back farther than that. Bean made no mention of how he arrived at the name, but Bishop David Evans of the White Mountain Mission of 1855 may have left a clue. Evans reported that the Indians in Snake Valley called themselves "Koonepanger," translated "Snake."[26] No doubt Bean, who was an excellent interpreter, made the same discovery and named the creek after the Indians. It seems this is the only one of Bean's appellations to survive to the present day.

There is a possibility that the Golden Gate Range is a survival of the name Dame applied to the canyon in the Grant Range. Carl I. Wheat claimed that the Golden Gate Range is "an interesting survival of the name of the pass [canyon]" designated by Colonel Dame.[27] Helen Carlson then adopted the idea from Wheat.[28] But Wheat misinterpreted Dame's "Journal," believing that Gray Head Mountain, where the Golden Gate was found, *was* the Golden Gate Range. A careful study of the company journals and maps reveals that Gray Head was the Grant Range. Since no other White Mountain names have survived anywhere near this remote region, and many a California miner could have named this small range after a more familiar Golden Gate in his home state, the name duplication may be coincidental.

Other White Mountain place names have long ago been erased from the maps of Utah and Nevada. Before the results of Wheeler's surveys were incorporated into the maps of the Great Basin, a few more of the White Mountain place names were in use. A. L. Bancroft's 1873 *Map of California, Nevada, Utah and Arizona* was probably using local information when it applied the terms "Desert Swamp" and "White Mountain Cave" to the same features named by the White Mountain explorers. This may have been the last published usage of the term "White Mountain." Curiously, Crystal Peak (which was the White Mountain of Evans's White Mountain Mission of 1855) was still known as "White Mountain Summit" by residents of Snake Valley as late as 1901,[29] even though they had no apparent knowledge of the expedition of the same name.

The White Mountain Expedition was the largest exploring enterprise ever promoted by the Mormon church. Despite a staggering outlay of time, talent, and manpower, very little was gained of material value. Only the miner and stockman have made this region pay. In later years, George W. Bean recalled: "We became well acquainted with south-east Nevada, but it was left for others to discover the rich mines of Pioche and Frisco. . . ."[30] The White Mountain explorers walked right over the ground where these rich lodes were eventually discovered. But mineral wealth meant little to the Mormons in 1858. Their duty was first to the kingdom of God, and they did not shrink from it no matter what the requirement—abandoning a gold mine or removing to the desert.

# AFTERWORD

With the White Mountain Expedition brought to a close and war tensions abated, the men of the expedition returned to their homes to pick up the threads of their lives—lives that had been in turmoil for a year. Some drifted off into relative obscurity, while others led colorful and notable careers. This was especially true of some of the expedition's leaders.

George W. Bean, the first to be called to the White Mountain Expedition, continued to lead a prominent career as a government scout and interpreter. Shortly after returning from the White Mountain country, Bean was hired by Capt. James H. Simpson, one of Johnston's engineers, to guide him across the desert west of Camp Floyd, the army post in Cedar Valley. Like Colonel Steptoe in 1855, General Johnston's situation in Utah made the establishment of a direct trail to California very desirable. Bean, who had also been Steptoe's guide in 1855, knew the western deserts as well as anyone. The company ventured out in late October, 1858, but returned without going far for lack of time and water. The big push was to be made in the spring.

Bean was undecided whether to accept Simpson's offer to guide him again. Counselling with Brigham Young on the matter in December, the president told him "he had no objection if he could get ten dollars per day, one half in advance, but it was not wisdom to be tramping around, when he should be putting in a spring crop, unless he was well paid for it."[1] It is not known whether he received his ten dollars per day or not, but he did guide the captain and his surveying party to Carson Valley and back in 1859, following his White Mountain trail from Steptoe Valley to Antelope Springs on the return trip, a distance of over one hundred miles.

George W. Bean's list of accomplishments is long and varied. Besides his periodic work as a guide, he became a prosecuting attorney for Utah County and later a probate judge in Provo for eight years. He also served in the latter capacity in Richfield, Utah, for six years, later in his career. In 1861 Bean was elected to the territorial legislature from Utah County. During the Black Hawk Indian War of the mid-1860s he served the territory as a lieutenant colonel of cavalry in the Nauvoo Legion. In 1872 he accompanied Dr. Dodge, the Utah Indian agent, and a delegation of Ute Indians to Washington, D.C., where he served as interpreter during an interview with President Grant. Bean was at times a United States revenue collector, tax assessor, and tax collector for Utah County, a high priest and patriarch, a farmer and stockman. In 1880 he was sustained as a member of the Sevier Stake presidency in Richfield. George W. Bean was the husband of three wives who bore him twenty-eight children, and in 1889 he was convicted of violating federal anti-polygamy laws. He died in 1897 at the age of sixty-six.[2]

Edson Barney, president of the Snake Creek farm, led a far more obscure life than George W. Bean after returning from the desert. He was an original pioneer of St. George in 1861, where he resided for some time. Barney was called to Escalante in 1882, and he later went to Bluff City in southeastern Utah. He returned to Provo late in life where he died in 1905.[3]

William H. Dame, the commander of the Southern Exploring Company, discovered upon his return to Parowan, after reporting his explorations to President Young, that charges had been leveled against him by the local high council accusing him of responsibility in the Mountain Meadows affair. It seems that he adequately defended himself before the investigating committee headed by Apostles George A. Smith and Amasa Lyman, because on August 12 the church exonerated him of all charges. Dame, however, was later indicted along with John D. Lee by a federal court on the charge of murder, but again the colonel was vindicated. Lee was not so lucky. William H. Dame was, in fact, the only church leader to be implicated in the crime and still retain his position in the church.[4]

Dame continued to lead a conspicuous life in southern Utah. In 1860 he was called by the church as a missionary to England. After serving for two and a half years he was released on account of bad health and returned to Parowan. Dame was appointed an agent for the presiding bishop of the church in 1866. In this capacity he organized the first cooperative store in Utah which he managed until his death in 1884. Although Dame had several wives, no record can be found of any children. Jenson says of him: "There are few men better known in the Church than Brother William H. Dame, being a man of great public worth and notable for his honesty and uprightness in all his business transactions with his fellow man."[5]

Dame's closest advisor on the White Mountain Expedition, James H. Martineau, became sheriff of Iron County shortly after returning from the desert. In 1860 he left Parowan to live in Salt Lake City, but on the advice of Brigham Young, he removed to Logan where his talents as a surveyor were needed. Logan was growing rapidly in the early sixties, and Martineau's abilities were not wasted. He located several large canals and installed the city's waterworks among other projects. His military career was not neglected either. As in Parowan, Martineau was appointed adjutant and military instructor of the Cache military district. He also served on the staff of Gen. Daniel H. Wells. During the Indian campaigns, he was called out on many missions.

In 1868 Martineau surveyed for the Union Pacific Railroad from Echo Canyon to Central, Nevada, and the following year he located the railroad from Ogden to Salt Lake City. In 1871–72 he surveyed the route of the Utah Northern Railroad from Ogden to Franklin, Idaho. Martineau also laid out the foundations and grounds of the Logan temple in 1877. During his years in Logan, he surveyed the town plats, pastures, and canals for many of the cities and towns of northern Utah and southern Idaho, including Idaho Falls and parts of Logan City. Martineau also became the county clerk of Cache County, county surveyor, U.S. deputy internal revenue collector, and city recorder of Logan—all while he ran a farm.

Accompanying Apostles Erastus Snow and Moses Thatcher to Mexico in 1882, he searched the State of Sonora for settlement sites for the Saints. Two years later Martineau was sent to southern Arizona to serve in the presidency of the St. Joseph Stake. During this time he continued his explorations in Mexico.

As a U.S. deputy surveyor in Arizona and Utah for many years, he surveyed over thirty-five townships. Martineau was also a county surveyor and a U.S. deputy land and mineral surveyor while living in Arizona.

In 1888 he removed to the Mormon settlement of Colonia Juarez in Chihuahua, Mexico, and surveyed the town plats there as well as at Dublan and Chuichupa. He also surveyed other large tracts of land in Mexico, one of which was eight hundred square miles of mountain timberland in the Sierra Madre Mountains for the California Land Company. While still in Mexico in 1898, Martineau was ordained a patriarch of the church.

Leaving his son to care for his home in Mexico, Martineau returned to Utah in 1908. In his absence, the revolution of 1912 forced his family to flee Mexico and abandon his estate. Unfortunately, Martineau's entire life savings of thousands of dollars was invested in his Mexico properties which he lost entirely. As a result, James H. Martineau died almost penniless in 1921. He was ninety-three. Martineau left a large posterity; his two wives bore him twenty-one children.[6]

Nephi Johnson continued his pioneering activities in southern Utah. Upon returning from the desert in 1858, he almost immediately organized an exploring expedition for the upper Virgin River Valley. On this trek he became one of the first white men to view Zion Canyon. They later built a road and founded Virgin City. For nearly eight years Johnson served as the presiding elder there.

In 1860 he went back to the Missouri River to aid in the Mormon emigration. Traveling with the William Budge ox train, his knowledge of the frontier was of great help to the captain.

Nephi Johnson's skills as an Indian interpreter were also utilized in 1862–63, when he accompanied Jacob Hamblin to the Moqui (Hopi) villages in present-day Arizona as a missionary.

Johnson moved to Kanab, Utah, in 1871 where he served in the bishopric and was later ordained a patriarch. While in Kanab, he was elected to three terms as a county commissioner. Johnson also served the community for various periods as town president, superintendent of waterworks, road commissioner, justice of the peace, and mail contractor. In addition, Johnson was a farmer. He was the husband of three wives and the father of twenty-seven children. Johnson died in Mesquite, Nevada, in 1919. He was eighty-five.[7]

Asahel Bennett, Dame's guide of 1858, did not stay long in Utah, and he quickly left the Mormon faith as well. According to Martineau, "Mr. Bennett was an educated man, and at the time [of the White Mountain Expedition] a Mormon, but subsequently he apostatized from what little Mormonism he possessed."[8] William Lewis Manly, a friend of Bennett's from their Death Valley ordeal, suggested that Bennett was "smarting under the terrible taxation [tithing] of one tenth of everything."[9] It is also possible that the Mountain Meadows Massacre incident affected his decision. On his way to Utah in the fall of 1857 he had witnessed the aftermath of the butchery. He reported to Manly in Los Angeles in 1860 that he had been appalled by what he saw.[10] In any event, Bennett left Utah soon after the completion of the White Mountain Expedition and returned to California.

Little is known about his later career. He may have worked in the mining camps for a time. One report had him living in the mining town of Belmont, Nevada.[11] In 1875 Bennett returned to Utah, briefly, to testify in the trial of John D. Lee, accused of murder in the Mountain Meadows affair. He had seen the bodies lying on the meadows shortly after the massacre.[12]

Asahel Bennett died in Idaho about 1891. He was said to be in his eighty-fourth year.[13]

Jesse N. Smith was one of the men who preferred charges against William H. Dame for complicity in the Mountain Meadows Massacre. With the investigation of Dame completed, George A. Smith called his cousin, Jesse, to head up an expedition to the Virgin River to locate a place for a cotton farm. After exploring the headwaters of the Virgin and Sevier rivers for nearly a month in the fall of 1858, the mission was abandoned.

The following February, Smith was elected mayor of Parowan for a term of two years, but he left the city in the spring to assist in founding the town of Minersville, Beaver County.

While residing in Beaver in 1860, he received a call from the church to serve a mission in Europe. Smith arrived in Copenhagen early in 1861, and by March of the following year, he was appointed president of the Scandinavian mission. Smith returned to Utah in the fall of 1864. Soon he was chosen regimental adjutant of the Iron military district and then county clerk. Both were positions previously held by James H. Martineau. In 1866 he was elected probate judge for Iron County.

During the Black Hawk War Smith served the territory as a colonel of militia, organizing and commanding the Piute military district. When the war ended, he was sent back to the Scandinavian mission for a second term as president. This tour extended from 1868 to 1870. Upon his return he picked up his old job as county clerk and also became a justice of the peace.

Jesse N. Smith then turned to the south, where he spent the rest of his life. With Apostle Erastus Snow he explored parts of Arizona Territory to locate settlement sites. Eventually, Smith settled at

Snowflake, Arizona, where he presided over the Eastern Arizona Stake of the church. In addition to taking some railroad grading contracts in Arizona and New Mexico territories, he was appointed to the office of probate judge by the governor of Arizona. Smith also served in the Arizona House of Representatives and returned to Utah, briefly, to serve one term in the Utah legislature.

Jesse N. Smith was still active in missionary labors as well. While working in the railroad camps, he was called to preach Mormonism to the camp laborers, and in 1883 he was called to be a missionary to the Indians.

Like Martineau, Smith was among those sent into Mexico to purchase lands for new settlements.

Despite his many civic and church positions, Jesse N. Smith was basically a farmer. He was the husband of five wives and the father of forty-four children. During the 1880s he became one of the first men in Arizona to be prosecuted for violation of the Edmunds–Tucker Act, which prohibited the practice of polygamy. Smith died at Snowflake in 1906, at the age of sixty-nine.[14]

Although they were not members of the White Mountain Expedition, Brigham Young, John C. Frémont, Elijah Barney Ward, and Albert Sidney Johnston played significant roles in its story. The careers of Young and Frémont are well known. The biographies of Johnston and Ward are of interest, although it is not likely either man was aware of the desert expedition in 1858. Both men met violent, premature deaths.

Johnston, whose zeal to chastise the Mormon "rebels" was a major factor in the decision to abandon Salt Lake City and search for a new gathering place, resigned from the U.S. Army in 1861 to take a commission in the Confederate army. Johnston's career was brilliant but short lived. While commanding the Southern forces at Shiloh, he was shot and killed on April 6, 1862.[15]

Barney Ward, the mountain man who promoted the "Oasis Theory" to almost everyone who would listen, was baptized into the Mormon church in 1850. In 1853 he was a settler of Fort Supply in present-day Wyoming. The place was abandoned and burned, however, in preparation for the approach of Johnston's army. Durin the Utah War, Ward moved south with the general tide and settled in Payson, Utah. Fearing for her life at this time. Ward's Indian wife returned to her people until the war was over. But while living among her people, she became sick and died, leaving her husband with the care of their two daughters. Ward later relocated at Fairview and Gunnison in Sanpete County.

On April 20, 1865, while looking for some lost cattle in Salina Canyon, Ward was surprised by a band of Ute warriors, and became one of the first casualties of the Black Hawk War in Utah. Ward's scalped and mutilated body was discovered the next day. The Utes had never forgiven him for his part in a battle with the Indians near Provo in 1850. He was fifty-two at the time of his death.

Barney Ward's two daughters were taken into the home of his beloved friend, Brigham Young. During the 1870s Young tried to locate Ward's unmarked grave so that a suitable monument could be erected over it. After several years, the site was found, and a monument was erected at the expense of the church.[16]

But the real heroes of the White Mountain Expedition were the explorers themselves. These were the men who had been ordered to be ready to march "at a moment's warning" to any part of the territory to meet the enemy, or to mobilize and lay waste to everything they owned, depending on the situation; these were the men who were taught to expect a worldwide millennial war at any moment, many of whom would be haunted the rest of their lives by the bloody scenes of Mountain Meadows. These were the men who spent three and four months scouring the bitter deserts of the Great Basin for a refuge that did not exist, in the name of a cause more real to them than the vast, barren land before them.

# APPENDIX A

## PERSONNEL OF THE
## WHITE MOUNTAIN EXPEDITION

I. George W. Bean's White Mountain Company

Bean's company comprised 104 men. The thirty-eight men named below have been identified from the sources referred to by number after each name. See list of sources below.

Salt Lake County (about 19 men)

    1. "Brother" Free, 1, 2

    2. "Father" Rhodes, 3

Utah County (about 24 men)

    3. George W. Bean (Provo) (Expedition captain), 4, 5, et al.

    4. Edson Barney (Provo) (Snake Creek president), 2, 6, et al.

    5. Joseph Stewart, 7

    6. John Riggs (Provo), 8, 9

    7. John Shelley (American Fork), 10

    8. David Wood (American Fork), 10

    9. David E. Bunnell (Provo), 2, 11

Fillmore (about 16 men)

    10. Orange Warner (company leader), 7, 21

    11. Mortimer W. Warner, 7

    12. Edwin Stott, 12

    13. William E. Bridges, 7

    14. Thomas Evans, 7

    15. Thomas Evans, Jr., 7

    16. John Niel, 7

    17. John Cavannah, 7

    18. Ransford Colby, 7

    19. John King, 7

    20. Henry Robison, 7

21. Wessley Dame, 7
22. Luke Nield, 13
23. Edwin Twitchell (Indian Creek), 7

Cedar City (16 men)

24. Charles Hopkins (company leader), 2, 14
25. James Haslam, 4
26. William Walker, 4, 15, 16
27. John Woodhouse, 17
28. Josiah Reeves, 16
29. _____ Day, 4
30. James Whitaker, 20
31. James Willard Bay, 20

Nephi

32. Miles Miller (?), 18

Beaver (17 men)

33. James Low (company leader), 2, 4
34. _____ Mathews, 4

Parowan (12 men)

35. Orson B. Adams (company leader), 2, 15, 16, 18
36. Urban Van Stewart, 12, 15, 16
37. William Roberts, 16
38. Lafayette Guyman, 16, 19

Others connected with George W. Bean's company were:
Mashoquab, the Indian guide, 7
Samuel P. Hoyt, who ran an express to Snake Creek, 7, 11

Sources
1. *A Series of Instructions and Remarks made by Brigham Young*, 21 March 1858.
2. "Biographical Sketch of Edson Barney."
3. George W. Bean to Brigham Young, 27 March 1858.
4. Bean, *Autobiography of George W. Bean.*
5. George W. Bean, Journal.
6. George W. Bean to Brigham Young, 2 April 1858.
7. King, "Millard County, 1851–1875," *Utah Humanities Review.*
8. John Riggs, Autobiography, L.D.S. Archives.
9. Dame, "Journal of Southern Exploring Company."
10. American Fork Ward Records, Minutes of Meetings, 7 March 1858.
11. Lewis Brunson to Brigham Young, 14 July 1858.

12. Jenson, *L.D.S. Biographical Encyclopedia.*

13. John Nield, "Extracts from the Journal of John Nield," typescript in possession of author.

14. John D. Lee, *Mormon Chronicle: The Diaries of John D. Lee.*

15. Jesse N. Smith, Journal.

16. Martineau, "History of the Mission Exploring the Southwest Deserts."

17. John Woodhouse, Autobiography, (Typescript), Brigham Young University.

18. "Autobiography of Orson Bennett Adams."

19. Joseph Fish, "History of Enterprise."

20. James Willard Bay, Journal.

21. Thomas W. Cropper, Autobiography.

II. William H. Dame's Southern Exploring Company
Dame's company consisted of sixty men, all from southern Utah. This roster of the company is contained in James H. Martineau's "History of the Mission Exploring the Southwest Deserts of Utah Territory &c in 1858." The list is considered complete.

From Parowan, Iron Co.,

| | | | |
|---|---|---|---|
| 1. | William Horne Dame | | President of the company—High Priest |
| 2. | John Topham | one wagon | Seventy |
| 3. | John Wardell | | Elder |
| 4. | Francis Tufts Whitney | | High Priest |
| 5. | James Henry Martineau | one wagon | High Priest |
| 6. | John W. Osburn | | member |
| 7. | Enoch Davis | | not a member |
| 8. | Charles Carter | one wagon | Elder |
| 9. | Thomas Durham | | Elder |

From Beaver, Beaver Co.,

| | | | |
|---|---|---|---|
| 10. | Ross R. Rogers | | High Priest |
| 11. | Andrew Patterson | one wagon | Elder |
| 12. | J. Ward Christian | | member |
| 13. | Robert Kershaw | | Seventy (no quorum) |
| 14. | Francis Brown | one wagon | Seventy 20th Q. |
| 15. | James Duke | | Seventy 25th Q. |
| 16. | Martin Taylor | | member |
| 17. | Nathan Pierce | one wagon | Seventy 42nd Q. |
| 18. | William Hulme | | member |
| 19. | Thomas Holliday | | member |
| 20. | Ansel Twitchell | one wagon | Elder |
| 21. | Henry Spears | | Seventy 42nd Q. |

22. Samuel Sheppard          )                    High Priest
23. Nathan Thomas            }    one wagon       Seventy 22nd Q.
24. Swan Arnell              )                    Priest


From Cedar, Iron Co.,

25. Isaac Turley             )                    member
26. James Cliff             }    one wagon       member
27. William Smith            )                    Deacon
28. Thomas Harwood           )                    Seventy 20th Q.
29. Samuel Hamilton          }    one wagon       Elder
30. Charles Wilden           )                    Deacon
31. John Kay                 )                    Seventy (no quorum)
32. Jesse B. Lewis           }    one wagon       Elder
33. Asahel Bennett           )                    member
34. Samuel D. White          )                    High Priest
35. Nephi Johnson            }    one wagon       Elder
36. Joseph Hunter            )                    Seventy 15th Q.
37. Robert Keys              )                    member
38. John Stoddard            }    one wagon       Elder
39. William C. Stewart       )                    Seventy 15th Q.


From Harmony, Washington Co.,

40. Don Carlos Shirts        )                    Deacon
41. Elisha Groves            }    one wagon       Teacher
42. Joseph Nelson            )                    Teacher


From Washington, Washington Co.,

43. George W. Sirrine        )                    Elder
44. John Woodruff Freeman    }    one wagon       Elder
45. James Alexander Mowry    )                    Seventy 11th Q.
46. Jabez Nowland            )                    High Priest
47. William Stevens          }    one wagon       Seventy 42nd Q.
48. William Duggins          )                    Seventy 42nd Q.
49. Lyman Curtis             )                    Seventy 9th Q.
50. James Pierce             }    one wagon       member
51. Joseph Smith Littlefield )                    Elder
52. John M. Lewis            )                    Elder
53. Samuel Newton Adair      }    one wagon       member
54. Silas Harris             )                    Seventy 28th Q.

55. John Couch                     ⎞                      High Priest
56. Robert Lloyd                   ⎬      one wagon        Seventy 11th Q.
57. Willis Young                   ⎠                      Seventy 34th Q.


From Fort Clara, Washington Co.,

58. John Crow                      ⎞                      not a member
59. Francis Hamblin                ⎬      one wagon        Deacon
60. George Day                     ⎠                      Deacon


The following men were part of a relief company of seven men to arrive at Meadow Valley on June 25, 1858:[1]

1. Jesse N. Smith, of Parowan
2. Marius Ensign, of Parowan
3. John Hunter, of Cedar City

# APPENDIX B

## GUIDE FOR THE DESERT CAMP
### By W. H. Dame[2]

Commencing at Parowan, Iron Co., U. T.

From — Parowan to Summit Creek       6 miles
           grass & water good — willow for fuel

From — Summit Creek to Cedar City       12 miles
           water good — feed scarce

From — Cedar City to Iron Springs       10 miles
           water & grass good, willow & sage for fuel

From — Iron Springs to Antelope Springs       15 miles
           water, grass & fuel good — willow & sage fuel

From — Antelope Springs to Pinta Creek       12 miles
           water up the Kanyon 1 ½ miles — grass good
           willow & sage brush for fuel

From — Pinta Creek to first water Shoal Creek Kanyon       18 miles
           in the Kanyon plenty of good grass & water for
           herding—no farming land—the creek sinks often

From—Shoal Creek Kanyon to Nephi Springs       11 miles
           springs very small—narrow—deep Kanyon
           grass & water good—cedar for fuel

From—Nephi Springs to Cave Spring wells       22 miles
           the road passes over the rim of the basin, rough and
           rugged—hills covered with good bunch grass, pinion pines
           & cedars—water not good

From—Cave Springs to Meadow Valley       33 miles
           rough road passing thro heavy growth of pinion pine &
           cedar timber—the valley 16 miles long, width from 5 to 20
           miles—300 acres of meadow grass, by extending down in
           Kanyon South many hundred acres of meadow grass at
           head of Valley a large warm Spring sufficient for a small
           grist mill—by taking 2 miles in a ditch can water 150 acres
           of land in east side of the Valley—2 miles N.W. from this
           spring is a small Kanyon spring Box Elder Creek able to
           water 20 acres good cool water. The warm water no fit to
           drink

From — Meadow Valley to Bennett Springs       12 miles
           sufficient water for 10 acres of land, feed, grass and wood
           plenty — cedar for fuel

From — Bennett Springs to Desert Spring Wells                         34 miles
    water all gone 1st of June 1858 — all desert — travelling
    camp can stay one night for grass and fuel — one man 5
    hours to dip water for 2 wagons 15[5] May 58

From — Desert Spring Wells to Desert Swamps                           38 miles
    water strong alkali — plenty grass — sage brush for fuel — no
    farming land in this neighborhood full of alkali beds —

From — Desert swamp to Desert Swamp springs                          17 miles
    some farm lands here, tho' very high & cold, heavy alkali
    beds all around —

From — Desert swamp Springs to Willow Springs                        18 miles
    Water for 20 acres of farm land — very frosty land which is
The End of the Wagon Trail

## PACK TRAIN EXPLORATIONS

Johnson's Lake Country
    Accessable for wagons good water & farm lands, sufficient to support 2000
    people — 18 May, occupied by a large number of Indians, farming,
    wheat — Leaving out at that date — they have squash, corn & water melons — they
    invited us to come & settle on a free land — this place within 2 days ride of the
    crossing of the Muddy, California road —

Golden Gate Country
    Water entirely in the Kanyons, sufficient to water 40 acres — the Kanyon & low
    hills on each side covered with rich bunch grass sufficient for several thousand
    head of cattle in the summer.

Eureka Creek Country
    High and cold, tho richly covered with grass for stock — abundance of
    water — extent from Willow Springs to Ruby Valley 72 miles.

Pack Trail
    Willow springs by Pockage Cave, Pockage Pass spring cricket spring, richly
    covered with bunch grass — small springs, simply for herding purposes, no
    farming — Cave springs a rich herd ground, & water for 5 acres of farming land.

# APPENDIX C

## GAZETTEER OF WHITE MOUNTAIN PLACE NAMES

| White Mountain Name | Present Name | Location | References |
|---|---|---|---|
| Altar Peak | Presently unnamed peak | Grant Range, near Cherry Creek Summit, Nevada | HM, 23 |
| Antelope Spring | Silver Springs | White River Valley, Lincoln Co., Nevada | HM, 29 |
| Badger Valley | Clover Valley | Lincoln Co., Nevada | HM, 13 |
| Bennett('s) Springs | Bennett's Springs | Lincoln Co., Nevada | HM, 16 |
| Big Warm Spring | Panaca Spring | Meadow Valley, Lincoln Co., Nevada | Smith, 29 |
| Box Elder Creek | Condor Creek | Lincoln Co., Nevada | GDC; Chart |

Abbreviations of References:

Adams . . . . . . . . . . . . . Orson B. Adams, "Map of the Desert, June 1858."
Bean . . . . . . . . . . George W. Bean Report, Manuscript History, 7 June 1858, pp. 610–16.
Bean/Young . . . . . . . George W. Bean to Brigham Young, 22 May 1858.
Chart . . . . . . . . . . . . James H. Martineau, "Chart Showing the Explorations of the Desert Mission."
Dame/Young . . . . . . . William H. Dame to Brigham Young, 3 May 1858.
GDC . . . . . . . . . . . . . William H. Dame, "Guide for the Desert Camp."
GWB . . . . . . . . . . . George W. Bean, *Autobiography of George W. Bean*.
HM . . . . . . . . . . . . . James H. Martineau, "History of the Mission Exploring the Southwest Deserts of Utah Territory."
JC . . . . . . . . . . . . . William H. Dame, "Journal of the Southern Exploring Company."
Map . . . . . . . . . . . . James H. Martineau, "Map Showing Explorations of Desert Camp," 24 June 1858.
Smith . . . . . . . . . . . Jesse N. Smith, *Journal of Jesse N. Smith*, ed. Oliver R. Smith.

| White Mountain Name | Present Name | Location | References |
|---|---|---|---|
| Cache Canyon | Dome Canyon Pass | House Range, Millard Co., Utah | Bean, 611 |
| Cane Spring Wells | poss. site of Acoma Res. | near Acoma, Lincoln Co., Nevada | HM, 13 |
| Cave Mountain | Schell Creek Range | Lincoln Co., Nevada | Adams |
| Cave Spring(s) | Cave Spring | near Barclay, Lincoln Co., Nevada | HM, 13 |
| Cave Spring Valley | Clover Valley | Lincoln Co., Nevada | HM, 42; Adams |
| Clover Valley | Clover Valley | Lincoln Co., Nevada | Smith, 29 |
| Cove Spring | Highland Spring | Lincoln Co., Nevada | HM, 40 |
| Cricket Spring | Pony Springs | Lake Valley, Lincoln Co., Nevada | HM, 39 |
| Crystal Spring | prob. Lion Spring | Egan Range, White Pine Co., Nevada | HM, 32 |
| Currant Spring | | near Lund, White Pine Co., Nevada | Chart |
| Deep Spring | poss. Indian Springs | White River Valley, White Pine Co., Nevada | HM, 31 |
| Desert Spring | Layton Spring | Spring Valley, White Pine Co., Nevada | Adams |
| Desert Spring | see Desert Spring Wells | | JC, 12 |
| Desert Spring Mountain | North Pahroc Range | Lincoln Co., Nevada | JC, 13 |
| Desert Spring Wells | prob. Black Rock Spring | west side Dry Lake Valley, Lincoln Co. | HM, 19 |
| Desert Swamp | sink of White River | White River Valley, Nye Co., Nevada | HM, 20 |
| Desert Swamp Springs | Flagg Springs | White River Valley, Nye Co., Nevada | HM, 26 |
| Eureka Creek | White River, Ellison Ck. | White Pine Co., Nevada | HM, 31, 33 |
| Eureka Mountain | White Pine Range | White Pine Co., Nevada | JC, 29 |
| Golden Gate | head of Cherry Ck. Canyon | Grant/Quinn Canyon Rg., Nye Co., Nevada | JC, 18 |
| Grand Echo Canyon | Meadow Valley Wash | Lincoln Co., Nevada | HM, 42 |
| Granite Spring | Big Spring | Egan Range, Lincoln Co., Nevada | HM, 35 |
| Grapevine Springs | prob. Ash Springs | Pahranagat Valley, Lincoln Co., Nevada | Chart |
| Gray Head (Greyhead) Mtn. | Grant, Quinn Canyon Rg. | Nye Co., Nevada | HM, 21 |
| Gunsight Mountain | Gap Mountain | Egan Range, Nye Co., Nevada | JC, 29 |
| Indian Spring | Tule Spring | Tule Valley, Millard Co., Utah | Adams |
| Indian Spring | | Pahranagat Valley, Lincoln Co., Nevada | Chart |
| Indian Springs | | Shingle Pass, Egan Range, Lincoln Co. | HM, 27 |

| White Mountain Name | Present Name | Location | References |
| --- | --- | --- | --- |
| Johnson's Lake | Lower Pahranagat Lake | Pahranagat Valley, Lincoln Co., Nevada | HM, 36 |
| Level Top Mountain | in Egan Range | White Pine Co., Nevada | JC, 26 |
| Lewis Spring | | Coal Valley, Lincoln Co., Nevada | Chart |
| Lone Rock Canyon | Murry Canyon | Egan Range, White Pine Co., Nevada | HM, 32 |
| Lone Rock Creek | Murry Creek | Murry Canyon, White Pine Co., Nevada | Chart |
| Long Valley | Snake Valley | Millard Co., Utah-White Pine Co., Nevada | Bean, 611 |
| Mahogany Spring | unnamed | south slope Patterson Peak, Lincoln Co. | Adams |
| Mammoth Cave | Cave Valley Cave | Cave Valley, Lincoln Co., Nevada | JC, 29 |
| Martineau's Peak | peak in Quinn Canyon Rg. | Nye Co., Nevada | JC, 29 |
| Meadow Creek | Baker Creek | Snake Valley, Millard Co., Utah | Adams |
| Meadow Valley | Meadow Valley | Lincoln Co., Nevada | HM, 13 |
| Meadow Valley Springs | Panaca Spring | Meadow Valley, Lincoln Co., Nevada | JC, 33 |
| Mount Lookout | peak of the Cedar Range | Lincoln Co., Nevada | HM, 14 |
| Mount Whitney | Whipple Peak | Egan Range, Lincoln Co., Nevada | JC, 29 |
| Nephi's Hole | Nephi Spring | Shoal Creek Canyon, Iron Co., Utah | Adams |
| Nephi('s) Spring(s) | Nephi Spring | Shoal Creek Canyon, Iron Co., Utah | GDC; Chart |
| Onion Canyon | poss. Rimrock Canyon | Grant Range, Nye Co., Nevada | JC, 15 |
| Onion Spring | | poss. in Rimrock Canyon, Nye Co., Nevada | HM, 22 |
| Pine Canyon | Shingle Pass | Egan Range, Lincoln Co., Nevada | HM, 27 |
| Pinnacle Peak | Patterson Peak | Schell Creek Range, Lincoln Co., Nevada | HM, 39 |
| Pockage Cave | Cave Valley Cave | Cave Valley, Lincoln Co., Nevada | HM, 38 |
| Pockage Pass | Patterson Pass | Schell Creek Range, Lincoln Co., Nevada | GDC; JC, 31 |
| Pockage Spring | Cave Springs | Cave Valley, Lincoln Co., Nevada | JC, 30 |
| Pockage Valley | Cave Valley | Lincoln Co., Nevada | Bean/Young |
| Rock Spring | | Coal Valley, Lincoln Co., Nevada | Chart |
| Rocky Point Hill | foothill, N. Pahroc Range | Dry Lake Valley, Lincoln Co., Nevada | HM, 17 |
| Rose Spring | unnamed | 5 miles s. Pony Springs, Lake Valley, Lincoln Co., Nevada | HM, 40; Map |

| White Mountain Name | Present Name | Location | References |
| --- | --- | --- | --- |
| Rush Lake | Upper Pahranagat Lake | Pahranagat Valley, Lincoln Co., Nevada | HM, 36 |
| Saleratus Valley | Tule Valley | Millard Co., Utah | Bean, 611 |
| Secret Spring | prob. Coal or Hamilton Sp. | Dry Lake Valley, Lincoln Co., Nevada | HM, 19; Chart |
| Shoal Creek | Shoal Creek | Shoal Creek Canyon, Iron Co., Utah | GDC |
| Snake Creek | Snake Creek | White Pine Co., Nevada; Millard Co., Utah | Bean, 611 |
| Soap Creek | Steptoe Creek | Steptoe Valley, White Pine Co., Nevada | Adams; Chart |
| South Creek | Murry Creek | Steptoe Valley, White Pine Co., Nevada | Adams |
| Stewart's Springs | Crystal Springs | Pahranagat Valley, Lincoln Co., Nevada | Chart |
| Three Butte Valley | Cave Valley | Lincoln Co., Nevada | JC, 21 |
| Toole Springs | Knoll Springs | Snake Valley, Millard Co., Utah | Adams |
| Well Spring | | Shingle Pass, Egan Range, Lincoln Co. | Map |
| West Mountain Range | House Range | Millard Co., Utah | GWB |
| White Mountain | Crystal Peak | Wah Wah Range, Millard Co., Utah | Adams |
| White Mountains | prob. peak in Ruby Range | Elko Co., Nevada | JC, 16 |
| White Mountains | Snake Range | White Pine Co., Nevada | Bean, 611 |
| White Mountains | Grant-Quinn Canyon Rg. | Nye Co., Nevada | Dame/Young |
| Wibe Creek | Cherry Creek | Garden Valley, Nye Co., Nevada | HM, 24 |
| Wibe Valley | Garden Valley | Nye Co., Nevada | HM, 21 |
| Willow Springs | Emigrant Springs | White River Valley, Nye Co., Nevada | HM, 28 |

# NOTES

## PREFACE

1. Samuel G. Houghton, *A Trace of Desert Waters: The Great Basin Story* (Glendale, Calif.: Arthur H. Clark Co., 1976), p. 194.

2. Three previous attempts to establish the White Mountain Expedition's geography have been published: Brigham H. Roberts, *A Comprehensive History of the Church of Jesus Christ of Latter-day Saints*, 6 vols. (Salt Lake City: Deseret Book Co., 1930), 4:361–63; Leonard J. Arrington, *Great Basin Kingdom: An Economic History of the Latter-day Saints, 1830–1900* (Cambridge: Harvard University Press, 1958), pp. 184–85; Carl Irving Wheat, *Mapping the Transmississippi West, 1540–1861*, 5 vols. (San Francisco: Grabhorn Press for the Institute of Historical Cartography, 1957–63), 4:122–36. The brief accounts of Roberts and Arrington are not geographically accurate. Wheat's account is the only intensive study of the White Mountain trails in print. Concerning himself primarily with the geographical aspects of the expedition, Wheat correctly identifies much of the route. There are, however, a number of inaccuracies, and no attempt has been made to establish certain segments of the route. All three accounts are based on incomplete evidence, and Roberts and Arrington were not particularly familiar with the territory, being more concerned with Mormon strategy than with geography.

## CHAPTER I: AN INTRODUCTION TO EXPLORATION IN THE GREAT BASIN

1. Gloria Griffen Cline, *Exploring the Great Basin*, 2d ed. (Norman: University of Oklahoma Press, 1972), p. 3.

2. For studies of the natural features of the Great Basin, see Houghton, *Trace of Desert Waters;* also Edmund C. Jaeger, *The North American Deserts* (Stanford: Stanford University Press, 1957), pp. 142–50.

3. The Garcés expedition of 1771 is chronicled in Herbert Eugene Bolton, *Anza's California Expeditions*, 5 vols. (Berkeley: University of California Press, 1930), 1:45–46, 5:3–7; also Robert Glass Cleland, *From Wilderness to Empire: A History of California*, ed. Glenn S. Dumke (New York: Alfred A. Knopf, 1959), pp. 38–39. Due to confusion over the Great Basin's southern borders, this expedition is sometimes considered not to have entered the basin. I have used Houghton's defini-

tion of the Great Basin, which extended as far south as the Laguna Salada in Baja California, in this work.

4. See Bolton, *Anza's California Expeditions* for details of other explorations in the Great Basin by Garcés and Anza.

5. An annotated account is Herbert S. Auerbach, ed. "Father Escalante's Journal with Related Documents and Maps," *Utah Historical Quarterly* 11 (1943):1–132. The Rio San Buenaventura was depicted on the expedition's map drawn by Don Bernardo Miera y Pacheco, a member of the party.

6. Joseph J. Hill, "Spanish and Mexican Exploration and Trade Northwest from New Mexico into the Great Basin, 1765–1853," *Utah Historical Quarterly* 3 (January 1930):17–19.

7. Robert Stuart, *The Discovery of the Oregon Trail: Robert Stuart's Narratives*, ed. Philip Aston Rollins (London and New York, Scribner's, 1935), p. 86.

8. A narrative of Mackenzie's expeditions is Alexander Ross, *The Fur Hunters of the Far West*, ed. Kenneth A. Spaulding (Norman: University of Oklahoma Press, 1956).

9. Accounts of the Ogden expeditions are Peter Skene Ogden, *Peter Skene Ogden's Snake Country Journals, 1824-25 and 1825-26*, ed. E. E. Rich (London: Hudson's Bay Records Society, 1950); T. C. Elliott, ed. "Peter Skene Ogden, Journals of Snake Expeditions, 1827–28; 1828–29," *Quarterly of the Oregon Historical Society* 11 (December 1910):355–97; John Scaglione, ed. "Ogden's Report of his 1829–30 Expeditions," *California Historical Quarterly* 28 (June 1949):117–24; Alice Bay Maloney, "Peter Skene Ogden's Trapping Expedition to the Gulf of California," *California Historical Quarterly* 19 (December 1940):308–16.

10. Dale L. Morgan, *Jedediah Smith and the Opening of the West* (Indianapolis: Bobbs-Merrill Co., 1953), pp. 161–70; *Niles' Weekly Register*, 9 December 1826, p. 229.

11. Jedediah S. Smith to William Clark, 12 July 1827 (photocopy of transcript), Utah State Historical Society. The journals of Smith's southwest expedition have only recently been discovered and published. For Smith's account of the expedition see *The Southwest Expedition of Jedediah S. Smith: His Personal Account of the Journey to California, 1826–1827*, ed. George R. Brooks (Glendale, Calif.: Arthur H. Clark Co., 1977). A good overall accounting of Smith's activities is Morgan's *Jedediah Smith and the Opening of the West*.

12. Washington Irving, *The Adventures of Captain Bonneville, U.S.A.* (New York: G. P. Putnam's Sons, 1868; Leland H. Creer, *The Founding of an Empire* (Salt Lake City: Bookcraft, 1947), pp. 94–100; Cline, *Exploring the Great Basin*, pp. 168–80.

13. John Bidwell, *Echoes of the Past about California* (Chicago: Lakeside Press, 1928). This volume includes Bidwell's narrative "The First Emigrant Train to California."

14. George C. Yount, "The Chronicles of George C. Yount," ed. Charles L. Camp, *California Historical Quarterly* 2 (April 1923):3–68; also Cline, *Exploring the Great Basin*, pp. 166–68.

15. John C. Frémont, *Report of the Exploring Expedition to the Rocky Mountains in the Year 1843, and to Oregon and North California in the Years 1843-'44.* (Washington, D.C.: Gales & Seaton, 1845), p. 205. See also pp. 196, 214, 219, 221, 226, 255.

16. Ibid., p. 276.

17. Ibid.

18. Besides Frémont's *Report* of his first and second expeditions to the Far West published in 1845, his *Geographical Memoir*, originally a Senate document in 1848, was published and distributed by several companies. Twenty thousand copies were printed by Tippin & Streeper in 1849.

19. Unfortunately Frémont made little note of his third expedition (1845–46). His *Geographical Memoir Upon Upper California in Illustration of His Map of Oregon and California* (Washington, D.C.: Wendell & Van Beathuysen, 1848) said little of the route which Frémont had only recently taken. For a documentary account, see Ferol Egan, *Frémont, Explorer for a Restless Nation* (Garden City, N.Y.: Doubleday & Co., 1977).

20. The best account of these groups is LeRoy R. Hafen and Ann W. Hafen, eds., *Journals of the Forty-niners Salt Lake to Los Angeles*, Far West and Rocky Mountain Series, vol. 2 (Glendale, Calif.: Arthur H. Clark Co., 1954). Ward's assertions are found on pp. 75, 198, 227–29. Volume 15 of the Far West Series contains a supplement to the *Journals of the Forty-niners*.

21. LeRoy R. Hafen and Ann W. Hafen, eds., *Supplement to the Journals of the Forty-niners Salt Lake to Los Angeles*, Far West and Rocky Mountain Series, vol. 15 (Glendale, Calif.: Arthur H. Clark Co., 1961), pp. 71–72.

22. A biography of Gunnison with details of his ill-fated expedition to the Sevier River is Nolie Mumey, *John Williams Gunnison (1812–1853), The Last of the Western Explorers: A History of the Survey through Colorado and Utah with a Biography and Details of his Massacre* (Denver: Artcraft, 1955).

23. Accounts of Frémont's fifth expedition (1853–54) are meager. See his report in *Alta California* (San Francisco), 24 April 1854 (copied into *Deseret News* [Salt Lake City], 8 June 1854); also U.S. Congress, Senate, *Letter of J. C. Frémont to the Editors of the National Intelligencer*, S. Doc. 67. 33d Cong., 1st sess., 1854. Letter was published in *Daily National Intelligencer* (Washington, D.C.), 14 June 1854.

24. James H. Simpson, *Report of Explorations Across the Great Basin of the Territory of Utah for a Direct Wagon Route from Camp Floyd to Genoa, in Carson Valley, in 1859* (Washington, D.C.: Government Printing Office, 1876), p. 24. The *Report* also includes a map of the Great Basin showing the routes of Beckwith, Gunnison, Frémont and others.

25. Oliver B. Huntington, Diary, 2 vols. (typescript), Brigham Young University, 2:83–89; entries are not precisely dated. *Deseret News Weekly*, 7 December 1854. John F. Bluth, "Confrontation with an Arid Land: The Incursion of Gosiutes and Whites into Utah's Central West Desert, 1800–1978" (Ph.D dissertation, Brigham Young University, 1978), pp. 30–43. Simpson, *Report of Explorations*, p. 24.

26. Simpson, *Report of Explorations*, pp. 24–25. A map indicating the route of Rockwell's reconnoitering party drawn by George W. Bean, a member of the expedition, and dated 20 April 1855, is lodged in the Church Historian's Archives of the Church of Jesus Christ of Latter-day Saints, hereinafter cited L.D.S. Archives.

27. Despite Steptoe's suspicions, Huntington's dairy is quite explicit on the matter of the trip to Carson Valley and would seem to indicate that Steptoe's doubts were unfounded. Rockwell's negative appraisal of the cutoff was determined in the spring of the year when the salt flats were, as usual during this time of year, wet and miry.

28. Howard Egan, *Pioneering the West, 1846–1878; Major Howard Egan's Diary*, ed. William M. Egan (Richmond, Utah: Howard R. Egan Estate, 1917), pp. 193–98.

29. Seth Blair, Diary, p. 18, 3 August–22 September 1856 (typescript), Brigham Young University.

30. David Evans, "Report of the White Mountain Mission," 17 July 1855, Journal History of the Church, (same date), p. 3, L.D.S. Archives. The entire "Report" is on pp. 2–11 inclusive. Other reports of the 1855 White Mountain Mission are E. G. Williams to Heber C. Kimball, 11 June 1855, Journal History, (same date), pp. 4–12; and Richard John Moxey Bee, "Autobiographical Sketch" (typescript), Brigham Young University, pp. 14–18. Bee was a member of the expedition. References are also found in Journal History, 24 May, p. 1; 27 May, p. 3; 29 May, p. 6; 3 July, p. 1; 31 August 1855, p. 5.

31. Williams to Kimball, Journal History, 11 June 1855, pp. 8–9.

32. Volney King, "Millard County, 1851–1875," *Utah Humanities Review*, 4 parts, 1 (January–October 1947):262–63.

33. Mention of the 1853 expedition in Edwin Stott affidavit, 5 January 1926, Indian Wars pension application, #7721, National Archives. Mashoquab's involvement in the Gunnison Massacre described in Roberts, *Comprehensive History*, 4:41–42, 45; King, "Millard County," pp. 148–50.

34. Isaac C. Haight, Diary, 10 March 1858 (typescript), L.D.S. Archives; John D. Lee, *A Mormon Chronicle: The Diaries of John D. Lee, 1848–1876*, ed. Robert Glass Cleland and Juanita Brooks, 2 vols. (San Marino, Calif.: Huntington Library, 1955), 1:154–55, entries for 14, 21 March 1858; Charles Lowell Walker, Diary, 21 March 1858 (typescript), Brigham Young University; David B. Adams, Diary, 1, 22 April 1858 (typescript), partial copy in possession of author; James Willard Bay, Journal, p. 200, L.D.S. Archives.

# CHAPTER II: THE GATHERING STORM

1. While some have maintained that Utah's population during the Utah War stood at about 50,000, it is highly unlikely. In 1860, two years after the war, federal census takers reported only 40,244 residents of Utah. For higher figure see Roberts, *Comprehensive History*, 4:514; Andrew Love Neff, *History of Utah* (Salt Lake City: Deseret News Press, 1940), p. 206.

2. In this work I have used the term "gentile" in the Mormon context, meaning persons who are not Latter-day Saints.

3. Accounts of the Mormon "restoration" movement from a Latter-day Saint point of view are numerous. See Ivan J. Barrett, *Joseph Smith and the Restoration* (Provo, Utah: Brigham Young University Press, 1967); Roberts, *Comprehensive History*, vols. 1, 2. A critical viewpoint is Fawn M. Brodie, *No Man Knows My History; The Life of Joseph Smith, the Mormon Prophet* (New York: Alfred A. Knopf, 1971). A sympathetic treatment that incorporates recent scholarship is Donna Hill, *Joseph Smith the First Mormon* (Garden City, New York: Doubleday & Co., 1977).

4. Polygamy was practiced at least as early as 1843 by the Mormon leadership, nine years before the official announcement after the Saints arrived in Utah. See Lawrence Foster, *Religion and Sexuality, Three American Communal Experiments of the Nineteenth Century* (New York/Oxford: Oxford University Press, 1981), pp. 123–39; Hill, *Joseph Smith*, pp. 335–43; Roberts, *Comprehensive History*, 2:93–110, 4:55–57.

5. Brigham Young, *Discourses of Brigham Young*, comp. John A. Widtsoe (Salt Lake City: Deseret Book Co., 1977), p. 354.

6. William Chandless, *A Visit to Salt Lake being a Journey across the Plains and a Residence in the Mormon Settlements of Utah*, reprint of 1857 edition (New York: AMS Press, 1971), pp. 177-78 contains the observations of an eyewitness to the Utah political scene shortly before the Utah War. Also see Furniss, *Mormon Conflict*, pp. 16-17; Neff, *History of Utah*, pp. 120-22; Klaus J. Hansen, *Quest for Empire, the Political Kingdom of God and the Council of Fifty in Mormon History* (East Lansing: Michigan State University Press, 1970), pp. 128-30, 137-38.

7. Furniss, *Mormon Conflict*, pp. 17-18.

8. Ibid., pp. 25-29; Neff, *History of Utah*, pp. 174-75.

9. Furniss, *Mormon Conflict*, pp. 57-58; Roberts, *Comprehensive History*, 4:198-99.

10. Furniss, *Mormon Conflict*, pp. 45-51. Although Hurt did not leave Utah until after the war had begun, his numerous letters to the Commissioner of Indian Affairs contributed to the opening of hostilities.

11. Ibid., pp. 54-57; Roberts, *Comprehensive History*, 4:200-206; Neff, *History of Utah*, pp. 447-51.

12. Furniss, *Mormon Conflict*, pp. 33-37, 45-46, 50-51, 87.

13. Ibid., p. 23-26; Roberts, *Comprehensive History*, 3:516-17.

14. Roberts, *Comprehensive History*, 4:200-202, 207n; Furniss, *Mormon Conflict*, pp. 54-55; Neff, *History of Utah*, pp. 447-48.

15. Furniss, *Mormon Conflict*, pp. 23-24, 53, 76. On July 26, 1857, Brigham Young declared: "Three years ago they appropriated $45,000 for the purpose of making treaties with the Indians. Has even that diminutively small sum ever been sent here? It is in the coffers of the Government to this day, unless they have stolen it out, or improperly paid it out for some other purpose." (*Journal of Discourses*, 26 vols., ed. George D. Watt, et al. [Liverpool: Church of Jesus Christ of Latter-day Saints, 1854-86], 5:78).

16. Furniss, *Mormon Conflict*, pp. 13-14, 45; Neff, *History of Utah*, pp. 435-38; Brigham Young, *Journal of Discourses* 5 (26 July 1857):78.

17. Furniss, *Mormon Conflict*, pp. 75-76.

18. John Taylor, *Journal of Discourses* 5 (23 August 1857):152.

19. Furniss, *Mormon Conflict*, pp. 92-94; Juanita Brooks, *The Mountain Meadows Massacre*, 2d ed. (Norman: University of Oklahoma Press, 1962), pp. 11-13.

20. Furniss, *Mormon Conflict*, p. 78.

21. Parley P. Pratt, *Autobiography of Parley P. Pratt*, ed. Parley P. Pratt, [Jr.] (Salt Lake City: Deseret Book Company, 1938), p. 444. Four months later Pratt was assassinated near Van Buren, Arkansas.

22. Furniss, *Mormon Conflict*, pp. 86-88.

23. Ibid., pp. 90-91; Richard D. Poll, "The Mormon Question, 1850-65: A Study in Politics and Public Opinion" (Ph.D. dissertation, University of California, Berkeley, 1948), pp. 73, 77, 78.

24. Poll, "Mormon Question," p. 75; Furniss, *Mormon Conflict*, p. 78.

25. This factor is considered by Neff, *History of Utah*, pp. 457-60; Poll, "Mormon Question," p. 75; Furniss, *Mormon Conflict*, pp. 74-75; Roberts, *Comprehensive History*, 4:223-24.

On August 23, 1857, John Taylor lashed out against the administration:

> The Democrats have professed to be our friends, and they go to work to sustain the domestic institutions of the South [slavery] and the rights of the people; but when they do that, the Republicans throw polygamy at them, and they are determined to make them swallow that with the other. This makes the Democrats gag, and they have felt a strong desire to get rid of the "Mormon" question. . . . (*Journal of Discourses* 5:153).

26. Complete instructions are found in U.S. Congress, House, *Utah Expedition*, H. Exec. Doc. 71, 35th Cong. 1st sess., 1858, pp. 7-9. Doc. 71 includes many pieces of correspondence relative to the Utah War.

27. U.S. Department of State Territorial Papers, Utah, 1853-1859, National Archives microfilm.

28. Everett L. Cooley, ed., *Diary of Brigham Young 1857* (Salt Lake City: Tanner Trust Fund, University of Utah Library, 1980), pp. 48-52.

29. Brigham Young, *Journal of Discourses* 5 (13 September 1857):226.

30. Jesse A. Gove, *The Utah Expedition, 1857-1858; Letters of Captain Jesse A. Gove to Mrs. Gove and the New York Herald*, ed. Otis G. Hammond (Concord: New Hampshire Historical Society, 1928), p. 175.

31. George Laub, Diary, 29 January 1858 (typescript), Utah State Historical Society.

32. Heber C. Kimball, *Journal of Discourses* 5 (20 September 1857):250. Also see ibid., 5:154, 233, 340, 353-54; Samuel Pitchforth, Diary, 1 February 1858 (typescript), Brigham Young University.

33. Perhaps the best example of Mormon thought along such lines is Wilford Woodruff's Tabernacle speech of December 6, 1857:

> The day of the Devil's power to prevail against the kingdom of God has passed away. . . . The nation does not know what it is doing nor comprehend the fearful results of the course they are pursuing. They are turning the last key to rend the nation asunder, and they will be broken as a potter's vessel, and cast down as a nation, to rise no more forever. (*Journal of Discourses*, 5:120-21.)

34. Brigham Young to John M. Bernhisel, 6 May 1858, Brigham Young papers, L.D.S. Archives.

35. For an extensive rebuttal to the charge of treason see "Who are the Rebels?" *Latter-day Saints' Millennial Star*, 20 (13-27 March 1858):161-64, 177-80, 193-96. Hereinafter cited *Millennial Star*.

36. Thomas B. H. Stenhouse, *Rocky Mountain Saints* (New York: D. Appleton & Co., 1873), p. 375.

37. Brigham Young, *Journal of Discourses* 5 (2 August 1857):98, 99.

38. Heber C. Kimball, *Journal of Discourses* 5 (30 August 1857):161, 164.

39. Brigham Young, *Journal of Discourses* 5 (18 October 1857):343. Numerous sources attest to the Saints' declared separation from the United States. See ibid., 5:251, 253, 257, 321, 369; 6:131; Hosea Stout, Diary, 6 September 1857, L.D.S. Archives; Laub, Diary, 29 January 1858.

40. Richard F. Burton, *The City of the Saints and Across the Rocky Mountains to California* (New York: Harper & Bros., 1862), pp. 239-40.

41. Cited in Neff, *History of Utah*, p. 567.

42. Young contended on September 13, 1857: "You might as well tell me that you can make hell into a powder-house as to tell me that you could let an army in here and have peace." (*Journal of Discourses* 5:231).

43. Brigham Young, *Journal of Discourses* 5 (18 October 1857):342.

44. Roberts, *Comprehensive History*, 4:259–63. On January 6, 1858, Young wrote:

Rather than see my wives and daughters ravished and polluted, and the seeds of corruption sown in the hearts of my sons by a brutal soldiery, I would leave my home in ashes, my gardens and orchards a waste, and subsist upon roots and herbs, a wanderer through these mountains for the remainder of my natural life. (Arrington, *Great Basin Kingdom*, p. 467n.)

45. Furniss, *Mormon Conflict*, pp. 123–24.

46. Brigham Young, *Journal of Discourses* 5 (13 September 1857):232–33.

47. Brigham Young, *Journal of Discourses* 5 (18 October 1857):338–39.

48. *Deseret News*, 23 September 1857, p. 231.

49. One colorful and apparently credible version of Mormon strategy, said to be received from "a priest high in authority at Salt Lake City," was published some time later by the *Alta California* (San Francisco):

Our plans are all matured and laid. If they enter these valleys, which will be most difficult, we propose caching, i.e., burying our grain, for we have an abundance of it, and then we'll make a Moscow of everything that will burn. Burn up the grass, and every mortal thing that will burn, and leave behind us nothing but desolation, upon which it is impossible to subsist. We shall retreat to the dense canons and places in the mountains, surrounded by natural barriers which render the interior impervious to all ingress, and which alone are accessible through narrow and almost impassable defiles, that can be successfully guarded by a few to the exclusion of thousands. It is impossible to introduce a large army into this Territory. They cannot bring sufficient food to last them more than one year, and if the grass is destroyed, how will the cattle subsist? We will destroy all the timber, and everything suitable for fuel, and when they come to the mountains and canons for something to cook their scanty meals with, they will find Mormon mountaineers there, and perhaps a thousand and one red men to pick them off on the right hand and on the left. (Reprinted in *Harper's Weekly*, 22 May 1858, p. 326).

50. Brigham Young, *Journal of Discourses* 5 (18 October 1857):339.

51. Daniel H. Wells to David Evans, 13 August 1857, David Evans papers, L.D.S. Archives.

52. Joseph Fish, Journal, pp. 32–39 (microfilm), Brigham Young University; James H. Martineau to Albert Carrington, 20 September 1857, Nauvoo Legion papers, correspondence, Utah State Archives.

53. *New York Herald*, 25 May 1858, p. 1.

54. James Pace, Autobiography, p. 11, L.D.S. Archives; Aaron Johnson to Daniel H. Wells, 11 December 1857, Nauvoo Legion papers, correspondence, Utah State Archives.

55. Junius F. Wells [Vaux], "Echo Cañon War," *Contributor* 3 (March 1882):177. Junius was the son of General Daniel H. Wells of Utah War fame.

56. James Ferguson to Brigham Young, 7 January 1858, Nauvoo Legion papers (microfilm), Brigham Young University. The Nauvoo Legion papers at Brigham Young University and at the Utah State Archives contain many muster rolls of the Utah militia. Others have contended the Nauvoo Legion stood at 4,000–5,000 troops during the Utah War. See Hubert Howe Bancroft, *History of Utah, 1540–1887* (San Francisco: The History Company, 1890), p. 509; Neff, *History of Utah*, p. 474n.

57. Young's proclamation is found in *Utah Expedition*, H. Exec. Doc. 71, pp. 33-35.

58. Daniel H. Wells and Brigham Young to David Evans, 16 September 1857, David Evans papers, L.D.S. Archives.

59. Dame's report of 23 August 1857 cited in Juanita Brooks, *John Doyle Lee— Zealot—Pioneer Builder—Scapegoat* (Glendale, Calif.: Arthur H. Clark Co., 1962), pp. 201-202. Returns of 10 October 1857 are found in the Nauvoo Legion papers, Brigham Young University.

60. Arrington, *Great Basin Kingdom*, pp. 176-77, 180; Roberts, *Comprehensive History*, 4:333; Kate B. Carter, comp., *Our Pioneer Heritage*, 23 vols. (Salt Lake City: Daughters of Utah Pioneers, 1958-80), 2:29-31.

61. Brigham Young, *Journal of Discourses* 5 (13 September 1857):235.

62. Heber C. Kimball, *Journal of Discourses* 5 (26 July 1857):95.

63. Best account of the massacre is Brooks, *Mountain Meadows Massacre*. Also see George A. Smith, *Journal of Discourses* 5 (13 September 1857):221-24 for comments about the high emotional state and mood for vengeance found in Iron County just prior to the massacre.

64. Neff, *History of Utah*, p. 479; Furniss, *Mormon Conflict*, p. 141.

65. Arrington, *Great Basin Kingdom*, pp. 179-80.

66. Charles A. Scott, Diary, 21 June 1858 (photocopy), Utah State Historical Society.

67. Gove, *Utah Expedition*, p. 176.

68. Arrington, *Great Basin Kingdom*, p. 178; Lot Smith's narrative of Mormon guerrilla activity is found in Wells, "Echo Cañon War," 4:27-29, 47-50, 167-69, 224-26.

69. Henry S. Hamilton, *Reminiscences of a Veteran* (Concord, N.H.: Republican Press Association, 1897), pp. 80-81.

70. Furniss, *Mormon Conflict*, p. 140; Neff, *History of Utah*, p. 478. Colonel Alexander commanded the expedition until the arrival of Colonel Albert Sidney Johnston. Johnston was designated by the War Department to replace Harney who was detained by a previous assignment in Kansas.

71. Furniss, *Mormon Conflict*, pp. 112-18.

72. Ibid., p. 116.

73. Scott, Diary, 7 November 1857. On January 1, 1858, Scott recorded: "Rather tough times now, not enough to eat and blest with a ravenous appetite. Intensely cold weather. Sentinels have to be relieved every hour to keep from being frost bitten. . . ."

74. *New York Herald*, 2 July 1858, p. 2; also see *New York Tribune*, 9 December 1857, p. 4 for references to the suffering of U.S. troops at the hands of the Mormons.

75. John Taylor, *Journal of Discourses*, 7 (10 January 1858):124.

## CHAPTER III: THE CRISIS

1. Stenhouse, *Rocky Mountain Saints*, pp. 371-72.

2. Wilford Woodruff, Diary, 1 January 1858 (microfilm), L.D.S. Archives.

3. *Deseret News*, 6 January 1858, p. 349. All mail for Utah arrived by way of California, the eastern mail having been severed during the summer.

4. Journal History, 27 December 1857, p. 9.

5. *Deseret News*, 6 January 1858, p. 349. The *News* of 27 January 1858 reprinted the article.

6. Lee, *Mormon Chronicle*, 1:141. Entry for 4 January 1858.

Threats of a southern invasion were not entirely unheard of earlier in the war. In mid-August 1857 the Iron Battalion scrambled into the mountains east of Parowan to meet 600 soldiers from the Utah expedition said to be penetrating the territory over Frémont's trail of 1854. The rumor proved unfounded. (James H. Martineau, Autobiography [typescript], pp. 13-14, Brigham Young University; Fish, Journal, p. 29; George A. Smith, *Journal of Discourses* 5 [13 September 1857]:223.) As early as October reports reached Salt Lake City that the government would attempt to navigate the Colorado River with light draught steamers in a military expedition against Utah, but this report seems not to have been taken seriously. (Journal History, 7 October 1857, p. 7).

7. Woodruff, Diary, 3 January 1858.

8. Ferguson to Young, 7 January 1858.

9. Cited in Brooks, *Mountain Meadows Massacre*, pp. 146-47.

10. Wall's report is found in Journal History, 12 December 1857, pp. 1-8. Also see Kate B. Carter, comp., *Heart Throbs of the West*, 12 vols. (Salt Lake City: Daughters of Utah Pioneers, 1939-51), 6:451.

11. Journal History, 12 December 1857, p. 6.

12. *Daily National Intelligencer* (Washington, D.C.), 1 April 1858, p. [3], declared: "The animals [camels] are now on their return to the Colorado River for the purpose of carrying provisions to Lieutenant Beale and the military escort, who, it is conjectured, will penetrate from thence, as far as possible into the Mormon country." The *Missouri Republican* (St. Louis), 9 April 1858, p. [2], published a letter from Beale to John B. Floyd, Secretary of War: "In a previous letter I informed you that I had sent the camels back to Fort Tejon from the Colorado river . . . that they might be used in the campaign against Utah." (Cited in Roberts, *Comprehensive History*, 4:371.)

13. The men accompanying Lyman were James Lewis, William H. Dame, Silas S. Smith, John M. Higbee, Nephi Johnson, Atha Carter, J. S. Walker, and W. H. Shearman. (Amasa Lyman, Diaries, 11 January 1858, pp. 99-100 [typescript], Brigham Young University. Originals in L.D.S. Archives.)

14. Amasa Lyman to Brigham Young, 20 January 1858, Brigham Young papers, L.D.S. Archives. Hamblin's encounter with Lyman in Lyman diary, 17 January 1858, p. 101.

15. Lyman to Young, 20 January 1858.

16. Lyman, Diary, 31 January 1858, p. 105.

17. Ibid., 13 February 1858, p. 107.

18. Joseph C. Ives, *Report upon the Colorado River of the West* (Washington, D.C.: Government Printing Office, 1861), p. 21. Johnson claimed he lost the appropriation because Ives married a niece of the secretary of war and used his influence to get the money. See Arthur Woodward, *Feud on the Colorado* (Los Angeles: Western Lore Press, 1955), p. 70.

19. Woodward, *Feud on the Colorado*, pp. 83-84. Weaver's name had been Hispanicized to "Paulino" and later Americanized to "Pauline." Ironically,

Weaver was one of the Mormon Battalion guides in 1846. (Roberts, *Comprehensive History*, 3:112.) An interesting biography of Weaver is Arthur Woodward, "Pauline Weaver of the Feet," *Desert Magazine* 1 (March 1938):4-6.

20. Ives, *Colorado River of the West*, p. 89.

21. The Ives and Johnson expeditions on the Colorado River are detailed in Woodward, *Feud on the Colorado*, pp. 61-104; Melvin T. Smith, "Colorado River Exploration and the Mormon War," *Utah Historical Quarterly* 38 (Summer 1970):207-23; Ives, *Colorado River of the West*, pp. 25-92.

22. Jacob Hamblin, Diary, [17 March 1858], p. 53, L.D.S. Archives; Ives, *Colorado River of the West*, p. 88.

23. Hamblin, Diary, [date unclear], pp. 54-55.

24. Ives, *Colorado River of the West*, p. 80.

25. Woodward, *Feud on the Colorado*, pp. 80-81, 104.

26. *Deseret News*, 17 February 1858, p. 398.

27. Manuscript History, 19 January 1858, pp. 155, 158. It has been deduced that the returned missionaries were the source of this disturbing news from the fact that the information was recorded in the church annals on the same day that Pratt, Benson, and other missionaries arrived from the States, and from the content of their speeches delivered within days of their arrival in Salt Lake City. The California mail, the Mormon's primary source of information from the outside world, had been received two weeks prior to the missionaries' arrival and was not received again until February 3.

28. Andrew Jackson Allen, Diary, 19 January 1858 (typescript), Brigham Young University.

29. Laub, Diary, 24 January 1858.

30. Brigham Young to Joseph Horne, 25 January 1858, Brigham Young papers, L.D.S. Archives.

31. Woodruff, Diary, 31 December 1857.

32. Young to Horne, 25 January 1858.

33. Lee, *Mormon Chronicle*, 1:149. Entry for 8 February 1858.

34. *Millennial Star* 11 (1 December 1849):362; *Times and Seasons* (Nauvoo, Ill.), 20 January 1846, p. 1096; Woodruff, Diary, 29 May, 24 July 1847.

35. Lee, *Mormon Chronicle*, 1:141. Entry for 4 January 1858.

36. "An Act, Granting unto Brigham Young Sen., and others, Aivenpah [Ibapah] Valley for a Herding Ground and other Purposes," Utah Legislative Assembly, 8 January 1858, Utah State Archives.

37. Brigham Young to W. G. Young, 10 March 1858, Brigham Young papers, L.D.S. Archives.

38. Woodruff, Diary, 21 December 1857.

39. James D. Richardson, comp., *Messages and Papers of the Presidents*, 18 vols. (New York: Bureau of National Literature, 1917), 6:2987.

40. Woodruff, Diary, 3 February 1858.

41. Samuel Pitchforth, Diary, 1 February 1858 (typescript), Brigham Young University.

42. Woodruff, Diary, 4 February 1858.

43. Brigham Young to Amasa Lyman, 4 February 1858, Brigham Young papers, L.D.S. Archives.

44. Brigham Young to Henry W. Bigler and John S. Woodbury, 4 February 1858, Brigham Young papers, L.D.S. Archives.

45. Woodruff, Diary, 6 February 1858.

46. Smith's remarks quoted in Lee, *Mormonism Unveiled*, pp. 221–22.

47. *Deseret News*, 17 February 1858, p. 397. Ives article p. 398.

48. Gove, *Utah Expedition*, p. 147.

49. Woodruff, Diary, 21 February 1858.

50. Historical Department Journal, 13 March 1858 (microfilm ), L.D.S. Archives.

51. Laub, Diary, 21 February 1858.

## CHAPTER IV: SEBASTOPOL

1. Brigham Young to Lewis Brunson, 23 February 1858, Brigham Young papers, L.D.S. Archives.

2. Brigham Young to W. G. Young, 10 March 1858.

3. Melvin T. Smith, "Colorado River Exploration," pp. 216, 221–22; details of the expedition are found in Lyman, Diary, 9 March–7 May 1858, pp. 110–26; also see Amasa Lyman to Brigham Young, 25 March 1858, Brigham Young papers, L.D.S. Archives.

4. Poll, "Mormon Question," pp. 109, 113–25; Furniss, *Mormon Conflict*, pp. 7, 8–9, 30, 61, 176–77. Utah's delegate in Washington, Dr. John M. Bernhisel, was also active in lobbying the government for modification of its Mormon policy. See Poll, "Mormon Question," p. 114.

5. Woodruff, Diary, 25 February 1858.

6. Roberts, *Comprehensive History*, 4:346, 349; Manuscript History, 15 August 1858, p. 927.

7. Poll, "Mormon Question," pp. 123–25; Furniss, *Mormon Conflict*, pp. 179–80.

8. George W. Bean, Journal, 5 vols., 4:62, Brigham Young University.

9. Historical Department Journal, 6 March 1858.

10. American Fork Ward Records, Minutes of Meetings, 7 March 1858 (microfilm), L.D.S. Archives.

11. Edson Barney, "Biographical Sketch" (microfilm of typescript), L.D.S. Archives.

12. Manuscript History, 7 March 1858, p. 225.

13. Historical Department Journal, 8 March 1858. George A. Smith was the church historian and the likely author of these lines. Also see Henry Ballard, Diary, 7 March 1858 (typescript), Utah State Historical Society. Ballard underscores the Mormon belief that the army was employing Indians against them.

14. Roberts, *Comprehensive History*, 4:353–54.

15. Hosea Stout, Diary, 10 March 1858 (microfilm), L.D.S. Archives.

16. The church declared in the *Deseret News* of April 14, 1857 (p. 35): "Governor Young and the 'Mormons' have ever counseled the Indians to remain strictly neutral."

The policy of the government, according to Commissioner of Indian Affairs J. W. Denver, was to "keep the Indians in a state of peace and quiet . . . and to spare no pains to keep them from attacking the whites. The object of the Government is to keep them as quiet as possible, but if this cannot be done, then to control them in such a manner as to direct their attacks against those savages who may take up arms against our people." (J. W. Denver to J. L. Collins, 24 Nov. 1857, [typescript] U.S. Dept. of Indian Affairs, selected correspondence, Utah State Historical Society.)

17. See, for example, Daniel H. Wells to David Evans, 13 August 1857, David Evans papers, L.D.S. Archives. Also see "Report of a Party of Observation," 18 August 1857, Nauvoo Legion papers, Brigham Young University, in which Marcellus Monroe describes the efforts of his militia unit to "instruct" the Indians in the mountains east of Ogden.

18. John Owens, *The Journals and Letters of Major John Owens, Pioneer of the Northwest, 1850–1871*, 2 vols., ed. Seymour Dunbar and Paul C. Phillip (New York: Edward Eberstadt, 1927), 1:189–93; Roberts, *Comprehensive History*, 4:365, 366n, 368–69; *Deseret News*, 17 March 1858, p. 13.

19. Manuscript History, 9 April 1858, pp. 340–41; 13 April 1858, p. 356.

20. Ibid., 18 March 1858, p. 266. Historical Department Journal, 18 March 1858, lists those present at the meeting: Brigham Young, Heber C. Kimball, Daniel H. Wells, Orson Hyde, Orson Pratt, Wilford Woodruff, George A. Smith, Franklin D. Richards, Erastus Snow, Ezra Taft Benson, Charles C. Rich, Albert Carrington, Hosea Stout, William H. Hooper, Nathaniel V. Jones, James W. Cummings, Alexander McRae, David J. Ross, John S. Fullmer, Jonathan Pugmire, Leonard W. Hardy, Alonzo H. Raleigh, Robert T. Burton, John D. T. McAllister, Harrison Burgess, F. Kesler, Jesse P. Harmon, Albert P. Rockwood, Hiram B. Clawson, Joseph M. Simmons, T. W. Ellerbeck, James Ferguson, Jesse C. Little, H. S. Beatie, and Elijah F. Sheets. Some of these men, like Charles C. Rich and George A. Smith, were both apostles and military officers.

21. Stout, Diary, 18 March 1858.

22. Manuscript History, 18 March 1858, p. 266.

23. Brigham Young to W. G. Young, 15 March 1858, Brigham Young papers, L.D.S. Archives.

24. Thomas L. Kane to Judge John K. Kane, [4 April 1858], Kane Collection, Brigham Young University. When Kane reached Camp Scott on March 12, he was rebuffed by Johnston, and Cumming, too, appeared unyielding. By March 19 Kane had concluded his mission was a practical failure. On March 17 the colonel had conferred with his Mormon escort stationed a few miles away and no doubt conveyed his disappointment to them. It is probable that news of the seemingly fruitless negotiations had reached Brigham Young before March 21, the day the prophet revealed his latest defense strategy to the Saints. See Furniss, *Mormon Conflict*, pp. 178–82.

25. All quotes from this speech from Brigham Young's pamphlet, *A Series of Instructions and Remarks by President Brigham Young at a Special Council, Tabernacle, March 21, 1858* (Salt Lake City: 1858). Originals of this rare pamphlet are located at University of Utah Library, Special Collections, and Yale University Library. A photocopy is at Brigham Young University.

26. Justin McCarthy, *History of Our Own Times*, 4 vols. (Boston: Estes and Lauriat, 1897), 2:253. Cited in Roberts, *Comprehensive History*, 4:364–65.

27. Manuscript History, 21 March 1858, pp. 269–72 contains a summary of Kimball's speech and others made that day.

28. *Deseret News*, 31 March 1858, p. 26.

29. Quotes from Brigham Young's second speech of 21 March 1858 also included in *A Series of Instructions and Remarks*, pp. 15–19.

30. Charles B. Hancock to Brigham Young, 29 March 1858, Brigham Young papers, L.D.S. Archives.

31. William Luck, Journal, 21 March 1858 (typescript), L.D.S. Archives.

32. Journal History, 23 March 1858, p. 1.

33. Roberts, *Comprehensive History*, 4:361. Hosea Stout also mentioned in his diary that he attended "Ward meeting" on the evening of 21 March 1858, where the subject of volunteers for the desert was taken up. Stout writes: "The brethren seemed some what loth to volunteer for which reason I gave my name to go in the first Company although I did not come in that class [those who had never been driven from their homes] who were called upon." See Hosea Stout, *On the Mormon Frontier: The Diary of Hosea Stout*, 2 vols., ed. Juanita Brooks (Salt Lake City: University of Utah Press, 1964), 2:655.

34. Historical Department Journal, 22 March 1858.

35. Manuscript History, 5 April 1858, p. 310.

36. Young, *A Series of Instructions and Remarks*, pp. 17–18; Arrington, *Great Basin Kingdom*, p. 186; Journal History, 22 March 1858, p. 1; Manuscript History, 13 April 1858, p. 355; Historical Department Journal, 25 March, 6 April 1858.

37. This circular is the already-mentioned *Series of Instructions and Remarks*.

38. Brigham Young to John D. Lee, 24 March 1958, Brigham Young papers, L.D.S. Archives.

39. Other letters were sent to Joseph Horne, Heberville (the cotton farm); Bishop John L. Butler, Spanish Fork; Bishop Aaron Johnson, Springville; Bishop Charles B. Hancock, Payson; Bishop Holman, Santaquin; Bishop Jacob Bigler, Nephi; Bishop Tarleton Lewis, Parowan; President Isaac C. Haight, Cedar City, Bishop Philo T. Farnsworth, Beaver. All correspondence in Brigham Young papers, L.D.S. Archives.

40. Young, *A Series of Instructions and Remarks*, pp. 18–19; Brigham Young to Officers north of G.S.L.C., 24 March 1858, Brigham Young papers, L.D.S. Archives.

41. Young, *A Series of Instructions and Remarks*, pp. 16, 17.

42. *Deseret News*, 24 March 1858, p. 20. The Sebastopol allegory continued in public usage for some time. The property of the emigrants massacred at Mountain Meadows was referred to in 1859 as the "property taken at the siege of Sevastopol." (Roberts, *Comprehensive History*, 4:158.)

43. Charles Lowell Walker is one who understood the inference in Young's speech. See Walker, Diary, 21 March 1858, where he correctly identifies the destination.

44. *New York Herald*, 31 May 1858, p. 5.

45. Ibid., 24 May 1858, pp. 1, 4; 25 May 1858, p. 1.

46. Ibid., 25 May 1858, p. 1. Gilbert stated that he left Salt Lake City on 31 March, but, since he mentioned seeing Brigham Young on the road south of Salt

Lake City, the correct date must have been 2 April. Manuscript History, 2 April 1858, p. 294 records the meeting.

47. "The Supposed Mormon Retreat," *Harper's Weekly*, 29 May 1858, p. 342.

48. [Albert G. Browne], "The Utah Expedition," *Atlantic Monthly*, April 1859, p. 483.

# CHAPTER V: TO THE WHITE MOUNTAINS

1. Brigham Young to George W. Bean, 21 March 1858, Brigham Young papers, L.D.S. Archives.

2. George W. Bean, Journals, 4:62.

3. For biographical information about George W. Bean, see Bean's *Autobiography of George W. Bean*, comp. Flora Diane Bean Horne (Salt Lake City: Utah Printing Company for Flora D. B. Horne, 1945); Harry C. Dees, ed., "Journal of George W. Bean," *Nevada Historical Quarterly* 15 (Fall 1972), pp. 2–29; Frank Esshom, *Pioneers and Prominent Men of Utah* (Salt Lake City: Western Epics, 1966), p. 744; Andrew Jenson, *Latter-day Saint Biographical Encyclopedia*, 4 vols. (Salt Lake City: Deseret News Press, 1901), 4:611; George W. Bean, Journals.

4. For biographical information about Edson Barney, see Jenson, *L.D.S. Biographical Encylopedia*, 4:687; Edson Barney, "Biographical Sketch" (typescript), L.D.S. Archives.

5. Young, *A Series of Instructions and Remarks*, p. 12.

6. Manuscript History, 7 June 1858, p. 610. Bean's report on pp. 610–16 inclusive. The report is also found in Journal History, 7 June 1858, pp. 2–4. The Journal History is a copy of the former record and a poor one, containing numerous errors and deletions. Unless otherwise noted, all references to Bean's exploring activities are from his report of 7 June 1858 as recorded in the Manuscript History.

7. Lewis Brunson to Brigham Young, 21 March 1858, Brigham Young papers, L.D.S. Archives.

8. George W. Bean to Brigham Young, 27 March 1858, Brigham Young papers, L.D.S. Archives.

9. Brigham Young to George W. Bean, 24 March 1858, Brigham Young papers, L.D.S. Archives.

10. Historical Department Journal, 29 March 1858.

11. Ibid., 5 April 1858.

12. Ibid., 3 April 1858. Curiously, when the national press became aware of the exodus, it was perceived by some editors to be a sign that the Mormons were preparing for a fight rather than flight. Some press reports interpreted the move south as an attempt to remove the women and children from the firing line.

13. Bean to Young, 27 March 1858.

14. Ibid., also see George W. Bean to Brigham Young, 2 April 1858, Brigham Young papers, L.D.S. Archives.

15. Chandless, *A Visit to Salt Lake*, p. 272.

16. Bean to Young, 2 April 1858.

17. Orson B. Adams, Autobiography, pp. 17–18, Brigham Young University. Biographical material about Adams found in Jenson, *L.D.S. Biographical En-*

*cyclopedia*, 4:728; Andrew Jenson, "Manuscript History of Parowan Ward," L.D.S. Archives; Nauvoo Legion Papers, Muster Rolls, Brigham Young University; Adams, Autobiography. Biographical data about Stewart in Jenson, *L.D.S. Biographical Encyclopedia*, 3:526-27.

18. Bay, Journal, pp. 200-201. James Willard Bay was a member of the Cedar City company but resided at nearby Ft. Johnson (now Enoch, Utah).

19. References to Hopkins's involvement at Mountain Meadows in John D. Lee, *Life, Confession, and Execution*, p. 6; *Congressional Globe*, 7 February 1863, Appendix, p. 123. Further biographical data in Charles Hopkins papers, Brigham Young University.

20. Biographical information about Woodhouse in his Autobiography (typescript), Brigham Young University; Carter, *Our Pioneer Heritage*, 2:29-31.

21. Isaac C. Haight, Diary, 10 March 1858 (typescript), L.D.S. Archives; Isaac C. Haight to Brigham Young, 24 March 1858, Brigham Young papers, L.D.S. Archives.

22. Haight to Young, 24 March 1858. Also see Bay, Journal, p. 200 for details of events relevant to the organization of the Cedar City company.

23. Bean to Young, 2 April 1858.

24. King, "Millard County," p. 265. Although King was not a member of the expedition, he was a resident of Fillmore during the Utah War and was acquainted with many of the particulars of the expedition and its personnel. Mashoquab variously spelled.

25. Ibid., pp. 262-63.

26. Bean to Young, 2 April 1858.

27. Adams, Autobiography, p. 18.

28. Simpson, *Report of Explorations*, p. 118.

29. Bay, Journal, p. 201.

30. Thomas W. Cropper, Autobiography, p. 68. Cropper was a teenager living in Fillmore at the time of the expedition but was not himself a participant.

31. Bean, *Autobiography of George W. Bean*, p. 132. Volney King called the range "Antelope Mountain." (King, "Millard County," p. 266.)

32. Manuscript History, 7 June 1858, pp. 610-11; Bay, Journal, p. 200; King, "Millard County," p. 265.

33. Bay, Journal, p. 201.

34. While following the Mormons' White Mountain trail in 1859, Captain Simpson of the Topographical Engineers discovered four large holes dug near the summit of Cooper Canyon in Nevada's Schell Creek Range, which he surmised had been dug by the Mormons for the purpose of caching supplies. (Simpson, *Report of Explorations*, p. 120.)

35. Cropper, Autobiography, p. 68. Cropper's account of the discovery of the skeletons is uncorroborated in any of Bean's letters or reports of the expedition. Most of the details of Cropper's narrative relating to the White Mountain Expedition can be verified, however, including the fact that the expedition's course brought them through Dome Canyon Pass, which, according to Cropper, is known as Death Canyon and Doom Canyon because of the finding of the skeletons. The Bureau of Land Management presently uses the Death Canyon designation.

36. Bean, *Autobiography of George W. Bean*, pp. 132-33; Barney, "Biographical Sketch," p. 4; King, "Millard County," p. 265-66.

37. Bay, Journal, p. 201.

38. Barney, "Biographical Sketch," p. 4.

39. King, "Millard County," p. 265.

40. Ibid., pp. 265-66.

41. The exact number to go from Fillmore is unknown. Brigham Young had requested "a party of fifteen or twenty men." Fourteen men, not including the two Indian guides, have been identified.

42. King, "Millard County," p. 265.

43. Bay, Journal, p. 200; Barney, "Biographical Sketch," p. 4.

44. Philo T. Farnsworth to Brigham Young, 24 March 1858, Brigham Young papers, L.D.S. Archives.

45. David B. Adams, Diary, 1 April 1858 (typescript), in author's possession.

46. Manuscript History, 7 June 1858, p. 611.

47. Despite Bean's exaggeration of the canyon's narrowness, there is little doubt that he was describing Dome Canyon. Bean led Captain James H. Simpson over his trail in 1859, and Simpson's map and report leave no question that Bean's Cache Canyon was indeed Dome Canyon. Simpson's map and *Report of Explorations* was of primary importance in solving much of Bean's route.

48. Manuscript History, 7 June 1858, p. 611. Apparently Bean considered the Burbank Meadows ten miles south of Snake Creek to be too distant to be convenient.

49. Brigham Young, *Journal of Discourses*, 7 (28 March 1858):43, 45-47.

50. "The Utah War: Journal of Captain Albert Tracy, 1858-1860," *Utah Historical Quarterly* 13 (1945):5-6.

51. Manuscript History, 1 April 1858, p. 293.

52. Ibid., 4 April 1858, p. 303.

53. Woodruff, Diary, 6 April 1858.

54. Historical Department Journal, 6 April 1858; also "Minutes of Conference," *Deseret News*, 14 April 1858, p. 35.

55. Historical Department Journal, 12 April 1858.

56. Brigham Young and Daniel H. Wells to David Evans, 16 September 1857, David Evans papers, L.D.S. Archives.

57. Stout, *On the Mormon Frontier*, 2:656. Entry for 2 April 1858. This was false reasoning on the part of the Mormons. It was only because of the sad state of the treasury and the Mormon problem's indirect entanglement with the Kansas and slavery issues that Buchanan's recommendations were rejected, not because of any lessening of hostility toward the Mormons in Congress. See Furniss, *Mormon Conflict*, pp. 174-75. Eventually two regiments were approved for Utah service late in the war.

58. Historical Department Journal, 6 April 1858.

59. Furniss, *Mormon Conflict*, p. 184.

60. Historical Department Journal, 12 April 1858.

61. Furniss, *Mormon Conflict*, p. 183.

62. Kane to Judge Kane, 4 April 1858; also see Thomas L. Kane to Robert P. Kane, 4 April 1858, and Thomas L. Kane to James Buchanan, 23 March 1858, Kane Collection, Brigham Young University.

## CHAPTER VI: THE SOUTHERN EXPLORING COMPANY

1. George A. Smith to Thomas B. H. Stenhouse, 5 April 1858, Manuscript History, 5 April 1858, p. 307.

2. John R. Young, *Memoirs of John R. Young, Utah Pioneer* (Salt Lake City: Deseret News Press, 1920), pp. 113-14.

3. Historical Department Journal, 6 April 1858.

4. Juanita Brooks, *John Doyle Lee—Zealot—Pioneer Builder—Scapegoat* (Glendale, Calif.: Arthur H. Clark Co., 1962), p. 209.

5. Brooks, *Mountain Meadows Massacre*, pp. 80, 81, 95, 111-12. Biographical material about Dame found in Harold W. Pease, "The Life and Works of William Horne Dame," (Master's thesis, Brigham Young University, 1971); Jenson, *L.D.S. Biographical Encylopedia*, 1:532.

6. Brigham Young to William H. Dame, 7 April 1858, Brigham Young papers, L.D.S. Archives.

7. Journal History, 7 April 1858, p. 1.

8. Lee, *Mormon Chronicle*, 1:158. Entry for 13 April 1858.

9. Journal History, 7 April 1858, p. 1.

10. Lee, *Mormon Chronicle*, 1:158. Of the four attempts mentioned by Young, only three are certain: Evans in 1855, and Bean and Dame in 1858. The other attempt to find the refuge is unknown, although Young may have been referring to the small, local searches conducted in the fall of 1857, Lyman's recent activities in the Mojave, Frémont's 1854 expedition, or perhaps the attempts to cross the region in 1849 by forty-niners and Mormon missionaries.

11. James H. Martineau, "History of the Mission Exploring the Southwest Deserts of Utah Territory &c in 1858," p. 3, L.D.S. Archives; hereinafter cited "History of Mission." This sixty-page manuscript is a day-by-day log of the activities of the expedition. Martineau, the historian of the company, apparently wrote this account from notes after his return from the desert, as a few retrospective comments are included. See footnote 29.

12. George A. Smith to William H. Dame, 24 February 1858 (typescript), William H. Dame papers, Brigham Young University.

13. Lee, *Mormon Chronicle*, 1:158. Entry for 13 April 1858.

14. James H. Martineau [Santiago], "Seeking a Refuge in the Desert," *Contributor* 11 (May-June 1890):249. Although written under the pseudonym "Santiago," there is little doubt that Martineau is the author of this two-part article. The author revealed on p. 249: "The writer, who was a member of Colonel Dame's party, was county and probate clerk, and Church recorder of Parowan ward." Also see "Who was Santiago?" *Deseret News* (Church News Section), 7 September 1957, p. 3.

15. Haight, Diary, 14 April 1858.

16. Simpson, *Report of Explorations*, p. 454. In contrast, Harmony had an estimated population of 600, and Fillmore and Parowan 800 apiece.

17. Haight, Diary, 14 April 1858.

18. Lee, *Mormon Chronicle*, 1:159. Entry for 16 April 1858.

19. For Lee's actions in helping the expedition, see ibid., 1:159-60.

20. Fish, Journal, p. 38.

21. For biographical information about James H. Martineau, see Jenson, *L.D.S. Biographical Encyclopedia*, 3:156–59; Esshom, *Pioneers and Prominent Men of Utah*, p. 1025; Martineau, "Autobiography" (typescript), Brigham Young University.

22. For biographical details of Nephi Johnson, see Jenson, *L.D.S. Biographical Encyclopedia*, p. 970; Esshom, *Pioneers and Prominent Men of Utah*, p. 970; Nephi Johnson, "The Life Sketch of Nephi Johnson (From his Diary,)" L.D.S. Archives.

23. Woodruff, Diary, 22 February 1858.

24. Ibid. It is not known if this company actually went.

25. For biographical details of Asahel Bennett, see Margaret Long, *The Shadow of the Arrow*, 2d ed. (Caldwell, Idaho: Caxton Printers, 1950), pp. 249–50; William Lewis Manly, *Death Valley in '49* (New York: Wallace Hebberd, 1929), pp. 393–95; and William Lewis Manly, *The Jayhawkers' Oath and Other Sketches*, ed. Arthur Woodward (Los Angeles: Warren F. Lewis, 1949), pp. 28–43.

26. Joseph Fish, *The Life and Times of Joseph Fish*, ed. John H. Krenkel (Danville, Ill.: Interstate Printers & Publishers, 1970), p. 64. This work is a condensation of the Fish journals.

27. Alfred M. Durham, "Sketch of the Life of Thomas Durham," contained in "Parowan and Iron County Biographies" (typescript), Brigham Young University.

28. The nonmembers were John Crow, of Fort Clara, and Enoch Davis, of Parowan. (Martineau, "History of Mission," pp. 4, 8).

29. William H. Dame, "Journal of the Southern Exploring Company for the Desert," p. 5, L.D.S. Archives. Hereinafter cited, "Journal of Company." This 40-page manuscript is very similar to Martineau's "History of Mission." Martineau actually wrote this account; however, it is believed that it was largely dictated by Dame. It was written in a small notebook belonging to Dame which contained a few pages of unrelated material in Dame's own hand from previous years. This was probably the original manuscript from which Martineau wrote his "History of Mission" when he returned. Dame's "Journal of Company" is included in the Journal History under the date 25 April 1858, pp. 6–20, but it has been altered to some extent. These two manuscripts, by Dame and Martineau, provide the primary documentation for the history of the Southern Exploring Company, except as noted.

30. Martineau, "Seeking a Refuge in the Desert," p. 250.

31. William H. Dame to Brigham Young, 3 May 1858, Brigham Young papers, L.D.S. Archives.

32. Brigham Young to William H. Dame, 14 April 1858 (typescript), William H. Dame papers, Brigham Young University.

33. Martineau, "Seeking a Refuge in the Desert," p. 250; Dame to Young, 3 May 1858; Martineau, "History of Mission," p. 8; Dame, "Journal of Company," inside front cover.

34. Martineau, "Seeking a Refuge in the Desert," p. 249.

35. Ibid., p. 250.

36. Martineau, "Autobiography," p. 41.

37. Mary Lee Spence, "The Frémonts and Utah," *Utah Historical Quarterly* 44 (Summer 1976):301.

38. Joseph Fish, "History of Enterprise and its Surroundings" (typescript), p. 29, Brigham Young University. An unpublished history of Enterprise, Utah.

39. Ibid.; Orson B. Adams, "Map of the Desert, June 1858" applies the name "Nephi's Hole."

40. Martineau, "History of Mission," p. 12. Entry for 29 April 1858.

41. Martineau, "Seeking a Refuge in the Desert," p. 297. J. W. Brier, a member of the Death Valley company, recalled in 1853 that the party cut a road through this cedar forest. See Brier's statement in Gwinn Harris Heap, *Central Route to the Pacific*, reprint edition with editing, introduction, and notes by LeRoy R. Hafen and Ann W. Hafen, Far West and Rocky Mountain Series, vol. 7 (Glendale, Calif.: Arthur H. Clark Co., 1957), p. 279.

42. Although it is true that the Southern Exploring Company had reached the boundary of the Great Basin at this point, the term "Rim of the Basin" is used indiscriminately throughout the writing of Dame and Martineau. It is clear that at this time the Mormons misconceived the true boundaries of the Great Basin. Martineau's maps indicate the belief that much of the Basin's interior was a part of the Muddy River drainage.

43. Martineau, "Seeking a Refuge in the Desert," p. 297.

44. Dame to Young, 3 May 1858. Neither Dame nor Martineau mention the origin of the name "Cave Spring." However, the U.S. Geological Survey 7½' quadrangle "Acoma, Nevada" identifies a Cave Spring about one mile northeast of Barclay, Nevada, which is situated near a cave. It is believed to be the same spring.

45. Dame to Young, 3 May 1858.

46. George C. Lambert to *Deseret News*, 7 March 1871, published in *Deseret News Weekly*, 29 March 1871, p. 87.

47. Dame to Young, 3 May 1858.

48. Martineau's "History of Mission," pp. 13–14 indicates only 27 miles, probably forgetting to add the six miles between Cane Spring Wells and Cave Spring.

49. William H. Dame, "Guide for the Desert Camp," p. 2 (typescript), William H. Dame Papers, Brigham Young University.

50. Martineau, "History of Mission," p. 15. Entry for 2 May 1858.

51. Dame to Young, 3 May 1858; Dame, "Guide for the Desert Camp," p. 2; Martineau, "History of Mission," p. 15. Entry for 2 May 1858.

52. Dame to Young, 3 May 1858.


## CHAPTER VI: THE MYTH AND THE SANCTUARY

1. *Millennial Star* 20 (24 July 1858):475.

2. Gove, *Utah Expedition*, p. 170.

3. Alfred Cumming to Lewis Cass, 2 May 1858, *Cessation of Difficulties in Utah*, H. Exec. Doc. 138, 35th Cong., 1st sess., 1858, p. 6.

4. Copied into the *Deseret News*, 17 February 1858, p. 398. The *New York Herald* of 2 July 1858, p. 2 reported, "Sonora, Mexico is considered to be their destination."

5. Cumming to Cass, 2 May 1858, *Cessation of Difficulties in Utah*, p. 6.

6. Gene A. Sessions and Stephen W. Stathis, "The Mormon Invasion of Russian America: Dynamics of a Potent Myth," *Utah Historical Quarterly* 45 (Winter 1977):22–35.

7. Orson Pratt, *New Jerusalem* (Liverpool: R. James, 1849), pp. 18–19; Orson Pratt, "Latter-day Kingdom, or the Preparations for the Second Advent," *A Series of Pamphlets by Orson Pratt* (Liverpool: Franklin D. Richards, 1852), pp. 123–24. For other references to the fulfillment of prophecy from modern L.D.S. authorities, see Bruce R. McConkie, *Mormon Doctrine*, 2d ed. (Salt Lake City: Bookcraft, 1966), pp. 517–18; Mark E. Petersen, *Isaiah For Today* (Salt Lake City: Deseret Book Co., 1981), pp. 54–56.

8. Brigham Young to William Cox, 5 November 1857, Brigham Young papers, L.D.S. Archives.

9. Brigham Young, *Journal of Discourses*, 5 (13 September 1957):231.

10. Manuscript History, 24 May 1858, pp. 563–66. Also see Woodruff, Diary, 24–26 May 1858.

11. John R. Young, *Memoirs*, pp. 114–15.

12. Woodruff, Diary, 26 May 1858.

13. Brigham Young, *Journal of Discourses*, 5 (18 October 1857):341.

14. Young, *A Series of Instructions and Remarks*, p. 7.

15. Lee, *Mormon Chronicle*, 1:158. Entry for 13 April 1858.

16. Young to Dame, 7 April 1858.

17. Bean, Journal, 4:62.

18. Young, *A Series of Instructions and Remarks*, p. 7.

19. For biographical information about Elijah Barney Ward, see Jenson, *L.D.S. Biographical Encyclopedia*, 3:553–54; LeRoy R. Hafen, "Elijah Barney Ward," *The Mountain Men and the Fur Trade of the Far West*, 9 vols., ed. LeRoy R. Hafen (Glendale, Calif.: Arthur H. Clark Co., 1969), 7:343–51.

20. *Missouri Republican*, 4 December 1849, p. [2]. In Journal History, same date.

21. Journal History, 15 December 1849, p. 2.

22. Ibid., 26 April 1951, p. 1.

23. Ibid., 9 June 1851, p. 1.

24. Ibid., 27 April 1852, p. 1.

25. Frémont, *Report*, p. 276. Also see Frémont's *Map of Oregon and Upper California* (Washington, 1848) which accompanied his *Geographical Memoir*. This map was drawn from Frémont's surveys by Charles Preuss.

26. Frémont, *Report*, p. 276.

27. Ibid. Frémont also said: "The structure of the country would require this formation of interior lakes; for the waters which would collect between the Rocky Mountains and the Sierra Nevada, not being able to cross this formidable barrier, nor get to the Columbia or Colorado, must naturally collect into reservoirs, each of which would have its little system of streams and rivers running into it." (*Report*, p. 275.)

28. Arrington, *Great Basin Kingdom*, p. 41; Roberts, *Comprehensive History*, 2:521.

29. John C. Frémont, *Geographical Memoir Upon Upper California in Illustration of his Map of Oregon and California*, Senate Misc. Doc. 148, 30th Cong., 1st sess. (Washington, D.C.: Wendell & Van Beathuysen, 1848), pp. 11, 13.

30. Ibid., p. 8.

31. U.S. Congress, Senate, *Letter of J. C. Fremont to the Editors of the Daily National Intelligencer*, S. Doc. 67, 33rd Cong., 1st sess., 1854. This letter was originally published in the *Intelligencer* of 14 June 1854.

32. Simpson, *Report of Explorations*, pp. 22-23.

33. Heap, *Central Route to the Pacific*, p. 277.

34. Ibid., pp. 230-31.

35. Ibid., p. 277.

36. Ibid., p. 280.

37. Ibid., pp. 278-81.

38. Ibid., p. 270.

39. Reproductions of these maps are found in Wheat, *Mapping the Transmississippi West*, vol. 4.

# CHAPTER VIII: A HUNGRY INDIAN

1. Dame to Young, 3 May 1858.

2. Manuscript History, 19 May 1858, p. 550.

3. William H. Dame to wives, 3 May 1858, William H. Dame papers, L.D.S. Archives.

4. Dame to Young, 3 May 1858.

5. Martineau, "Seeking a Refuge in the Desert," p. 250.

6. A good view of this desert valley can be obtained from U.S. Highway 93 about eighteen miles south of Dame's crossing.

7. The distances given in the accounts of Dame and Martineau often tend to be a little overstated. According to Martineau, "distances were estimated by the time of travel and judgements of distance combined." ("History of Mission," p. 57.)

8. Martineau, "History of Mission," pp. 57-58.

9. Martineau, "Seeking a Refuge in the Desert," p. 251.

10. Perhaps not so coincidently, the Paiute word "pahroc" is translated to mean "underground water." See Helen S. Carlson, *Nevada Place Names, A Geographical Dictionary* (Reno: University of Nevada Press, 1974), p. 185.

11. Martineau, "Seeking a Refuge in the Desert," p. 251.

12. William H. Dame to Brigham Young, 26 May 1858, Brigham Young papers, L.D.S. Archives.

13. Martineau, "Seeking a Refuge in the Desert," p. 251. Black Rock Spring is shown on today's maps where Dame's Desert Spring Wells were located.

14. Ibid.

15. Martineau, "History of Mission," p. 19. Dame's "Journal of Company," pp. 12-13 claims the spring was west of Desert Spring Wells, but Martineau's maps show it north of the wells. Secret Spring may possibly be Coal or Hamilton Spring on the maps of today.

16. Martineau, "Seeking a Refuge in the Desert," p. 250.

17. Ibid.

18. Ibid., p. 251. Here Martineau infers that this Indian was the same who showed Johnson how to dig for water. Martineau's "History of Mission," pp. 18–19 says that the Indian was only suspected of murdering his wife, whom he admitted cannibalizing. Simpson detailed another incidence of suspected cannibalism among these people in 1859. (*Report of Explorations*, p. 58.)

19. Martineau, "Seeking a Refuge in the Desert," p. 251; also see Dame, "Journal of Company," p. 13; and Martineau, "History of Mission," p. 18.

20. Jedediah S. Smith to General William Clark, 12 July 1827 (photocopy of transcript), Utah State Historical Society.

21. Frémont, *Report*, p. 276.

22. Simpson, *Report of Explorations*, p. 56.

23. A good study of these Indians is Catherine S. Fowler and Don D. Fowler, "Notes on the History of the Southern Paiutes and Western Shoshonis," *Utah Historical Quarterly* 39 (Spring 1971), pp. 96–113.

24. Bean's report, Manuscript History, 7 June 1858, p. 616. "Piede" is another term for "Southern Paiute."

25. Martineau, "Seeking a Refuge in the Desert," p. 251.

26. Ibid., p. 298.

# CHAPTER IX: THE NEW POLICY

1. Manuscript History, 9 April 1858, pp. 341–43, 349.

2. Historical Department Journal, 12 April 1858.

3. Manuscript History, 28 April 1858, p. 466.

4. Furniss, *Mormon Conflict*, p. 182.

5. Letter reproduced in full in Hafen, *Utah Expedition*, p. 304.

6. Furniss, *Mormon Conflict*, p. 182.

7. Neff, *History of Utah*, pp. 491–92.

8. Gove, *Utah Expedition*, pp. 134, 136.

9. Ibid., pp. 145, 155–56.

10. Alfred Cumming to A. S. Johnston, 15 April 1858, *Cessation of Difficulties in Utah*, H. Exec. Doc. 138, 35th Cong., 1st sess., 1858, pp. 2–3.

11. Furniss, *Mormon Conflict*, pp. 185–87; Roberts, *Comprehensive History*, 4:383–85.

12. Manuscript History, 14 April 1858, p. 361.

13. Ibid., 20 April 1858, p. 422.

14. Ibid., 30 April 1858, pp. 469–70.

15. Arrington, *Great Basin Kingdom*, p. 187; Roberts, *Comprehensive History*, 4:397–98.

16. Journal History, 5 April 1858, p. 2.

17. Manuscript History, 19 April 1858, p. 397.

18. Alfred Cumming to Lewis Cass, 2 May 1858, *Cessation of Difficulties in Utah*, H. Exec. Doc. 138, 35th Cong., 1st sess., 1858, p. 5.

19. Manuscript History, 25 April 1858, p. 443.

20. Ibid., p. 439. This statement is not true. See speech of Heber C. Kimball, *Journal of Discourses*, 5 (30 August 1857):164, when he declared: "We will have you, brother Brigham, as our Governor just so long as you live. We will not have any other Governor."

21. Woodruff, Diary, 25 April 1858. Ironically, this was the same location chosen for settlement by Evans in 1855 that displeased Brigham Young.

22. George W. Bean to Brigham Young, 26 April 1858, Brigham Young papers, L.D.S. Archives.

23. Brigham Young to George W. Bean, 28 April 1858, Brigham Young papers, L.D.S. Archives.

24. Alfred Cumming to A. S. Johnston, 21 May 1858. Cited in Hafen, *Utah Expedition*, pp. 315–16.

25. Orson B. Adams, "Map of the Desert, June 1858." Originally housed in the Historical Archives, L.D.S. Church, this hand-drawn map has become lost or misfiled. Wheat, who reproduced the map in 1960 in *Mapping the Transmississippi West*, 4:129 (facing page), describes it as 13½ x 10½ inches drawn on blue paper with pen and pencil.

26. Barney, "Biographical Sketch," p. 3; Edson Barney and George W. Bean to Brigham Young, 22 May 1858, Brigham Young papers, L.D.S. Archives.

27. Simpson, *Report of Explorations*, p. 120. As Simpson followed the Mormon road in 1859 from Steptoe Valley to Antelope Springs, his observations and descriptions of the country are considered valid for the period and are used occasionally to describe the physical features of this leg of the expedition. See pp. 62, 118–25.

28. Ibid., p. 118.

29. The movements of the Iron County company in Steptoe Valley are confirmed by an Indian who resided in the valley at the time of the Mormons' entrance. In 1859 the native recalled to Captain Simpson that "the Mormons came into Steptoe Valley from the east; had about 50 wagons [probably only about ten], and after proceeding north of our camp [near present-day Ely] some 8 or 12 miles, turned into a canyon of the Un-go-we-ah [Schell Creek] range, whence they turned back and retraced their old route to the settlements." See Simpson, *Report of Explorations*, p. 118.

30. Barney and Bean to Young, 22 May 1858.

31. Bean, *Autobiography of George W. Bean*, p. 133.

32. Bean's report, Manuscript History, 7 June 1858, p. 611.

33. Barney and Bean to Young, 22 May 1858.

34. Barney, "Biographical Sketch," p. 4.

## CHAPTER X: MIRACLE ON ALTAR PEAK

1. Martineau, "History of Mission," p. 28. This is one of the retrospective entries in Martineau's account which indicates it was written later.

2. Dame, "Journal of Company," p. 14. Entry for 7 May 1858.

3. Martineau, "Seeking a Refuge in the Desert," p. 299.

4. Ibid., p. 250.

5. Martineau, "History of Mission," p. 20. Entry for 7 May 1858. Wire grass is another name for rushes and sedges.

6. Ibid.

7. William H. Dame to Brigham Young, 26 May 1858, Brigham Young papers, L.D.S. Archives.

8. This is according to interviews with present residents of White River Valley. In June 1979 the author found the creek bed only damp with grass growing in it.

9. Martineau, "History of Mission," p. 20. Entry for 7 May 1858. A part of the White River Valley north of Dame's Desert Swamp is now a wildlife refuge managed by the Nevada Department of Fish and Game.

10. Ibid., p. 21. Todd I. Berens located this arch in 1975 while conducting on-location research of the White Mountain trail. The arch is found in a remote region 21 miles southwest of Sunnyside, Nevada, at a place known locally as "the pinnacles." The discovery of this arch, which is not well known even among local residents, was a significant factor in establishing the White Mountain trail.

11. Dame, "Journal of Company," p. 15. Entry for 7 May 1858. The present term for wibe grass is unknown. Other early historical accounts verify that tall grasses once covered parts of this area. One account claims that when white men viewed the White River Valley in the 1860s, "it was an ocean of undulating wheat grass standing as high as a horse's belly." See Effie O. Read, *White Pine Lang Syne, A True History of White Pine County* (Denver: Big Mountain Press, 1965), p. 50. This was certainly not true of the entire valley, but from the White Mountain journals it is apparent that parts of this region were indeed covered with tall grass.

12. Martineau, "History of Mission," p. 22. Entry for 8 May 1858.

13. Although I originally concluded that this mountain was Troy Peak, Todd I. Berens has thrown considerable doubt on this hypothesis. While in Nevada researching the White Mountain trail in 1975, Berens came to the conclusion that this peak was a smaller, unnamed peak about ten air miles southwest of Troy peak. Among other evidence was his discovery of a group of flat stones on the summit arranged in the configuration of the points of the compass and lying on a true north-south axis. This peak also strongly resembles the small sketch of Altar Peak Martineau drew on his expedition map.

14. Dame, "Journal of Company," p. 16; Martineau, "History of Mission," p. 23. Entries for 8 May 1858. The frequent and indiscriminate usage of the term "White Mountains" by Dame and Bean is evidence that its meaning broadened considerably from its original application to Crystal Peak. While Bean applied the name to the Snake Range on the Utah-Nevada border, Dame's approach seems to have been to attach the name to any high, snowy mountain range in Utah's southwestern desert country. Further evidence of the dispersion is found in Brigham Young's "Sebastopol" speech. Here he criticized Evans for not going to where he was sent in 1855, despite the fact that Evans did locate the White Mountain (Crystal Peak). Clearly, Young was using the term for a multiplicity of ranges in 1858, for he sent Bean back to the White Mountains to find the desired refuge. From his instructions to Bean it is evident that this region was well beyond Crystal Peak, the original White Mountain of 1855.

15. Dame, "Journal of Company," p. 16. Entry for 8 May 1858. Martineau, like Frémont and others of this period, applied the term "Wasatch" to the entire chain of mountains extending from Idaho to Washington Co., Utah. Today the term is technically accurate only for that portion from Sanpete Co. north.

16. Martineau, "Seeking a Refuge in the Desert," p. 299.

17. "For the Strength of the Hills We Bless Thee," was published in the *Deseret News*, 6 January 1858, p. 352. Reference was made to this issue of the *News* in Dame's journal, 8 May 1858, p. 17. The hymn, written by Felicia D. H. Brown, was adapted by Edward L. Sloan. The music was by Evan Stephens.

18. Dame, "Journal of Company," p. 17; Martineau, "History of Mission," p. 23. Entries for 8 May 1858.

19. Martineau, "Seeking a Refuge in the Desert," p. 299.

20. Dame, "Journal of Company," p. 17. Entry for 8 May 1858.

21. Martineau, "History of Mission," p. 24. Entry for 8 May 1858.

22. Dame, "Journal of Company," p. 18. Entry for 8 May 1858. These narrow quartz ledges can be seen today at the mouth of Cherry Creek Canyon.

23. Martineau, "History of Mission," p. 24. Entry for 8 May 1858.

24. Manuscript History, 22 April 1858, p. 425.


# CHAPTER XI: RENDEZVOUS IN WHITE RIVER VALLEY

1. Estimates of the water flow from these springs varied greatly. Despite Rogers's estimate, Dame reported, "Desert Swamp Springs affords water enough for 1000 acres of land." ("Journal of Company," p. 23. Entry for 13 May 1858.)

2. Dame, "Journal of Company," p. 20. Entry for 12 May 1858.

3. Ibid.

4. Ibid.

5. Dame, "Guide for the Desert Camp," p. 3.

6. Martineau, "History of Mission," pp. 28-29. Entry for 13 May 1858.

7. Dame, "Journal of Company," p. 23. Dame also disagreed with Martineau's estimate of the amount of water. Dame believed Willow Springs afforded only enough water to irrigate fifty to seventy-five acres.

8. Martineau, "History of Mission," p. 27. Entry for 13 May 1858.

9. Ibid., p. 28. Entry for 13 May 1858.

10. Dame, "Journal of Company," p. 21. Entry for 13 May 1858.

11. Martineau claimed Johnson had seven men with him. ("History of Mission," p. 30.) Dame, however, asserted that "Johnson . . . started with five other brethren." ("Journal of Company," p. 24.) Johnson himself recalled in later years that he took six men with him to the South. ("Life Sketch," p. 2.)

12. Dame, "Journal of Company," p. 24. Entry for 14 May 1858. Martineau claimed the party carried a ten days' supply of provisions. ("History of Mission," p. 30.)

13. Martineau, "History of Mission," p. 31. Entry for 14 May 1858. Presumably, many of these men had not been on the previous exploration of Gray Head and Wibe Creek.

14. Ibid.

15. Ibid., p. 32. Entry for 15 May 1858.

16. Effie O. Read, the historian of White Pine County, Nevada, sent me a photograph of this once prominent landmark near Ely which she entitles "General Deterioration Through the Years." Mrs. Read contends that the rock was greatly reduced in size when the road bed was elevated in 1932, burying the base, and by "general deterioration with elements, children playing, guns used as target practice, etc." The rock had been a favorite picnic spot from the 1870s through the early 1900s when a nearby spring was covered over to make way for the roadbed up Murry Canyon.

17. Dame, "Journal of Company," p. 25. Entry for 15 May 1858.

18. Ibid., p. 26. Entry for 17 May 1858.

19. Dame used the terms "White Mountain Company" and "White Mountain Camp" to describe George W. Bean's expedition, while his own expedition was the "Southern Exploring Company."

20. Martineau, "History of Mission," p. 35. Entry for 19 May 1858.

21. Barney, "Biographical Sketch," p. 4.

22. Jenson, L.D.S. Biographical Encyclopedia, 3:530.

23. Simpson, Report of Explorations, p. 460. Simpson, who called these Indians "To-si-witches," agreed that "they are a very treacherous people."

24. Edson Barney and George W. Bean to Brigham Young, 22 May 1858, Brigham Young papers, L.D.S. Archives.

25. Johnson, "Life Sketch," p. 2. Johnson alleged that his party traveled without food for four days on the return march. This is subject to doubt, as Johnson's party was supplied with a week's rations before leaving camp, and they were gone for seven days. Other discrepancies also appear in Johnson's manuscript, which was obviously written from memory some years after the fact. Johnson claimed that after leaving the Pahranagat Valley, they went west "to wher [sic] Rhylite [Rhyolite, Nevada] now stands." This is doubtless the source for Jenson's claim that "Bro. Johnson led some of the party as far west as Death Valley." (L.D.S. Biographical Encyclopedia, 3:131.) Rhyolite, now a ghost town, is near Death Valley, far from Pahranagat Valley. Johnson was obviously in error, as he could not have deviated that far from his direct course in seven days. The contemporary accounts and maps of the expedition also indicate only a direct course. It is probable that Johnson did not know the location of Rhyolite (built many years after the White Mountain Expedition) in relation to his own explorations, just as Bean mistook Steptoe Valley for Ruby Valley.

26. Dame, "Guide for the Desert Camp," p. 3. Also see William H. Dame to Brigham Young, 26 May 1858, Brigham Young papers, L.D.S. Archives.

27. Martineau's maps do not accurately portray the extent of Johnson's southern penetration. Since Martineau was not a member of Johnson's exploring party, he could only attempt to reconstruct the route from the reports he received.

## CHAPTER XII: THE GREAT CAVE

1. William H. Dame to Brigham Young, 26 May 1858, Brigham Young papers, L.D.S. Archives.

2. Ibid. Dame apparently failed to mention Eureka Creek to Barney. Perhaps he considered it insignificant because it lay outside of Young's proposed settlement perimeter.

3. Ibid.

4. Ibid.

5. Bean's Report, Manuscript History, 7 June 1858, p. 612.

6. Ibid.

7. Dame to Young, 26 May 1858.

8. Could be either John M. Lewis, of Washington, or Jesse B. Lewis, of Cedar City.

9. Dame, "Journal of Company," p. 29. Entry for 20 May 1858.

10. Bean's Report, Manuscript History, 7 June 1858, pp. 614-15. In a letter to Brigham Young dated 22 May 1858, Bean described the cave as follows:

> We found a Large cave about a mile from our present camp. it has a small opening about 3½ feet high. soon opens out into large appartments. the route is very winding for half a mile has many pockets or side caves. the first part is dry and pleasant but further is muddy. a few springs toward the head of the cave. the air is wholesome and pure within. (Brigham Young papers, L.D.S. Archives.)

11. Martineau, "History of Mission," p. 38. Entry for 21 May 1858. On his compass diagram of 20 May Martineau called the cavern "Mammoth Cave," but on his "Chart" he used Bean's appellation.

12. Ibid., p. 37. Entry for 21 May 1858.

13. Bean, *Autobiography of George W. Bean*, p. 133.

14. Bean's Report, Manuscript History, 7 June 1858, p. 615. Martineau's account was similar except he recorded that the subterranean inhabitants *were* white men. ("History of Mission," p. 38. Entry for 21 May 1858.)

15. Martineau, "History of Mission," p. 38. Entry for 21 May 1858.

16. *Reese River Reveille* (Austin, Nevada), 2 March 1866.

17. Martineau, "Seeking a Refuge in the Desert," p. 299.

18. Bean, *Autobiography of George W. Bean*, p. 133.

19. Bean's Report, Manuscript History, 7 June 1858, pp. 615-16.

20. The author personally explored the cave in May 1977 and has no hesitation in declaring that Cave Valley Cave is indeed the cave discovered by the White Mountain Expedition. From the letters and journals, to the maps and compass headings, and even to the tenacious clay on the cave's floor, it can be confirmed in almost every detail.

21. The first part of the walk through the cave is easy and pleasant, and was made easier by the excavation of much of the clay by a commercial enterprise during the early 1930s. Two hundred feet into the passage the diggings end, and the cave assumes its natural appearance. As one proceeds deeper into the cavern, the passage broadens, becoming fifty feet wide, but the ceiling lowers to only three to six feet.

Good time can be made only by walking upright in the stream cut deep into the clay bottom, even though the incredibly sticky clay is sometimes over the tops of the boots. This trench is over four feet deep in places. There are two large chambers, over two hundred feet across, where the ceiling is considerably higher. It was doubtless in one of these chambers that Dame's men sang "For the Strength of the Hills. . . ." The cave contains numerous sodastraw stalactites and the evidence of some larger ones which have apparently been broken off by vandals. There are also several large columns and stalagmites which are a beautiful pink and orange color.

22. Edson Barney and George W. Bean to Brigham Young, 22 May 1858, Brigham Young papers, L.D.S. Archives.

23. Dame, "Journal of Company," p. 32. Entry for 23 May 1858.

24. This was their own estimate as recorded by Martineau and Dame. See Martineau, "History of Mission," p. 40, and Dame, "Journal of Company," p. 32. In reality they had traveled only about 31 miles. It seems that the longer and more difficult the journey, the more the mileage for that day was exaggerated.

## CHAPTER XIII: THE MEADOW VALLEY FARM

1. Barney, "Biographical Sketch," p. 4.

2. Barney and Bean to Brigham Young, 22 May 1858.

3. Bean's Report, Manuscript History, 7 June 1858, p. 613.

4. Ibid.

5. George M. Wheeler, *Preliminary Report upon a Reconnaissance through Southern and Southeastern Nevada made in 1869* (Washington: Government Printing Office, 1875), p. 61.

6. Bean's Report, Manuscript History, 7 June 1858, p. 613. Bean later told Wilford Woodruff, "The lower Beaver is one of the best vallies in the mountains." (Woodruff, Diary, 7 June 1858.) This valley was, of course, much too close to existing settlements to be considered for the refuge. Paradoxically, the White Mountain Mission of 1855 contended the lower Beaver Valley was worthless. Evans reported that with the exception of a few spots, "I consider the balance a desert and if it is not a desert there is no desert to be found in this region of country." ("Report of the White Mountain Mission," Journal History, 17 July 1855, p. 10.) This report probably impeded the development of lower Beaver Valley. Minersville was founded in the valley shortly after Bean's positive report, with the first settlers arriving in March, 1859.

7. Bean's Report, Manuscript History, 7 June 1858, p. 613.

8. Ibid., pp. 613–14.

9. Woodruff, Diary, 7 June 1858.

10. Dame to Young, 26 May 1858. Dame had accompanied Young on a tour of the Salmon River country in the spring of 1857.

11. Martineau mentioned finding an area in White River Valley on May 16 where the ground was covered with small crystals. See "History of Mission," p. 34.

12. Susan E. Martineau to James H. Martineau, 30 May 1858, James H. Martineau collection, L.D.S. Archives.

13. Lounna Dame to William H. Dame, May 1858, William H. Dame papers, L.D.S. Archives.

14. Dame, "Journal of Company," p. 34. Entry for 28 May 1858.

15. Martineau, "History of Mission," p. 44. Entry for 29 May 1858.

16. Manuscript History, 24 June 1858, p. 724.

17. Martineau, "History of Mission," p. 49. Entry for 7 June 1858.

18. Ibid., p. 50. Entry for 17 June 1858.

19. Dame to Young, 26 May 1858.

20. Martineau, "History of Mission," p. 56.

21. Brigham Young to William H. Dame, 9 June 1858, Brigham Young papers, L.D.S. Archives.

22. Brigham Young to Tarleton Lewis, 9 June 1858, Brigham Young papers, L.D.S. Archives.

## CHAPTER XIV: A PLAN FOR PEACE

1. Martineau drew two very similar maps—a large one on a scale of ten miles per inch and a small one on a scale of twenty miles per inch. It was the large map, entitled "Chart Showing Explorations of the Desert Mission," that Dame took to Provo. Martineau's "Chart" is now deposited in the L.D.S. Church Historian's Archives. The smaller map, entitled "Map Showing Explorations of Desert Camp," is generally less detailed; however, it does show the position of Rose Spring in present-day Lake Valley which is absent from Martineau's "Chart." It also includes extensive "Explanations" not included on the "Chart," which give a detailed description of the country explored by Colonel Dame. This map, dated "Meadow Valley, June 24, 1858," is now deposited in the Archives and Manuscript Department of the Lee Library, Brigham Young University.

2. This account was no doubt Dame's "Guide for the Desert Camp." Typescript copy in William H. Dame papers, Brigham Young University.

3. Roberts, Comprehensive History, 4:371-72; Neff, History of Utah, pp. 480-81; Poll, "Mormon Question," pp. 113-14.

4. The party consisted of: Amasa Lyman, Robert Clift, Ira Hatch, Freeman Tanner, John D. Holladay, David H. Holladay, Marion Lyman, Henry G. Boyle, Walter E. Dodge, William G. Warren, Marchs L. Shepherd, Cunningham Mathews, Howard T. Mills, Henry Jennings, Fred T. Perris, Taylor Crosby, Norman Taylor, Harvey Clark, William H. Shearman. (Lyman, Diary, 3 April 1858, pp. 111-12.)

5. Lyman, Diary, p. 115. Entry for 13 April 1858.

6. Ibid., p. 117. Entry for 17 April 1858.

7. Stout, On the Mormon Frontier, 2:658. Entry for 3 May 1858.

8. Furniss, Mormon Conflict, p. 175.

9. Cessation of Difficulties in Utah, H. Exec. Doc. 138, 35th Cong., 1st sess., 1858, pp. 6-7; also published in Hafen, Utah Expedition, p. 313.

10. Ironically, Johnston joined the Confederacy in 1861.

11. Furniss, *Mormon Conflict*, p. 193.

12. Poll, "Mormon Question," p. 111–12.

13. Roberts, *Comprehensive History*, 4:409, 411. Examples of press criticism are found on pp. 405–10, 416–18; also see Poll, "Mormon Question," p. 112.

14. Furniss, *Mormon Conflict*, pp. 62, 168–74.

15. Ibid., pp. 174–75.

16. Ibid., pp. 192–93; Roberts, *Comprehensive History*, 4:410–11. The commissioner's instructions from Secretary of War John B. Floyd are found in Hafen, *Utah Expedition*, pp. 329–32.

17. Furniss, *Mormon Conflict*, p. 194; Roberts, *Comprehensive History*, 4:419–20.

18. Roberts, *Comprehensive History*, 4:420–22; Furniss, *Mormon Conflict*, pp. 197–98. Governor Cumming angrily wrote to Johnston on June 15 about this apparent breach of faith. In response the general explained: "I did say, as represented by you, that 'I would delay the march of the troops until I heard from them [the peace commissioners];' but by no means did I intend to give to what I said the binding force of a pledge, should it be in confliction with good military reason for pursuing a different course, nor did I suppose the Commissioners and yourself so understood it." (*Comprehensive History*, 4:422.)

19. U.S. Congress, House, *By James Buchanan, President of the United States of America, A Proclamation*, H. Exec. Doc. 2, 35th Cong., 2d sess., 1858, pp. 69–72; also published in Roberts, *Comprehensive History*, 4:425–28; Hafen, *Utah Expedition*, pp. 332–37.

20. The Mormon attitude is expressed by Roberts: "Then without investigation and without official notification of its intention—much less explanation of its purposes—the administration sends an army to Utah, which by popular rumor, by declaration of the press of the country, as well as the braggadocio of the teamsters and camp followers, the purpose of the army for Utah is declared to be to make a war of conquest upon the saints, to whip them into submission, to crush out a 'rebellion' which, up to that time, really had no existence." (*Comprehensive History*, 4:412.)

21. Furniss, *Mormon Conflict*, pp. 195–96; Roberts, *Comprehensive History*, 4:422–25; Neff, *History of Utah*, pp. 508–9.

22. U.S. Congress, House, *Official Report of Governor Cumming to General Cass*, H. Exec. Doc. 78, 36th Cong., 1st sess., 1860, p. 42. Recent reports of army depravity included Lyman's discovery that soldiers from Beale's and Ives's forces on the Colorado had "seduced many of the [Mojave] women, and sewed disease among them." (Manuscript History, 22 May 1858, p. 560).

A few days prior to Lyman's arrival with news from the Colorado, a Dr. Clinton reached Provo after spending some time in the soldiers' camp on Black's Fork. Reporting to the church historian, he recalled asking a sergeant at Camp Scott, "How many out of one thousand, if they were permitted to go to Great Salt Lake City, would abstain from seducing the women, if they got the chance."

"About fifteen," replied the sergeant.

When Clinton asked, "How many would abstain from getting drunk, and . . . taking the Lord's name in vain?" the soldier answered, he thought "not any."

To this the doctor replied, "These were the kind of men President Buchanan sent to put things right in Utah." (Manuscript History, 18 May 1858, p. 547.) Indeed, the Mormon leaders seemed almost obsessed with this fear.

23. Furniss, *Mormon Conflict*, p. 196; Neff, *History of Utah*, pp. 510–11; Roberts, *Comprehensive History*, 4:428, 439. In response to the commissioner's letter expressing the Mormons' anxiety over the army's conduct, Johnston issued a proclamation which stated: "I . . . assure those citizens of the territory who, I learn, apprehend from the army ill treatment, that no person whatever will be in any wise interfered with or molested in his person or rights, or in the peaceful pursuit of his avocations." (Cited in Roberts, *Comprehensive History*, 4:439.)

24. Journal History, 12 June 1858, pp. 5–7.

25. Woodruff, Diary, 12 June 1858.

26. Journal History, 12 June 1858, pp. 8–9.

27. Scott, Diary, 26 June 1858.

28. Gove, *Utah Expedition*, pp. 177–78.

29. Brigham Young to James Ferguson, 27 June 1858, Brigham Young papers, L.D.S. Archives.

30. William C. Staines to Brigham Young, 17 June 1858, Brigham Young papers, L.D.S. Archives.

31. Furniss, *Mormon Conflict*, pp. 188, 202–203.

32. Ibid., pp. 187–88; Neff, *History of Utah*, p. 502; Manuscript History, 17 May 1858, p. 547.

33. Furniss, *Mormon Conflict*, p. 203.

34. Scott, Diary, 6 July 1858.

35. Furniss, *Mormon Conflict*, p. 211.

## CHAPTER XV: ABANDONMENT

1. Martineau, "History of Mission," p. 50. Entry for 15 June 1858.

2. Ibid., pp. 50–51. Entry for 17 June 1858.

3. It is not recorded when Sirrine and Carter left Meadow Valley, but it was apparently a few days after Dame departed for Parowan.

4. Jesse N. Smith, Journal, 22 June 1858. L.D.S. Archives. This journal was published under the title, *Journal of Jesse N. Smith*, ed. Oliver R. Smith (Salt Lake City: Publishers Press for Jesse N. Smith Family Association, 1970). Entries for June 1858 are mistakenly printed as "May," however.

5. It is possible that Smith used the term "Adams' Camp" because he was acquainted with Adams, who was also from Parowan. Hopkins was from Cedar City.

6. Brigham Young to Lewis Brunson and Philo T. Farnsworth, 21 June 1858, Brigham Young papers, L.D.S. Archives.

7. Philo T. Farnsworth to Brigham Young, 12 July 1858, Brigham Young papers, L.D.S. Archives.

8. Lewis Brunson to Brigham Young, 14 July 1858, Brigham Young papers, L.D.S. Archives.

9. Jesse N. Smith, Journal, 10 July 1858.

10. Farnsworth to Young, 12 July 1858. This comparison may not have been entirely fair, as Parowan had other men enlisted who could not go because either they or their animals were in Salt Lake City helping with the exodus at the time. Parowan had also been called upon to aid Joseph Horne's cotton mission on the Rio Virgin, with the removal of the Saints from San Bernardino, and for Lyman's expedition to the Mojave in January. The *New York Herald* of 31 May 1858, p. 5, carried a report that, "The people of the southern [Utah] settlements are almost in open rebellion against the church. They are taxed so enormously for the support of their army that their substance is nearly eaten up." Although the case for "open rebellion" was a gross overstatement, it is possible that the *Herald* had heard some of the grumblings from Beaver about which Farnsworth wrote to Young.

11. Martineau, "History of Mission," p. 54. It is also possible that these men dared not leave their post without Colonel Dame's permission because he was their commanding officer in the Nauvoo Legion.

12. Martineau, "History of Mission," p. 52. Entry for 27 June 1858; Jesse N. Smith, Journal, 10 July 1858.

13. Jesse N. Smith, Journal, 18-19 July 1858.

14. Ibid., 10 July 1858.

15. Ibid., 13 July 1858.

16. Martineau, "History of Mission," pp. 52-53.

17. William H. Dame to Brigham Young, 31 July 1858, Brigham Young papers, L.D.S. Archives.

18. Martineau, "History of Mission," p. 53.

19. Ibid., p. 52. Jesse N. Smith's journal for 19 July 1858 claims Orson B. Adams and John M. Lewis carried the mail.

20. Martineau, "History of Mission," p. 55.

21. Fish, "History of Enterprise," p. 29.

22. Jesse N. Smith, Journal, 20 July 1858.

23. Ibid., 22-23 July 1858.

24. Ibid., 23 July 1858. All quotes from this episode in Meadow Valley Wash are from the Smith journal, this date.

25. Dame to Young, 31 July 1858.

26. Jesse N. Smith, Journal, 25 July 1858.

27. Orson B. Adams, "Autobiography," p. 18.

28. James H. Martineau, "Map Showing Explorations of Desert Camp," Brigham Young University.

29. Brunson to Young, 14 July 1858.

30. King, "Millard County," p. 266.


# CHAPTER XVI: SUMMARY AND CONCLUSIONS

1. Examples are found in Roberts, *Comprehensive History*, 4:517, 5:201.

2. Jedediah S. Smith, *Southwest Expedition*, pp. 180-84.

3. Replacements sent to the Snake Creek and Meadow Valley farms probably brought the total to nearly two hundred men.

4. Simpson, *Report of Explorations*, p. 118.

5. *New York Herald*, 2 July 1859, p. 3.

6. Burton, *City of the Saints*, pp. 449–50.

7. Local tradition holds that the first permanent settlers of Snake Creek were emigrants passing through the country in 1869 destined for California. See Stella H. Day and Sabrina C. Ekins, comp., *Milestones of Millard* (Springville, Utah: Art City Printing Co., 1957), p. 180.

8. Simpson, *Report of Explorations*, p. 61.

9. Burton, *City of the Saints*, p. 450.

10. Wheeler, *Preliminary Report*, p. 61.

11. Fish, "History of Enterprise," p. 29.

12. Johnson, "Life Sketch," p. 2.

13. Andrew Jenson, "Manuscript History of Panaca Ward," L.D.S. Archives; Ruth Lee and Sylvia Wadsworth, comp. and ed., *A Century in Meadow Valley, 1864–1964* (Salt Lake City: Panaca Centennial Book Committee, 1966), p. 1.

14. Juanita Brooks, "A Place of Refuge," *Nevada Historical Society Quarterly* 14 (Spring 1971), p. 22.

15. Stout, *On the Mormon Frontier*, 2:655n. This is an editorial comment by Brooks.

16. Jenson, "Manuscript History of Panaca Ward"; Fish, "History of Enterprise," p. 29.

17. Fish, "History of Enterprise," p. 29.

18. Lee and Wadsworth, *A Century in Meadow Valley*, p. 1.

19. The Mormon settlement of Spring Valley was in Spring Valley Wash between the Wilson Creek Range and the White Rock Mountains in Lincoln County, and is not to be confused with the much larger Spring Valley primarily in White Pine County.

20. Read, *White Pine Lang Syne*, p. 135, quoting from the *Ely Record* of 7 February 1873.

21. Andrew Jenson, *Encyclopedic History of the Church of Jesus Christ of Latter-day Saints* (Salt Lake City: Deseret News Publishing Company, 1941), p. 947.

22. *Deseret Evening News*, 9 November 1917, p. 16.

23. Adams, "Autobiography," p. 18.

24. Jesse N. Smith, Journal, 24, 27 June; 10 July 1858.

25. Helen S. Carlson, *Nevada Place Names, A Geographical Dictionary* (Reno: University of Nevada Press, 1974), p. 219.

26. "Report of the White Mountain Mission," Journal History, 17 July 1855, p. 4.

27. Wheat, *Mapping the Transmississippi West*, 4:131.

28. Carlson, *Nevada Place Names*, p. 122.

29. Elias M. Smith, Diary, 30 July 1901, photocopy in possession of author.

30. Bean, *Autobiography of George W. Bean*, p. 134.

## AFTERWORD

1. Journal History, 26 December 1858, p. 1.

2. For biographical details of George W. Bean, see references listed in footnote 3, chapter IV.

3. For biographical details of Edson Barney, see references listed in footnote 4, chapter IV.

4. Brooks, *Mountain Meadows Massacre*, pp. 180, 184.

5. For biographical details of William H. Dame, see references listed in footnote 5, chapter V.

6. For biographical details of James H. Martineau, see references listed in footnote 21, chapter V. Also see Family Group Record Archives, L.D.S. Genealogical Department Library, Salt Lake City, sheets for James H. Martineau.

7. For biographical details of Nephi Johnson, see references listed in footnote 22, chapter V; also Family Group Records, L.D.S. Genealogical Department Library.

8. Martineau, "Seeking a Refuge in the Desert," p. 297. Manly contradicts Martineau, calling Bennett an "uneducated" man. See William Lewis Manly, *The Jayhawkers' Oath and Other Sketches*, Arthur Woodward (Los Angeles: Warren F. Lewis, 1949), p. 40.

9. William Lewis Manly, *Death Valley in '49* (New York: Wallace Hebberd, 1929), p. 394; Manly, *Jayhawkers' Oath*, p. 34.

10. Manly, *Jayhawkers' Oath*, pp. 33-40; Manly, *Death Valley in '49*, p. 394.

11. Manly, *Death Valley in '49*, pp. 394-95.

12. Brooks, *Mountain Meadows Massacre*, p. 192.

13. For biographical details of Asahel Bennett, see references in footnote 25, chapter V.

14. For biographical details of Jesse N. Smith, see Jesse N. Smith, Journal, L.D.S. Archives; Oliver R. Smith, ed., *Journal of Jesse N. Smith* (Salt Lake City: Publishers Press for Jesse N. Smith Family Association, 1970); Jenson, *L.D.S. Biographical Encyclopedia*, 1:316-23, Family Group Record Archives, L.D.S. Genealogical Department Library, sheets for Jesse N. Smith.

15. Roberts, *Comprehensive History*, 4:253-54, 312-13. A biography of Johnston is William Preston Johnston, *The Life of General Albert Sidney Johnston* (New York: D. Appleton & Co., 1878).

16. For biographical details of the life of Elijah Barney Ward, see references listed in footnote 19, chapter VI.

## APPENDICES

1. Jesse N. Smith, Journal, 21 June 1858.

2. William H. Dame papers (typescript), Brigham Young University.

# BIBLIOGRAPHY

## UNPUBLISHED MANUSCRIPTS

Adams, David B. "Diary." Partial copy of typescript in possession of author.

Adams, Orson B. "Autobiography of Orson Bennett Adams." Brigham Young University. Includes important details of the White Mountain Expedition by a member.

_____. "Map of the Desert, June 1858." According to Carl I. Wheat the original map was located in the Archives of the Church of Jesus Christ of Latter-day Saints (cited, L.D.S. Archives); however, the document has either become lost or misfiled. A reproduction is found in Wheat's *Mapping the Transmississippi West*, 4:129 (facing page), plate 938.

Allen, Andrew Jackson. "Diary." Typescript. Brigham Young University. Allen reveals the feelings of the Mormon people during the Utah War.

American Fork L.D.S. Ward Records. Minutes of Meetings, 1857–58. Microfilm. L.D.S. Archives.

Ballard, Henry. "Diary." Typescript. Utah State Historical Society.

Barney, Edson. "Biographical Sketch of Edson Barney." Microfilm of typescript. L.D.S. Archives. Barney was a member of the expedition. Although short, his "Biographical Sketch" contains a number of important details.

Bay, James Willard. "Journal." L.D.S. Archives. Bay was a member of the expedition from Fort Johnson. His journal includes a detailed description of the beginning of the expedition, but, unfortunately, the record concludes before his company got far onto the desert.

Bean, George W. "Journals." 5 vols. Brigham Young University. Bean's account of the expedition is disappointing, consisting of only one short paragraph about the expedition he commanded.

Bee, Richard John Moxey. "Autobiographical Sketch." Typescript. Brigham Young University. Bee was a member of the White Mountain Mission of 1855.

Blair, Seth. "Diary." Typescript. Brigham Young University. Contains a brief account of Blair's expedition to the western desert in 1856.

Bluth, John Frederick. "Confrontation with an Arid Land: The Incursion of Gosiutes and Whites into Utah's Central West Desert, 1800–1978." Ph.D. dissertation, Brigham Young University, 1978.

Cropper, Thomas W. "Autobiography." Brigham Young University.

Dame, William H. "Journal of the Southern Exploring Company for the Desert." L.D.S. Archives. This forty-page document is a daily diary of the Dame expedition. Although written in the hand of James H. Martineau, the company historian, it is believed to have been largely dictated by Dame. The "Journal" is very similar to Martineau's "History of the Mission Exploring the Southwest Deserts," which was apparently written from notes—probably Dame's "Journal"—immediately after the expedition.

_____. "Papers." Photocopy. L.D.S. Archives. Contains numerous documents, papers, and letters, several of which relate to the White Mountain Expedition.

_____. "Papers." Typescript. Brigham Young University. Basically typewritten copies of the same papers located in L.D.S. Archives with the exception of the inclusion of Dame's "Guide for the Desert Camp," a traveler's guide to the White Mountain country.

Durham, Alfred M. "Sketch of the Life of Thomas Durham." Parowan and Iron County Biographies. Typescript. Brigham Young University. Brief mention of the White Mountain Expedition of which Durham was a member. Good for biographical details.

Evans, David. "Papers." L.D.S. Archives. Of particular interest are the letters received from Nauvoo Legion headquarters in 1857 while Evans was a district military commander. Nothing about Evans's involvement with White Mountain Mission of 1855.

Family Group Record Archives. L.D.S. Genealogical Department Library. Helpful for establishing biographical data about members of the expedition.

Fish, Joseph. "History of Enterprise and its Surroundings." Typescript. Brigham Young University. Contains references to the White Mountain Expedition in relation to Enterprise, Utah, which was later built on the trail of 1858.

_____. "Journal." Microfilm of holograph. Brigham Young University. Fish was a resident of Parowan at the time of the expedition, but not himself a member.

Haight, Isaac C. "Diary." Typescript. L.D.S. Archives. Haight was the L.D.S. stake president of Cedar City during Utah War.

Hamblin, Jacob. "Diaries." 6 vols. Microfilm. L.D.S. Archives. Contains details of the southern invasion threat.

Hansen, Ralph. "Administrative History of the Nauvoo Legion in Utah." Master's thesis, Brigham Young University, 1954.

Historical Department Journals of the Church of Jesus Christ of Latter-day Saints. Microfilm. L.D.S. Archives. A day book of appointments and events of the first presidency of the church. Kept primarily by George A. Smith, the church historian, during the Utah War.

Hopkins, Charles. "Papers." Brigham Young University. Contains biographical information about this member of the expedition from Cedar City, but little is said of the expedition itself.

Huntington, Oliver B. "Diaries." 2 vols. Typescript. Brigham Young University. Huntington led an expedition across the Great Basin in 1854.

Jenson, Andrew. "Manuscript History of Clover Valley." Microfilm. L.D.S. Archives.

_____. "Manuscript History of Panaca, Nevada." Microfilm. L.D.S. Archives. Also contains historical sketch of Spring Valley, Nevada ward.

_____. "Manuscript History of Parowan Ward." Microfilm. L.D.S. Archives.

Johnson, Nephi. "The Sketch of Nephi Johnson, (From His Diary)." Microfilm of typescript. L.D.S. Archives. Although allegedly "From His Diary," the details of Johnson's participation in the White Mountain Expedition are obviously written from memory long after the fact.

Journal History of the Church of Jesus Christ of Latter-day Saints. Microfilm. L.D.S. Archives. Primarily a scrapbook of newspaper clippings, letters, and transcribed documents chronologically arranged in a daily journal format.

Kane, Thomas L. "Collection." 21 boxes. Brigham Young University. Box 3, fold ers 3–6. This valuable collection was recently acquired by Brigham Young University, and at the time of writing was still uncatalogued. Permission to use the Kane collection was kindly granted by Dennis Rowley, curator of archives and manuscripts.

Laub, George. "Diaries." 3 vols. Typescript. Utah State Historical Society. Important for the frequent commentary about events during the Utah War. Laub's diaries reflect the typical attitudes of the Mormon people.

Luck, William. "Journal." Typescript. L.D.S. Archives.

Lyman, Amasa M. "Diaries." 3 vols. Typescript. Brigham Young University. Contains important information relative to the proposed southern invasion of Utah Territory during the winter of 1858 and Mormon reactions to the same.

Manuscript History of the Church, Brigham Young Period, 1844–1877. Microfilm. L.D.S. Archives. A day-by-day history of the church compiled by the church historian and various clerks in the church historian's office. Much material derived from the church's historical journals, above.

Martineau, James H. "Autobiography." Typescript. Brigham Young University. Contains a few details of the expedition of which Martineau was a member.

_____. "Chart Showing the Explorations of the Desert Mission." L.D.S. Archives. This map was prepared by Martineau in 1858 while still on the desert with Dame's exploring party. It is indispensable for locating the trails of the White Mountain explorers.

_____. "History of the Mission Exploring the Southwest Deserts of Utah Territory &c in 1858." L.D.S. Archives. This is a daily account of the travels of the Southern Exploring Company under Dame. This sixty-page document is complete with sketches and diagrams. It closely resembles Dame's "Journal of the Southern Exploring Company," but extends over a longer period of time and is slightly more detailed. A few retrospective entries assure that the history was written after the completion of the mission, although the writing could not have been delayed for long, as the manuscript was deposited in the church historian's office in April 1859. Dame's "Journal" is supposed to be the basis of this history.

_____. "Map Showing Explorations of Desert Camp." Brigham Young University. Dated 24 June 1858, the map is very similar to Martineau's "Chart" but on half the scale and less detailed.

_____. "Collection." Microfilm. L.D.S. Archives.

Nauvoo Legion Papers. Microfilm. Brigham Young University.

Nauvoo Legion Papers. Muster rolls and Correspondence. Utah State Archives.

Pace, James. "Autobiography." Microfilm. L.D.S. Archives.

Pease, Harold W. "The Life and Works of William Horne Dame." Master's thesis, Brigham Young University, 1971. An excellent biography of Dame. Chapter five, "Mission to the Desert," is an account of the Southern Exploring Company commanded by Dame. No attempt was made to fix the routes used by the company.

Pitchforth, Samuel. "Diary." Typescript. Brigham Young University. An interesting commentary on the Utah War as seen through the eyes of a Utah Mormon.

Poll, Richard D. "The Mormon Question, 1850–65: A Study in Politics and Public Opinion." Ph.D. dissertation, University of California, Berkeley, 1948. Contains a study of the Utah War as a national political event.

Reinwand, Louis G. "An Interpretive Study of Mormon Millennialism during the Nineteenth Century with Emphasis on Millennial Developments in Utah." Master's thesis, Brigham Young University, 1971. Reinwand develops the concept that Mormon millennial beliefs were the primary motivating factors in many of the decisions and perceptions of the Latter-day Saints. Of particular interest is chapter five, "Millennialism and the Utah War," which deals with Mormon perceptions of the war as a millennial event.

Riggs, John. "Autobiography." Photocopy. L.D.S. Archives. Riggs was a member of the expedition.

Scott, Charles A. "Diary." Negative photostat. Utah State Historical Society. Scott, a soldier in Johnston's army, frequently mirrored the feelings of the soldiers toward the Mormon people and the Utah War.

Smith, Elias M. "Diary." Photocopy in possession of author.

Smith, Jedediah S. Letter to William Clark, 12 July 1827. Jedediah S. Smith Collection. Photocopy of transcript. Utah State Historical Society. Smith describes his travels across the Great Basin in 1826–27, partially the same country traversed by the White Mountain Expedition.

Smith, Jesse N. "Journal." Microfilm. L.D.S. Archives. Smith was a member of the relief company for Meadow Valley and commanded the operation after Dame's departure from the project.

Staines, William C. "Diary." Microfilm. L.D.S. Archives.

Stout, Hosea. "Diaries." 9 vols. Microfilm. L.D.S. Archives. Stout was a member of the "inner circle" in Salt Lake City during the Utah War. Diaries contain important remarks relative to the actions and thoughts of church leaders during the Utah War.

Utah Legislature, Acts and Resolutions, 1858. Utah State Archives.

Woodhouse, John. "Autobiography." Typescript. Brigham Young University. Woodhouse was a member of the expedition.

Woodruff, Wilford. "Diaries." 15 vols. Microfilm. L.D.S. Archives. Detailed accounts of events taking place in Salt Lake City and church headquarters during the Utah War. Woodruff often reports the comments, feelings, and decisions of L.D.S. authorities.

Young, Brigham, "Papers." Microfilm. L.D.S. Archives. Very important to this study. Of particular interest is the correspondence. Young's letterbooks give valuable insight into the thought of the Mormon leader during the Utah War. Incoming correspondence contained several reports from the White Mountain Expedition with details of routes, events, and discoveries. The incoming correspondence was also useful for determining the type and accuracy of information reaching Young in 1857–58, on which many of his decisions were based.

# PUBLISHED BOOKS, ARTICLES, AND PAMPHLETS

Anderson, Nels. *Desert Saints*: The Mormon Frontier in Utah. Chicago: University of Chicago Press, 1942.

Angel, Myron, ed. *History of Nevada*. Oakland, Calif.: Thompson & West, 1881.

Armijo, Antonio. "Armijo's Journal." Ed. LeRoy R. Hafen. *Huntington Library Quarterly* 11 (November 1947):87–101. Armijo led a party of traders into the Mojave Region in 1830.

Arrington, Leonard J. *Great Basin Kingdom: An Economic History of the Latter-day Saints, 1830–1900*. Cambridge: Harvard University Press, 1958.

Bancroft, Hubert Howe, *History of Utah, 1540–1887*. San Francisco: The History Co., 1890.

Barrett, Ivan J. *Joseph Smith and the Restoration*. Provo, Utah: Brigham Young University Press, 1967.

Bean, George W. *Autobiography of George W. Bean*. Comp. Flora Diana Bean Horne. Salt Lake City: Utah Printing Co. for Flora Diana Bean Horne, 1945. Contains a brief account of the expedition of 1858. Several important details are included which are not found elsewhere.

Bidwell, John. *Echoes of the Past about California*. Chicago: Lakeside Press, 1928. Includes Bidwell's narrative, "The First Emigrant Train to California."

Bolton, Herbert Eugene. *Anza's California Expeditions*. 5 vols. Berkeley: University of California Press, 1930.

Brooks, Juanita. *John Doyle Lee—Zealot—Pioneer Builder—Scapegoat*. Glendale, Calif.: Arthur H. Clark Co., 1962.

_____. *The Mountain Meadows Massacre*. 2d ed. Norman: University of Oklahoma Press, 1962.

_____. "A Place of Refuge." *Nevada Historical Society Quarterly* 14 (Spring 1971):13–24. One of only two published accounts dealing strictly with the White Mountain Expedition prior to this work. No attempt to fix routes.

[Browne, Albert G.] "The Utah Expedition." *Atlantic Monthly* 3 (March-May 1859): 361–76, 475–95, 569–84.

Burton, Richard F. *The City of the Saints and Across the Rocky Mountains to California*. New York: Harper & Bros., 1862.

Carlson, Helen S. *Nevada Place Names, A Geographical Dictionary*. Reno: University of Nevada Press, 1974.

Carter, Kate B., comp. *Heart Throbs of the West*. 12 vols. Salt Lake City: Daughters of Utah Pioneers, 1936–51.

_____. comp. *Our Pioneer Heritage*. 23 vols. Salt Lake City: Daughters of Utah Pioneers, 1958–80.

_____. comp. *Treasures of Pioneer History*. 6 vols. Salt Lake City: Daughters of Utah Pioneers, 1952–57.

Chandless, William. *A Visit to Salt Lake being a Journey across the Plains and a Residence in the Mormon Settlements of Utah*. Reprint 1857 edition. New York: AMS Press, 1971.

Cleland, Robert Glass. *From Wilderness to Empire: A History of California*. Ed. Glenn S. Dumke. New York: Alfred A. Knopf, 1959.

Cline, Gloria Griffen. *Exploring the Great Basin*. 2d ed. Norman: University of Oklahoma Press, 1972.

Cooley, Everett L., ed. *Diary of Brigham Young 1857*. Salt Lake City: Tanner Trust Fund, University of Utah Library, 1980.

Corbett, Pearson H. *Jacob Hamblin Peacemaker*. Salt Lake City: Deseret Book Co., 1976.

Creer, Leland H. *The Founding of an Empire*. Salt Lake City: Bookcraft, 1947.

Day, Stella H., and Sabrina C. Ekins, comps. *Milestones of Millard*. Springville, Utah: Art City Printing Co., 1957.

Dees, Harry C., ed. "The Journal of George W. Bean." *Nevada Historical Society Quarterly* 15 (Fall 1972):2-29.

*Doctrine and Covenants of the Church of Jesus Christ of Latter-day Saints*. Salt Lake City: Church of Jesus Christ of Latter-day Saints, 1973. A collection of revelations and other documents considered sacred by the Latter-day Saints. The *Doctrine and Covenants* is fundamental to an understanding of Mormon doctrine, practices, and perceptions of the world.

Edwards, Elbert B. *200 Years in Nevada*. Salt Lake City: Publishers Press, 1978. Pages 129-36 contain a brief history of the White Mountain Expedition. There is little attempt to fix the explorers' routes.

Egan, Ferol. *Fremont, Explorer for a Restless Nation*. Garden City, N.Y.: Doubleday & Co., 1977.

Escalante, Silvestre Vélez de. "Father Escalante's Journal with Related Documents and Maps." Ed. Herbert S. Auerbach. *Utah Historical Quarterly* 11 (1943):1-132.

Esshom, Frank. *Pioneers and Prominent Men of Utah*. Salt Lake City: Western Epics, 1966.

Fish, Joseph. *The Life and Times of Joseph Fish*. Ed. John H. Krenkel. Danville, Ill.: Interstate Publishers, 1970. This work is an edited version of Fish's journals.

Foster, Lawrence. *Religion and Sexuality, Three American Communal Experiments of the Nineteenth Century*. New York: Oxford University Press, 1981.

Fowler, Catherine S., and Don D. Fowler. "Notes on the History of the Southern Paiutes and Western Shoshonis." *Utah Historical Quarterly* 39 (Spring 1971): 96-113.

Furniss, Norman F. *The Mormon Conflict 1850-1859*. New Haven: Yale University Press, 1960. Used extensively for Utah War background.

Goetzman, William H. *Exploration and Empire*. New York: Alfred A. Knopf, 1966.

Gove, Jesse A. *The Utah Expedition, 1857-1858; Letters of Captain Jesse A. Gove to Mrs. Gove and the "New York Herald."* Ed. Otis G. Hammond. Concord: New Hampshire Historical Society, 1928. Through the letters of Captain Gove, it is possible to ascertain the extent of intelligence the army possessed about Mormon defense plans as well as the soldiers' feelings toward the Mormon people and leaders.

Hafen, LeRoy R., ed. *The Mountain Men and the Fur Trade of the Far West*. 9 vols. Glendale, Calif.: Arthur H. Clark Co., 1969. Important for the sketch of Elijah Barney Ward, 7:343-51.

Hafen, LeRoy R., and Ann W. Hafen, eds. *Journals of the Forty-niners Salt Lake to Los Angeles*. Far West and Rocky Mountain Series, vol. 2. Glendale, Calif.: Arthur H. Clark Co., 1954. Volume 15 of the Far West and Rocky Mountain Series contains a supplement to the *Journals of the Forty-niners*.

_____. *The Utah Expedition, 1857-1858*. Far West and Rocky Mountain Series, vol. 8. Glendale, Calif.: Arthur H. Clark Co., 1958.

Hamilton, Henry S. *Reminiscences of a Veteran*. Concord, N.H.: Republican Press Association, 1897.

Hansen, Klaus J. *Quest for Empire, the Political Kingdom of God and the Council of Fifty in Mormon History*. East Lansing: Michigan State University Press, 1970. A fascinating study of Mormon millennialism and its manifestations in the organization of the political kingdom of God.

Heap, Gwinn Harris. *Central Route to the Pacific*. Ed. LeRoy R. Hafen and Ann W. Hafen. Far West and Rocky Mountain Series, vol. 7. Glendale, Calif.: Arthur H. Clark Co., 1957. A reprint of Heap's original 1854 book with editing, notes, and introduction added by the Hafens.

Hill, Donna. *Joseph Smith the First Mormon*. Garden City, N.Y.: Doubleday & Co., 1977.

Hill, Joseph J. "Spanish and Mexican Exploration and Trade Northwest from New Mexico into the Great Basin, 1763-1853." *Utah Historical Quarterly* 3 (Jan. 1930):3-23.

Houghton, Samuel G. *A Trace of Desert Waters: The Great Basin Story*. Glendale, Calif.: Arthur H. Clark Co., 1976.

Hulse, James W. *Lincoln County, Nevada, 1864-1909: History of a Mining Region*. Reno: University of Nevada Press, 1971.

Irving, Gordon. "Encouraging the Saints: Brigham Young's Annual Tours of the Mormon Settlements." *Utah Historical Quarterly* 45 (Summer 1977):233-51.

Irving, Washington. *The Adventures of Captain Bonneville, U.S.A.* New York: G. P. Putnam's Sons, 1868.

Jaeger, Edmund C. *The North American Deserts*. Stanford: Stanford University Press, 1957.

Jenson, Andrew. *Church Chronology*. 2d ed. Salt Lake City: Deseret News, 1899.

_____. *Encyclopedic History of the Church of Jesus Christ of Latter-day Saints*. Salt Lake City: Deseret News Publishing Co., 1941.

_____. *Latter-day Saints Biographical Encyclopedia*. 4 vols. Salt Lake City: Deseret News Press, 1901.

Johnston, William Preston. *The Life of General Albert Sidney Johnston*. New York: D. Appleton & Co., 1878.

*Journal of Discourses*. 26 vols. Ed. George D. Watt et al. Liverpool: Church of Jesus Christ of Latter-day Saints, 1854-86. A collection of speeches made by authorities of the church. Important for an understanding of the L.D.S. beliefs and policies during the Utah War. Of particular interest are volumes 4-7.

King, Volney. "Millard County, 1851-1875." *Utah Humanities Review* 1 (Jan.-Oct. 1947): 18-37, 147-65, 261-78, 378-400. Of particular interest is part 3 which deals with the White Mountain Expedition. Although King was not a member of the expedition, he was a resident of Fillmore at the time and seems to have acquired some knowledge of it. King gives a near complete list of those who participated in the expedition from Fillmore.

Lee, John D. *Life, Confession and Execution of Bishop John D. Lee the Mormon Fiend!* Comp. William W. Bishop. Philadelphia: Old Franklin Publishing House, 1877.

_____. *A Mormon Chronicle: The Diaries of John D. Lee, 1848–1876*. Ed. Robert Glass Cleland and Juanita Brooks. 2 vols. San Marino, Calif.: Huntington Library, 1955.

_____. *Mormonism Unveiled: Or the Life and Confessions of the Late Mormon Bishop, John D. Lee*. Ed. William W. Bishop. St. Louis: Bryan, Brand & Co., 1878.

Lee, Ruth, and Sylvia Wadsworth. *A Century in Meadow Valley, 1864–1964*. Salt Lake City: Panaca Centennial Book Committee, 1966.

Little, James A. *Jacob Hamblin, A Narrative of His Personal Experiences, as a Frontiersman, Missionary to the Indians and Explorer*. Salt Lake City: Juvenile Instructor Office, 1881.

Long, Margaret. *Shadow of the Arrow*. 2d ed. Caldwell, Idaho: Caxton Printers, 1950.

Lyman, Albert R. *Amasa Lyman, Trailblazer and Pioneer from the Atlantic to the Pacific*. Delta, Utah: Melvin A. Lyman, 1957.

Maloney, Alice Bay. "Peter Skene Ogden's Trapping Expedition to the Gulf of California." *California Historical Quarterly* 19 (Dec. 1940):308–16.

Manly, William Lewis. *Death Valley in '49*. New York: Wallace Hebberd, 1929. Contains a sketch of the life of Asahel Bennett.

_____. *The Jayhawkers' Oath and Other Sketches*. Ed. Arthur Woodward. Los Angeles: Warren F. Lewis, 1949. Contains more on Asahel Bennett.

Martineau, James H. [Santiago]. "Seeking a Refuge in the Desert." *Contributor* 11 (May–June 1890):249–51, 296–300. A valuable sketch of the events which transpired in Dame's Southern Exploring Company of 1858. One of only two published accounts dealing specifically with the White Mountain Expedition, and the only published account by a participant. Martineau makes no attempt to establish the route.

McConkie, Bruce R. *Mormon Doctrine*. 2d ed. Salt Lake City: Bookcraft, 1966.

Morgan, Dale L. *The Humboldt, Highroad of the West*. Rinehart & Co., 1943.

_____. *Jedediah Smith and the Opening of the West*. Indianapolis: Bobbs–Merrill Co., 1953.

Mumey, Nolie. *John Williams Gunnison (1812–1853), The Last of the Western Explorers; A History of the Survey Through Colorado and Utah with a Biography and Details of His Massacre*. Denver: Artcraft, 1955.

Neff, Andrew Love. *The History of Utah*. Salt Lake City: Deseret News Press, 1940.

Ogden, Peter Skene. "Ogden's Report of His 1829–30 Expeditions." Ed. John Scaglione. *California Historical Quarterly* 28 (June 1949): 117–24.

_____. "Peter Skene Ogden, Journals of Snake Expeditions, 1827–28; 1828–29." Ed. T. C. Elliott. *Quarterly of the Oregon Historical Society* 11 (Dec. 1910): 355–97.

_____. *Peter Skene Ogden's Snake Country Journals, 1824–25 and 1825–26*. Ed. E. E. Rich. London: Hudson's Bay Records Society, 1950.

Owens, John. *The Journals and Letters of Major John Owens, Pioneer of the Northwest, 1850–1871*. 2 vols. Ed. Seymour Dunbar and Paul C. Phillip. New York: Edward Eberstadt, 1927.

Poll, Richard D., ed. *Utah's History*. Provo, Utah: Brigham Young University Press, 1978.

Pratt, Orson. *The Kingdom of God*. Liverpool: R. James, 1848–49.

_____. *New Jerusalem*. Liverpool: R. James, 1849.

_____. *A Series of Pamphlets*. Liverpool: Franklin D. Richards, 1852. Of particular interest is chapter 7, "Latter-day Kingdom or the Preparations for the Second Advent."

Pratt, Parley P. *Autobiography of Parley P. Pratt*. Ed. Parley P. Pratt, [Jr.] Salt Lake City: Deseret Book Co., 1938.

Read, Effie O. *White Pine Lang Syne, A True History of White Pine County*. Denver: Big Mountain Press, 1965. Contains early sketches of Snake Valley and White River Valley.

Richardson, James D., comp. *Messages and Papers of the Presidents*. 18 vols. Washington, D.C.: Bureau of National Literature, 1917.

Roberts, Brigham H. *A Comprehensive History of the Church of Jesus Christ of Latter-day Saints*. 6 vols. Salt Lake City: Deseret Book Co., 1930. A rich source of quoted documents and Mormon thought; heavily biased toward the church. Volume 4 contains a brief account of the White Mountain Expedition.

Ross, Alexander. *The Fur Hunters of the Far West*. Ed. Kenneth A. Spaulding. Norman: University of Oklahoma Press, 1956.

Sessions, Gene A., and Stephen W. Stathis. "The Mormon Invasion of Russian America: Dynamics of a Potent Myth." *Utah Historical Quarterly* 45 (Spring 1977):22–35.

Smith, Jedediah S. *The Southwest Expedition of Jedediah S. Smith, His Personal Account of the Journey to California, 1826–1827*. Ed. George R. Brooks. Glendale, Calif.: Arthur H. Clark Co., 1977.

Smith, Jesse N. *Journal of Jesse N. Smith*. Ed. Oliver R. Smith. Salt Lake City: Publishers Press for Jesse N. Smith Family Association, 1970. An edited version of the Smith journal, above. Some misplaced dates, but, on the whole, a helpful work. Smith commanded the Meadow Valley relief company in 1858.

Smith, Joseph, Jr. *History of the Church of Jesus Christ of Latter-day Saints*. 6 vols. Introduction and notes by B. H. Roberts. 2d ed. revised. Salt Lake City: Deseret Book Co., 1978. A seventh volume was compiled by Brigham Young after the death of Smith.

_____. *Teachings of the Prophet Joseph Smith*. Comp. Joseph Fielding Smith. Salt Lake City: Deseret Book Co., 1979.

Smith, Melvin T. "Colorado River Exploration and the Mormon War." *Utah Historical Quarterly* 38 (Summer 1970):207–23. An excellent overview of the southern invasion threat during the Utah War.

Spence, Mary Lee. "The Frémonts and Utah." *Utah Historical Quarterly* 44 (Summer 1976):286–302.

Stansbury, Howard. *Exploration and Survey of the Valley of the Great Salt Lake of Utah in 1849*. Philadelphia: Lippincott, Grambo & Co., 1852.

Stenhouse, Thomas B. H. *Rocky Mountain Saints*. New York: D. Appleton & Co., 1873.

Stout, Hosea. *On the Mormon Frontier: The Diary of Hosea Stout*. 2 vols. Ed. Juanita Brooks. Salt Lake City: University of Utah Press, 1964.

Stuart, Robert. *The Discovery of the Oregon Trail: Robert Stuart's Narratives*. Ed. Philip Ashton Rollins. London and New York: Scribner's, 1935.

"The Supposed Mormon Retreat." *Harper's Weekly*, 29 May 1858, p. 342.

Tracy, Albert. "The Utah War, Journal of Albert Tracy, 1858–1860." *Utah Historical Quarterly* 13 (1945):1–128.

Wells, Junius F. [Vaux]. "The Echo Cañon War." *Contributor* 3 (1881–83):50–54, 84–86, 102–5, 146–49, 177–79, 215–17, 270–74, 296–99, 339–43, 380–83; 4 (1883):27–29, 47–50, 167–69, 224–26, 381–83. Lot Smith's narrative contained in vol. 4.

Wheat, Carl I. *Mapping the Transmississippi West, 1540–1861.* 5 vols. San Francisco: Grabhorn Press for Institute of Historical Cartography, 1957–63. Wheat includes a description of the White Mountain trails of 1858 with moderate accuracy in vol. 4:122–36.

Woodward, Arthur. *Feud on the Colorado.* Los Angeles: Western Lore Press, 1955. A good documentary account of the Ives and Johnson expeditions of 1857–58.

_____. "Pauline Weaver of the Restless Feet." *Deseret Magazine*, March 1938, pp. 4–6.

Young, Brigham. *Discourses of Brigham Young.* Comp. John A. Widtsoe. Salt Lake City: Deseret Book Co., 1977.

_____. *A Series of Instructions and Remarks by President Brigham Young at a Special Conference, Tabernacle, March 21, 1858.* Reported by George D. Watt. [Salt Lake City: Church of Jesus Christ of Latter-day Saints, 1858]. This nineteen-page pamphlet was distributed throughout Utah in 1858 to the leading ecclesiastical, civil, and military authorities. Copies of this rare document are located at University of Utah special collections, and Yale University. A photocopy is available at Brigham Young University. This was the important policy speech which decreed the Mormons would flee to the deserts rather than fight the U.S. troops, giving the White Mountain Expedition added significance.

Young, John R. *Memoirs of John R. Young.* Salt Lake City: Deseret News Press, 1920.

Yount, George C. "Chronicles of George C. Yount." Ed. Charles L. Camp. *California Historical Quarterly* 2 (April 1923):3–68.

# GOVERNMENT DOCUMENTS

Frémont, John Charles. *Geographical Memoir upon Upper California in Illustration of his Map of Oregon and California.* S. Misc. Doc. 148, 30th Cong., 1st sess., Washington, D.C.: Wendell & Van Beathuysen, 1848.

_____. *Report of the Exploring Expedition to the Rocky Mountains in the Year 1843, and to Oregon and North California in the Years 1843–'44.* Washington, D.C.: Gales & Seaton, 1845.

Ives, Joseph C. *Report upon the Colorado River of the West.* Washington, D.C.: Government Printing Office, 1861.

Simpson, James H. *Report of Explorations across the Great Basin of the Territory of Utah for a Direct Wagon Route from Camp Floyd to Genoa, in Carson Valley, in 1859.* Washington, D.C.: Government Printing Office, 1876. Important for its comments about the "Mormon Road" which was a part of the White Mountain trail of the previous year. The *Report* and the accompanying maps make it possible to identify a segment of the White Mountain route between Antelope Springs and Steptoe Valley, otherwise unknown. Simpson also included an extensive introduction with a valuable summary of previous exploration in the Great Basin (although the introduction makes no mention of the White Mountain Expedition). Also valuable are the appendices which include notes on the Mormon settlements, Indians, native vegetation, etc.

U.S. Congress. House. *Cessation of Difficulties in Utah.* H. Exec. Doc. 138, 35th Cong., 1st sess., 1858.

U.S. Congress. House. *By James Buchanan, President of the United States of America, A Proclamation.* H. Exec. Doc. 2, 35th Cong., 2nd sess., 1858.

U.S. Congress. House. *Letter from the Secretary of War in Answer to a Resolution of the House calling for a Statement of all Contracts made in connection with the Utah Expedition.* H. Exec. Doc. 99, 35th Cong., 1st sess., 1858.

U.S. Congress. House. *Memorial of the Members and Officers of the Legislative Assembly of the Territory of Utah.* H. Misc. Doc. 100, 35th Cong., 1st sess., 1858.

U.S. Congress. House. *Report of Governor Cumming to General Cass,* 2 February 1860. H. Exec. Doc. 78, 36th Cong., 1st sess., 1860.

U.S. Congress. House. *Report of the Secretary of War.* H. Exec. Doc. 2, 35th Cong., 1st sess., vol. 2, 1858.

U.S. Congress. House. *Utah Expedition.* H. Exec. Doc. 71, 35th Cong., 1st sess., 1858. A large collection of documents relating to the Utah War.

U.S. Congress. Senate. *Letter of J. C. Fremont to the Editors of the National Intelligencer,* 13 June 1854. S. Doc. 67, 33rd Cong., 1st sess., 1854. Washington, D.C.: Beverly Tucker, 1854. Frémont's report of his fifth expedition which penetrated the Great Basin west of Cedar City, Utah.

U.S. Department of Indian Affairs. Correspondence. Utah State Historical Society. A typescript of selected letters from the National Archives.

U.S. State Department. Utah Territorial papers, 1853–1859. Microfilm. National Archives.

U.S. War Department. Utah letters sent, 1857–1860. National Archives.

Wheeler, George M. *Preliminary Report upon a Reconnaissance through Southern and Southeastern Nevada made in 1869.* Washington, D.C.: Government Printing Office, 1875.

————. *Report upon the U.S. Geographical Surveys West of the One Hundredth Meridian.* 7 vols. Washington, D.C.: Government Printing Office, 1889. Volume one, the "Geographical Report," is of primary interest.

# NEWSPAPERS

*Congressional Globe.* Washington, D.C.

*Daily National Intelligencer,* Washington, D.C. Microfilm.

*Deseret News.* Salt Lake City. Microfilm.

*Latter-day Saints Millennial Star.* Liverpool.

*Missouri Republican*. St. Louis. Microfilm.

*New York Daily Tribune*. Microfilm.

*New York Herald*. Microfilm.

*New York Times*. Microfilm.

*Niles' Weekly Register*. Baltimore. Microfilm.

*Reese River Reveille*. Austin, Nevada. Selected articles sent to author in 1975 by John L. Schippleck from files of Lehman Caves National Monument, Baker, Nevada.

*Times and Seasons*. Nauvoo, Illinois. Photocopy.

*Union Vedette*. Camp Douglas, Utah. Microfilm.

# INDEX